FLYING AND OTHER DOCTORING

Peter Morton

Copyright: Peter Morton 2018
Fourth Edition 2021

ISBN: 978-0-6450901-4-7

CONTENTS

Chapter 1	Pre-birth and Early Childhood	1
Chapter 2	Goodbye to School.	21
Chapter 3	Final Year	35
Chapter 4	Broken Hill	46
Chapter 5	Broome	61
Chapter 6	Port Hedland	86
Chapter 7	Woomera	105
Chapter 8	Warrnambool	140
Chapter 9	Port Lincoln	158
Chapter 10	Northern Territory	211
Chapter 11	Gladstone	249
Chapter 12	Excitement and Wonder	259
Chapter 13	2010	296
Chapter 14	2011	302
Chapter 15	2012 Tennant Creek	313
Chapter 16	2013 RAAF Wagga	325
Chapter 17	2014 Portland	335
Chapter 18	A Bridge Too Far	343
Chapter 19	Our World Changed	352
Chapter 20	Reflections	357

FOREWORD

Many years ago I started writing the story of my background, early life, school, university, my marriage to Leonore and our life together in rural Australia that I hope will reach 50 years in 2019. The intent was to produce something like Albert Facey's beautiful story, "A Fortunate Life", a simple reflexion on my life and times, for our family.

Somehow this turned into a book for publication and I can thank my friends Christine Stevens, Val Redding, Peter Harvey, Bob Hutchinson, Brian and Pam Murray, John Granger and our children and in laws for encouraging me to take that step into the unknown.

I was reluctant at first to do this as I thought it was arrogant but Val Redding suggested that I was the vehicle for such a story about a time when doctors and places were so different than today and that is what I have tried to be.

So I started writing and writing and produced something that reminded me of spilling water on a shiny table. It pooled in places but ultimately it ran off the edge.

In May 2017 I attended a Writers Week in Port Lincoln and found it most stimulating. I was fortunate to spend time with the guest speaker Bill "Swampy" Marsh who came to our house to interview me about a book he was writing and we discussed my dilemma.

A few minutes with him was like turning on a light. He essentially said that life was a series of stories that people could remember. This fitted very well with my belief that perception is reality.

I have had 25 stories published in outdoor magazines so was comfortable writing stories of 1-2000 words.

He explained that all I had to do was divide the chapters I had envisaged into stories. With those simple words I was up and running.

I hope it is an interesting read.

Thanks Bill and to Rory Barnes who has edited and produced this work.

Last but never least is my wife Leonore who has helped with proof reading, encouragement and patience and as always been an island of tranquillity in my sometimes turbulent life.

DEDICATION

This book is dedicated to each and every one of our four children, four in laws and 10 grandchildren. They are a cohesive, loving and loyal group but I cannot avoid a special mention about Harry and Laila, Tim and Lisa's children. Harry is the bravest boy I have known and Laila has been a caring and loving big sister.

CHAPTER ONE
PRE-BIRTH AND EARLY CHILDHOOD

I was born in Adelaide in 1943 of Scottish and Welsh descent. I grew to be tall with black hair and fair skin so maybe Viking genes were mixed with the Celtic.

My father's family arrived in Australia in 1860. So, if we include our grandchildren, we have been here for seven generations.

Mum was born to Morgan and Ruth Roberts in Wales and came to Australia with her parents, sister and brother in 1912. So there are four generations on that side. Both of my parents had a brother and sister.

Mum and Dad were both born in 1911 and they were married in 1940. Not long after the wedding Dad joined the Royal Australia Air Force (RAAF). Fortunately he was found to be colour blind which made him unacceptable for flight crew. There is a high probability that this saved his life as the losses of planes and crew were very high early in the war.

He was posted to Darwin and survived the bombing. The same aircraft carriers and planes that attacked Pearl Harbour on December seventh 1941 bombed Darwin on February nineteenth 1942. It is not well known that there were more bombs dropped on Darwin than Pearl Harbour with 246 people killed. Those who died were later reburied at the peaceful and manicured Adelaide River Cemetery.

If the reader imagines the cemetery as the page of a book and the words as graves the very first word is the grave of Wing commander Archibald Tindal after whom the RAAF base at Katherine is named.

Dad was Tindal's Adjutant and together they were sheltering in a slit trench during an air raid. Tindal jumped from the trench with a Vickers machine gun and fired at the attacking fighters. He was killed.

Later in 1942 Dad was transferred to Geelong for Officer training and was posted to the Middle East late in 1942. Mum accompanied him to Geelong and at the time he went overseas she did not know she was pregnant.

I have had a lucky life and it started in Geelong. Mum and Dad were unable to have any more children.

Dad parted from his wife and mother on the Adelaide railway station, taking the express to Melbourne. All his life he remembered the looks of grief on their faces. His Commanding Officer could have given him a job in Melbourne but he had been posted to the Middle East and this was held to be a privilege.

At the Adelaide station he did not see it that way but later - having survived the war - he realise that overseas service had been of great benefit to him.

He left Melbourne on Christmas Eve 1942 on the freighter

"Tanda". The vessel was unaccompanied, full of ammunition and at risk of submarine attack and indeed on its return voyage it was torpedoed and sunk.

Dad's unit disembarked at Madras and had a dreadful train trip to Bombay which lasted four days and needed a team approach to protecting their possessions. Dad had sickened on the ship and train and was left in India to recover from malaria while his companions went on to Egypt.

He duly recovered and found his way to Cairo where no one knew what to do with him - so he was sent on holiday.

Dad was well known in South Australia as an Australian Rules footballer and he was also a good cricketer. He belonged to the Gezira Sporting club in Cairo where he played a lot of cricket of quite a high standard against some very good players. One of them was Jim Laker. For those who do not know, Laker took nineteen, yes nineteen, wickets playing for England against Australia in 1956 in ONE test match. Dad made particular friends with a Spen Cama who was in charge of organising cricket in the Middle East.

Once he was fielding in the slips and commented to a fellow fielder that an English batsman "could play a bit". No wonder. He was Norman Yardley who later was the English captain who called for three cheers for Sir Donald Bradman in his last test match in 1948. I cannot comment on the claim that Yardley told his team that "We will give the bastard three cheers but that is all we will give him"

It was not all fun and games. Dad was sent to do something

in Alexandria for the Royal Air Force for which he was Mentioned in Despatches. I do not why but I'm trying to find out.

In 1945, when hostilities were over, Dad and another officer had the job of arranging postings home for RAAF personnel. Ever resourceful Dad and his mate swapped pads and posted each other home.

In five years of marriage Dad and Mum had spent six months together and he did not see me until I was two years old. A virtually identical scenario happened to my future in laws.

This must have been utterly dreadful for my mother and those like her but I believe that Mum derived some solace from having part of Dad to love, cherish, play with and care for in those long years of uncertainty and very real fear.

The good thing for Mum and I was that she stayed with her parents, her in –laws or her sister Sallie whose husband was also away serving in New Guinea with the Australian Army.

I was a very lucky little boy surrounded by so many loving and caring people for the first two years of my life and whilst I cannot remember most of it there are bits I can.

I remember my second birthday at Aunty Sallie's and a day at Grandpa Morton's house when I ran down the hallway and had my photograph taken with Grandma and Grandpa sitting on a white garden seat which is now in our backyard.

Grandpa had worked as a groundsman at the Adelaide Oval and had some role in the "Bodyline" series. In his retirement he maintained the Kingswood Oval opposite the Unley High School, a job which included cutting the grass with a horse drawn mower. The horse's name was "Sally" and I can remember the feel and smell of her and her leather harness. I remember him putting her into a yard the size of a house block diagonally opposite the oval.

I have a picture of me sitting on Grandpa's knee helping to hold the reins. I appear to be about eighteen months old. Maybe it was another time but I only remember one occasion with the horse and Grandpa.

Obviously it was a difficult time for Mum but the care and love lavished on me by Aunty Sal, Grandpa and Grandma Morton and Nana and Ga Roberts lasted all their lives and was a model for my parents and myself as grandparents. God only knows how others without such loved ones managed.

OUR MOVE TO GLENELG AND PRIMARY SCHOOL

We lived with Grandpa and Grandma Morton when Dad came home. He and Mum went to the Blue Mountains for six weeks and I remember staying with Nana at that time.

Dad had previously worked at the State Bank but soon went to work at Robern Dried Fruit Company owned by Edgar Sims, a Sturt footballer who he had played with.

A major event for us in 1947 or early 1948 was moving into a brand new house on Tapleys Hill Road in what is now North Glenelg. This place was the forerunner of modern houses with gas, electricity, hot water on tap, sewerage of course, a telephone, a V8 car and a wireless for entertainment. This was a quantum shift from the homes my parents and especially my grandparents had known as children. It must have been a much greater change than the shift in the standard of living that occurred in the half century from 1950 to 2000.

Somehow or other Dad acquired a share in a dairy farm that I believe he sold to pay for our house. I well remember the mud, manure and smell of the cows.

Soon after settling in Mum took me to a kindergarten but this ended when I took some blocks home. Naturally I took them back and instead of the teacher thanking me she told me I was a thief and the police would get me. This upset me and boy did Mum have a piece of the teacher. She made it clear that she tried very hard to imprint on me that the police were our friends and the people to go to if in trouble. She took me away from the kindergarten.

In 1949 I started at St Leonard's Primary School and enjoyed it very much. I must have coped well because I went from Grade three to four in the same year of 1951. I made a lot of friends, in particular Peter and Janet Buttery, Ian Chappell and David Combe. Peter is eighteen months older than the rest of us who are all the same age. Peter was "big" and I was "little" Peter but that changed in due course. In those days he used to protect me when playing football; but more importantly, as an adult, he has been a wonderful friend, mentor and guide in business and many other things. I was his best man.

Janet was the sister I never had although that relationship became somewhat blurred in our teenage years.

Ian Chappell and I met and became good friends and later saw quite a lot of each other - but that is to come later in this story.

David was in a different class but I knew that he was offered scholarships at every private school in Adelaide to which he applied.

It was a good experience to meet these boys and later we all attended Prince Alfred College (PAC).

MY WORLD OF SPORT

I had a wonderful time in my childhood at school and home and soon realised just how well known Dad was in the Sturt Football Club and the Adelaide football scene in general. He was club chairman and chairman of selectors for Sturt Football Club, wrote for the newspapers and broadcast football on 5KA, and was on the panel answering questions on a radio football show. I sent a question in which the panel could not answer and won some William Butler cigarettes.

Later Dad was a panellist on the Channel Nine Football show for many years and was selected in the Sturt Team of the Century and the South Australian Hall of Fame. He was awarded an Order of Australia for services to the sports of football and golf. Perhaps the most special honour of all is that the best Sturt player each year is awarded the P.T. Morton medal – not a common practice in the AFL world.

A further honour was to be asked to contribute to "Late Pickings" edited by Stella Guthrie. This book was part of South Australia's 150th Jubilee and contains 48 stories and predictions written by the great and famous people of South Australia. Dad wrote the chapter on Australian Rules Football. His predictions about how the game would progress were amazingly accurate.

Almost every day I would do something with a bat and or ball and most days after work Dad would hit balls for fielding practice, bowl a cricket ball or kick a football with me and was always patient. Indeed he was patient with my follies and failures all his life.

It was extraordinary how well he was known at the Adelaide Oval and other grounds. I met many well- known sporting people. Former test cricketer Gavin Stevens is our daughter's godfather, Jack Butler the Captain of Glenelg Cricket Club helped me enormously in my life, "Blue" Johnston a Magarey medallist was often at our place as was Len Fitzgerald. I met Ken Farmer and Bob Quinn the best full forward and rover in Dad's time and perhaps ever.

I even met "Jumping" Johnny Wilson, an Harlem Globetrotter basket-ball player and tried to teach him cricket unsuccessfully but he did buy me a Schweppes Palato orange drink the first I had ever tasted.

I went to a party with Mum and Dad and met Lindsay Hassett and Bill Johnston who were members of Bradman's

1948 team and another time I met Sir Donald Bradman himself - he was padded up with Dad in an informal game.

Allan Aylett from North Melbourne came to our house when Dad tried to woo him unsuccessfully to Sturt (and also tried to get "Butch" Gale senior with a similar result). Aylett was the man who put the very successful North Melbourne team of the 1970s together and later served as the first president of the AFL.I played football against Ross Oakley the second president and also with Wayne Jackson the third president. Now there is some trivia!

Dad's mate from Cairo Spen Cama often came to Australia with the English cricket team. He bowled a few left arm spinners to my mate and me in the back yard and commented how good we were and had the ability to play for Australia. He was a good judge as my mate was Ian Chappell.

Spen took me to dinner at the London Sheraton in 1974.There were 1000 elite ex sportsmen there and Prince Phillip, sitting about 15metres from our table, was a guest speaker. That was special.

One of Dad's proudest moments was going to a game of cricket with Spen in Oxford and deputising for the absent umpire adding International Cricket Umpire to his sporting CV. Oh he could play tennis and swim well also!!

MY WORLD AT HOME

It was often said that behind every great man was a great woman and Mum was the perfect mate for Dad. She was a woman of her time in that she was very houseproud, loved her garden, knitted for Dad and I (I still have a couple of those jumpers) and looked after the shopping and other home duties as they used to say.

Mum, her sister, brother, mother and father were the only members of their family in Australia so they were very close. Mum had a little Austin she called "Rosemary". It was probably 20 years old, but she used it to help Nana and Aunty Sal with the shopping every week.

Later she shared the care of Dad's father and her mother when their wife and husband respectively died.

She was not only kind to me and her family she was a volunteer at The Queen Elizabeth Hospital and delivered Meals on Wheels for many years and was always thoughtful about her friends and indeed mine.

She cared about boys away from home and even made jumpers, socks and pies for her favourites. I well remember Ian Longmire turning up from the south east for weddings and such. He was incredible in that he could have a shower and shave get dressed in a suit and tie, put on clean shoes in the bedroom and by the time he got to the kitchen his tie was undone, three buttons of his shirt likewise, his shoes filthy, his shirt hanging out and his hair everywhere. With a handful of Dad's studs and safety pins she would fix him up. Sadly he is no longer with us.

I do not think Dad ever lost his temper with me, Mum or anyone else for that matter, but Mum used to get cross. I must have been about 14 and six foot plus and did something wrong and Mum made to hit me with a wooden spoon, undoubtedly well deserved, I threw up my arm and accidentally hit her under the chin so that was the end of the wooden spoon.

She was a lady through and through and Dad at her funeral said she was the purest girl he had ever met. She was his life-long partner friend and wife in every sense of the words. As in Kipling's poem "If" they both could and did "Walk with kings but not lose the common touch".

Mum was by far the best poker player I ever saw and she played for relatively small stakes in a school of seven women that played draw or "ordinary" poker. They consistently played a hand a minute. That is mercurial.

Mum could talk to anyone and was the life of a party whereas Dad with all his experience sometimes was out of his depth.

My wife Leonore became the daughter Mum never had and a true friendship developed between them. When grandchildren came along this relationship was very precious. She and Dad were besotted by our pair of girls and then a pair of boys six years later and I am not about to judge who they fancied the most.

They cared for the girls aged three and one when we went overseas for three months. I took it for granted and when I was the same age as them, sixty-three, I could not believe how hard it would have been. They continued to be a huge part of our lives, visiting our various homes, particularly Port

Lincoln and welcoming us in their home even arranging beds at their neighbours on occasions.

In June 1994 Leonore and I celebrated our 25th wedding anniversary with a Murder Mystery at Peterborough. The night before this we met various guests at Clare and Mum and Dad joined us.

Alf Laslett, Allan Byers and Phillip Stain were there. Alf, Allan and I had played in one of the best Adelaide University AFL teams of all times, and Phillip and I were in the PAC team in 1960 that was one of the best schoolboy teams in Australia. Also prominent was Chris Stain, Leonore's best mate, who was a mad keen Norwood barracker.

Dad talked footy with these guys all night and Mum talked and laughed with everyone as well. It was night to remember.

Both Dad and Nana had an Abdominal Aortic Aneurysm (AAA). This is a weakening in the main artery of the body that results in a swelling that can burst. This is an ultra-serious condition, and it killed Nana.

Dad's was slowly getting bigger and reached a certain size where something had to be done and the risky operation was considered safer than doing nothing.

On July 31 1994 he was taken to theatre and had this operation. Mum and I sat up most of the night making phone calls to the hospital. He slowly recovered over a few weeks but it was incredibly slow and painful. I was pleased I could be there. Mum had done everything for me and now I could do something for her.

Actually there was one experience that could be considered funny.

I visited Dad one day and he was chatting away telling me about Geoff Noblet, an ex-Glenelg, State and Test cricketer who played with Jack Butler and Gavin Stevens and who I knew). I thought that he had suffered brain damage from all the drugs, trauma etc and was quite sad.

Lo and behold Geoff Noblet walked past the door and said "Good day" etc.

I couldn't help but jump up and grab him and slap him on the back.

Dad continued to improve but Mum was struggling and I kept encouraging her to get through the day. Eventually Dad was discharged to a convalescent place at Glenelg.

Mum was talking to Dad about his lunch and was it ok and other caring comments. I cannot remember how or why but Mum started crying and said something like "I don't know what to say I am only a woman".

This was like a knife in my chest. How such a fine, wonderful, loved and loving woman would feel like that hurt me very much and still does.

Dad improved and I went home to Port Lincoln.

A week or so later Mum rang and said that Dad had come home and that she "Felt like she had won the lottery and had bought a bottle of champagne to celebrate".

An hour later Dad rang and told me she had collapsed from a stroke and an ambulance officer confirmed it.

She eventually was transferred to Port Lincoln and although she was conscious she could not move her right side or talk. I just cannot comprehend how awful that must have been for her as she loved a chat.

She spent a few hours at home with us on Christmas Day and reacted well to our newly painted kitchen.

I went back to hospital with her that night. I think her wedding ring was removed when she was pregnant and Dad replaced it when he came home from the War. As a little boy and adult I always said I would wear it when the time came. That night at the hospital she tried to push it off her finger and I helped her put it on my unadorned ring finger.

She died in March 1995. Dad spent the next few months with us and, as much as he could, he enjoyed the time in the bosom of his family which included his mate Tessa, our Labrador.

Dad was courageous and uncomplaining as always and dealt with the next problem. The relatively low grade bladder cancer he had had for years flared up and he died in my arms at home in on Fathers' Day in September 1995.

Game, set and match. It was all over

The Port Lincoln Hospital had a fund raising appeal at the time and as an incentive donors could have various hospital units named how they chose. The tributes of their family and others are recognised by a "Morton Building" at that hospital.

Leonore was a daughter and friend to them until the end and words cannot convey how she cared for me. It reinforced what I thought the first week we met: that she was the person I wanted to spend my life with.

In the last conversation I had with Mum, just before Dad came home, she said that she was brought up to read, write and spell well, to be honest and kind and to follow the golden rule of treating others as you would like them to treat you.

I learned about care, gentleness, the importance of family, how to behave as a parent and grandparent and a person, love and duty from my parents.

Dad lived by a code ascribed to Grantland Rice, the first great sporting journalist in the USA, who penned "When that one great scorer comes to write the score against your name he marks not whether you won or lost but how you played the game."

I read a lot and words meant a lot to me and still do, particular the words of heroes and those that are consistent with the ideals that are expressed in Rice's words. The ultimate poem about courage in life is "If" written by Rudyard Kipling. I was given a copy by Jack Butler and have passed it on to my sons and one grandson so far.

Words I held dear from when I was a child to the present were "To strive to seek to find and not to yield" from Tennyson's "Ulysses" and "It is better to attempt mighty things and fail than to live in an eternal twilight where there is no victory and no defeat" adapted from "Teddy" Roosevelt's "Man in the Arena".

In "Julius Caesar" Shakespeare claimed the evil ways of

men live on but that the good is "Oft interred with their bones".

This is not so with Mum and Dad, I can see their good points in me, my wife and our children every time I care to look.

The good things I have done have come from Mum and Dad, the bad are self-made!

Finally, my mother passed on a priceless gift in that I married a girl, "Just like the girl that married dear old Dad".

PRINCE ALFRED COLLEGE

Prince Alfred College was a Methodist private school opened in 1869 by Prince Alfred who left after 20 minutes. He soon boarded the Royal Navy ship of which he was Captain and steamed to Melbourne where he obeyed advice to not attend the one and half million pounds (three million dollars) celebration arranged on the banks of the River Yarra by the gold engorged city fathers.

He then steamed to Sydney and attended a similar but smaller public function where he was shot in the back at point blank range by an Irishman. Somehow the bullet ran around his rib cage and exited from the front of his body and he survived.

Later he wrote to the College and complimented it on their policy of allowing Catholics to attend the school. South Australia was known as the "Dissenters Paradise" and this sort of religious tolerance may have been unique.

I entered grade six at PAC in 1953 and left in 1960. Robert Angel also went to PAC the same year and we became inseparable for the rest of our school days and I was his best man. He has had an incredible international career with Mobil Oil and only recently returned to Australia and we have rekindled our friendship.

There was barely a day I did not enjoy. The teachers were excellent and one, Bill Leak, played for Sturts when Dad was captain coach. The headmaster Jack Dunning played Test cricket for New Zealand and Chester Bennet was a very good cricketer and footballer..

One of the many men I found helpful was an Englishman David Mattingly, who taught history who died in his nineties in 2016.

It was only at the 50th anniversary of leaving school, which David attended, that I found out that he had restricted or maybe no movement in one arm due to a bullet wound he received while nursing a Lancaster bomber home during World War Two. Somehow he managed to save this stricken aircraft and his crew.

The only bad experience I had with teachers concerned a Mr Johnston. My mother had made me a two metre long scarf in the school colours of red and white that I still have. Waiting to go into class one morning I had doubled and knotted it and was chastising some miserable specimen of a schoolboy when Mr Johnstone came along and chided me for using my lovely scarf that way.

He then dropped dead right in front of me. No social worker on site in those days!

The teaching was designed for a range of future jobs so students could pick what they and their parents thought appropriate. Beyond the educational "nuts and bolts" needed to go to University, I sensed there was more.

There was an expectation that everyone would be employed, which of course was possible in post war Australia. There was also the tacit understanding that we would be honest, courageous, kind, charitable and in a word honourable. In my experience most people I know from schooldays have met those standards and have contributed much to business, the professions, the sporting field, the defence forces, and to their communities and families.

I had a wonderful time playing football, cricket and doing athletics and received a Merit Badge for success in these three sports. I got my build and ball sense from Dad, but Mum once won every event at her school sports and was an interstate basket ball player so her genes helped.

More to the point she was one who washed all my dirty clothes, endured the endless thumps of bat on ball when I was hitting a ball hanging in a stocking and other practice activities.

Dad did not see me play much as he played golf on Saturday mornings and in the afternoon in the winter he had media commitments and often in the summer went to the races.

Mum was the one from the under thirteens to University football ten years later who took me and often Nana and Ga all over Adelaide to cricket and football games. She was a real Mum and in gratitude I laid my Merit Badge on her coffin because she had earned it as much as I did.

Last but not least a story about Ian Chappell. The PAC first cricket team played in the South Australian Cricket Association B grade competition as did Saint Peters instead of the normal school competition.

In 1960 there was an epidemic of fast bowlers "chucking". Incidentally the rules about what constituted a no ball were different in those days and fast bowlers let go of the ball a metre nearer the batsman than they do today. Other than gloves, leg pads and a "box" protecting the genitals there was no protective equipment

The two opening bowlers for the South Australian team had been Trethewey and Hitchcock, the latter being seriously quick and they both "chucked". Predictably they were known has "Trethrowey" and "Pitchcock"

Hitchcock had been dropped from the State team to B grade and Ian Chappell and I opened the batting against him. I have never been anywhere near as scared of anything or anyone as I was that day.

Chappell was taunting him. I will never forget hitting a four. It was a delicious feeling. The ball exploded off my bat and seemed to instantly be four behind square leg. The bowler knew that it was more arse than class and I agreed with him and sort of apologised. Chappell taunted him even more. "What a useless bastard can't even get schoolboys out" or similar. It made the bowler angrier and scared me even more but fortunately I managed to get out, leaving Ian to belt him all around the ground.

Another quickie about Ian in fact I think it is the last time I spoke to him, well after he retired. We were watching Muralitharan bowl for the first time in Adelaide. I couldn't believe my eyes. He appeared to throw the ball. "No he doesn't" said Ian. "Yes he does" I said.

Ian had the last word. "Well it doesn't matter he is no effing good anyway". In case a reader does not know the bowler got 800+ test wickets.

CHAPTER TWO
GOODBYE TO SCHOOL

In the 1960s matriculation was determined on year 11 results. Year 12 was for people who wanted to gain extra knowledge or to do specific subjects required for courses at university such as maths for engineering studies. Effectively all people planning on going to university did year 12 and it was not long before this silly system was abandoned. I was only 15 when I entered year 12 having passed year 11 and matriculated.

I had wanted to do medicine since the day, as a little boy, I had stopped wanting to be a train driver. I believe I was deeply affected by my maternal grandfather's severe rheumatoid arthritis which was a disfiguring, distressing, debilitating, painful and worsening condition he had patiently borne for the 15 years I remember him.

I also read many books about the history of medicine, true and fictional novels about the Reverend Flynn and the Royal Flying Doctor Service (RFDS), David Livingstone in Africa and so on. And I thought it would be nice to help people.

It was all going to plan so in year 12 I took Biology a subject that was completely new to me and which I later failed at university. I also studied Physics, Chemistry and English. I planned to repeat year 12 as I was only 15.

During that year I felt unsure about medicine so when repeating year 12 I dropped biology and studied maths and in due course was accepted to study chemical engineering.

After leaving school in January 1961 I stayed with my friend Dick Bagshaw at his farm in the south east of South Australia and while there read an autobiography by Clyde Fenton, or maybe it was his biography by Ernestine Hill, they have very similar titles. He was nothing less than a legend. As a doctor he flew his own plane all around the Northern Territory and even to China and he served in the RAAF.

The founder of the RFDS, Reverend Flynn, believed in one man one job. To this day, unless it has changed in the last few years, there is no RFDS in the Northern Territory other than some aircraft based at Alice Springs belonging to Port Augusta RFDS. Fenton's legacy is the Northern Territory Aerial Health Services

Fenton only did medicine because he had won a scholarship to university and all his friends were doing medicine so he joined them.

This was like a star burst to me as I clearly wanted, despite my doubts, to do medicine more than he did, so I returned to Adelaide and enrolled to study medicine.

In 1961 there were 100 students accepted into medicine. In 1962 a quota of 100 students was in place but there were only 100 applicants. In 1963 there were 300 applicants. I have never forgotten how lucky I was to get into medicine but also how lucky I was to get out of doing engineering - because I had about as much chance of passing the necessary maths as making a hundred against that fast bowler I mentioned.

A WORLD OF DREAMS, THE BIG U

University was a wonderful experience of football, girls, learning, parties, bridge games and much study.

We had lectures in the morning, practical sessions in the afternoon and study at night so it was a hard slog. The first year subjects were physics, chemistry and biology.

I was selected for the University's Amateur League A1 football team and had a wonderful year being the highest goal kicker and being the highest point scorer, from our team, in the best and fairest medal for that competition. I also played in the South Australian Amateur League State and All Australian University team and we won the A1 premiership. This was one of the best ever university teams so being full forward I had plenty of opportunity to kick goals.

There were a lot of social activities generally and more with the football club. Lunches and coffee breaks were great with friends from football and other friends both male and female. There were at least six members of the football team who eventually married their girlfriends of those days.

At the time all of the lectures and practical sessions were in the main part of the Adelaide University as we had not yet crossed Frome road to the Medical School.

By the way a lot of us smoked and I did so for 20years but while that was certainly a hazard, alcohol put us and our girlfriend passengers at great risk.

Certainly in my last year at school there was no alcohol at school dances, Debutante Balls, sporting dinners or any other parties as far as I knew. After a very important football win four of us shared two bottles of beer with the mother of one.

The age limit for drinking alcohol was 21, the pubs shut at six pm and alcohol was not available within 500metres of a ball, but cabarets were usually held in hotels and so were able to serve alcohol if I remember correctly. So what was the problem one might ask?

Simply put we were and still are a high alcohol consuming society and part of the fun and comradeship of a footy team of alpha males were the parties that included girls, beer, mates and bawdy songs.

All good fun but the pubs shut at six o'clock there was what was known as the six o'clock swill. Thirsty footballers had an hour at best so five or six schooners were swallowed on an empty stomach into a dehydrated body because no water during a game was the custom.

The alternative, or maybe just the continuation of festivities, involved going to a house or pub before a ball and having another hour of drinking. But then at the ball there was no alcohol - pigs' bottom.

Hip flasks could hold all sorts of goodies that were mixed in coffee cups with coke or whatever. We were 17-18 years old inexperienced drinkers. Of course boys drove. There were no seat belts and as a mark of intimacy girls often cuddled up to a boy on the front bench seat.

Years later in our clinical years we were sickened by the facial injuries girls received in low speed crashes whilst the boy was usually protected by holding onto the steering wheel.

These injuries almost disappeared with the installation of seatbelts.

I talked my dad into putting seat belts in our car in 1960.

I did mention that the age limit for drinking was 21. We were careful where to go and I think that the police may have been pleased that university students were in relatively few places but maybe it was trickier than that.

In the 1960s there were 3000 people killed on the roads from a population of 10 million, now there are 1500 from nearly 25 million.

As the Americans might say "Go figure."

CROSSING FROME ROAD

There is no doubt that I was seduced by the life at university and probably did not do enough work but I had made a huge mistake by not repeating Biology at school.

As a general rule girls' schools taught Botany and Zoology and boys' Physics and Chemistry so boys were at a disadvantage when passing Biology was required.

The other mistake I made was overestimating how much Physics and Chemistry I knew from the two years I had studied them in year 12.

The result was that I failed first year but in 1962 I got my act together and passed. I still held my place in the A1 football team but did not do anywhere near as well as in 1961. There was a message there.

So in 1963 I was off to Medical School on the same North Terrace block as the, now old, Royal Adelaide Hospital on the eastern side of Frome Road.

Before we did anything Professor A.A. Abbie, a noted anatomist welcomed us to the Medical School and discussed privilege and behaviour. The boys were to wear slacks, shirt and tie, appropriate shoes and a jacket (often Harris Tweed). The girls had to wear dresses or skirts and I think stockings. This was the Frome Road East kit circa 1963. Later for what it is worth we were the first group to wear shorts in hospitals.

We now started to study Anatomy, Histology (which is the microscopic study of tissues), Physiology and Biochemistry and again these were eight hour days with study at night.

There was a lot of practical work in all subjects and much was sanitised but Anatomy was something else. We all knew what was to happen. We formed small groups and were given a body preserved in formalin to dissect. The body was to take three terms and the head and neck two terms the following year so second and third year studies were examined at the end of term two in third year.

Few if any of us had seen a dead person so it was quite confronting to see maybe 20 bodies on stainless steel tables.

There were probably 15 for medical and the rest for physiotherapy or dental students. As an aside Jan Shaw a physiotherapy student on the next body to ours became our daughter's mother-in-law in the distant future.

The dissection of a person is a challenge to say the least and whilst flippancy was common we did respect these depersonalised bodies who had been living breathing people and we treated them accordingly.

When we started dissecting it was necessary to concentrate on the few square centimetres we were working on whilst following the instructions of our designated colleague who was reading out loud from the dissecting manual. So we soon learned to cope with the new situation and I was to notice the same thing when we were dealing with live people in clinical years.

It was wonderful to get to the "real stuff" of medicine such as Anatomy and to have our own locker rooms, library, lecture theatres, laboratories and common rooms. We had a sense of direction and belonging.

When writing about this period I couldn't avoid the thought that I was looking through the wrong end of binoculars at a tiny scene far away or escape thinking about the opening paragraph of "A Tale of Two Cities" by Charles Dickens. "It was the best of times, it was the worst of times" and concluding with "It was the spring of hope, it was the winter of despair."

I had decided to play with the Sturt Football Club in 1963

and played mainly in the second 18 but did make the A grade team to play against West Torrens. Unfortunately the last thing I remember was watching *Ben Casey* about a neurosurgeon on TV on a Friday night and the next memory being Sunday morning waking up in hospital.

I have been told that I took a big mark and crashed to ground and got up holding my shoulder also that I was punched by a certain player. Sturt had a chance of making the finals but when West Torrens hit the lead I started clapping so someone realised there was a problem and I was taken off the ground.

I was not allowed to play for six weeks and strangely enough my next game was against the same team. I wasn't hurt but the only memory of that game was tapping the ball along the ground trying to pick it up in front of the Adelaide Oval scoreboard with Bob Shearman (who transferred to Sturt the next year) tackling me from one side and Freddy Bills from the other. These were two of the toughest guys playing and surprisingly once I had unwrapped my legs from around my head and had a shake I was ok.

The next year was 1964 and I played mainly in the seconds but this was when we had our exams in July. Sadly, I failed Anatomy and Histology for several reasons that do not really matter. About the only good thing about 1964 is that I got the first of seven black Labradors I and then my wife have owned to the time of writing.

We did move to fourth year for the last term and I was

allowed to do a supplementary exam so I worked incredibly hard and after God knows how many hours studying I would give myself a reward of an hour or so to study Microbiology and/or General Pathology that were fourth year subjects. The bitter irony was that I failed the supplementary exam but came top of the whole year in one fourth year subject and seventh in another in the end of term exams.

After I failed the supplementary exam I realised that I should give away league football as if I failed again I would be out of medicine. Ross Sawley was the full forward for Sturts and was retiring so it was not unreasonable to assume that I would take his place in what became perhaps the best Sturt team ever. I could have played in what would have been the first (of many) premierships since Dad was Captain Coach of the last premiership team in 1940. I was not prepared to take that risk. Being in a premiership team/s and failing medicine altogether would have been a far bitter pill to swallow than the reverse.

Dad was never critical of my choice in any way, in fact later in life he commented publicly that I had showed a lot of courage in making that decision In the light of modern knowledge having had the degree of head injury I did it may have been wise to finish on that account alone.

I ran into Malcolm Jones at University one day and told him I was quitting and he decided he would have a run with Sturts and played in several premierships and for SA.

If there is anything that I eventually found funny it was the time I told Jack Oatey the Sturt coach I was giving it away. I mentioned fourth year subjects. I was 21 in August 1964 and was given a large pigskin briefcase that I filled with newly purchased big fat books. Jack Oatey worked in the basement of News Limited opposite the railway station so I went to see him. He was sympathetic as he had a son who was doing medicine. So my resignation was done and dusted and I left his office and climbed the stairs towards the street with my thoughts far away.

I was puzzled to see a box like thing on the top stair so made the effort to step over it. It was part of the opening and closing mechanism of the door. I then found myself in North Terrace with shards of glass cascading past me and shattering on the footpath. I had walked through the glass door and suffered a one cm cut in my trousers and knee and a small bump on my head. It was a master piece of applied physics and athletic ability. I sort of lurched over the box thing and my right knee and the swinging heavy briefcase in my left hand and my head all had considerable momentum and they hit the door simultaneously and in an instant the door shattered. I must have walked through it before it had time to fall on me. Hell I should have kept playing footy as with that sort of luck passing exams would have been a cinch.

Eventually in 1965 I passed all the exam subjects I sat for as well as the clinical work. I entered fourth year with a flying start. I enjoyed fourth year as although we studied Applied Physiology, Pathology and Microbiology we made a start on

Medicine and Surgery and that was where I wanted to be. Most importantly I started studying on day one of fourth year.

I resumed football with the University and was still full forward in A1 in 1965 and 1966 and as I recall we played in two grand finals and won one of them. I remember the players in the team but little of what I did as my heart was not really in it.

I had a big chance in football and was not good enough to grasp it. Goodness me I forgot: it must have been 1964 when Sturt got into a final and I was 21st man but that meant little as I was in the crowd with everyone else.

Last but not least in this tale: in 1967 I intended playing but in a trial game a guy was very much under the ball and backing towards me. I did not want to hurt him by climbing all over him to mark so I more or less sneaked up to him and jumped with my legs straight and my chin came down on his head. Being a child of my time I had a lot of fillings in my back teeth and five or six of these teeth were split requiring lots of dental work some of which I still have. I had to spray my mouth with local anaesthetic to eat for some weeks. So good bye footy.

CLINICAL YEARS

These years were all about clinical training and involved attending lectures, ward rounds, post mortems, clinical lectures and so on at the Royal Adelaide (RAH) or The Queen Elizabeth Hospitals (TQEH). I preferred the latter as it was better designed and only built in 1953 with young guns as specialist staff. I lived at Glenelg so it was also much closer and easier to park than at the RAH.

The model of service provision and teaching was based on the English system of having surgical and medical units headed by Honorary Staff who would donate half their time to caring for poor patients and teaching students in public hospitals. Their reward was professional status and satisfaction and to interact with colleagues and trainee doctors so as to get patient referrals. Under them were salaried registrars, resident medical staff and interns.

TQEH had four general medical and four general surgical units. There was a professor leading a unit in each of those specialties to keep an eye on academic performance. The others were led by private practitioners. Fourth year students were allocated to these general units

There was formal and informal teaching and often nurses were involved. Sir Rupert Magarey had a list of 10 procedures that students had to do such as suturing, male and female catheterisation, application of plasters and so on. It was not easy to learn how to examine patients, particularly to do rectal or vaginal examinations but politeness, respect and explanations helped. Most people in public hospitals cooperated as they were aware that students were there to learn.

A lot of the names and certainly working conditions have changed but the general principles are still the same and particularly in intern years are underpinned by the concept of "see one, do one, teach one". The next step on the journey was fifth year and that continued this model of teaching but in different fields.

There were three terms. One included Ear, Nose and Throat surgery, Ophthalmology and Dermatology, the other two terms were Obstetrics and Gynaecology and Paediatrics. Examinations in these subjects were held in fifth year leaving final year free for Medicine and Surgery. This was very exciting as we were dealing with real people and were beginning to feel that we were on our way to being real doctors, but there was still time for fun.

Obstetrics was a great thing to do for obvious reasons and done in small groups so we learnt a lot particularly from the late Harvey Radden who was a terrific teacher and was the only surgeon I have seen who was truly ambidextrous

Chris Heinrich, whose dad was the Director of the Woomera Rocket Range made a catapult that could fling a water bomb made from two rubber finger stalls, one inside the other to avoid mid-air explosions, more than 100metres. There were four sets of four very large rubber bands joined together and joined to four points on the rim of a plastic bowl.

It was operated by three people. Two were outside on the external passage way to our rooms each holding two sets of rubber bands with one hand in the air and the other knee high with the leading foot on the parapet. The launch controller, obviously Chris, held the bowl and walked backwards into the doorway for two metres and released the missile. We became so good that the nurses had to walk in the wet weather underground tunnel to get from the nurses home to the main building in a dry state. Unfortunately we put one through a window so we were disarmed.

Paediatrics was next at the Adelaide Children's Hospital and again that was interesting and tested us even more because we had no experience with children. I am hazy about the details but I seem to recall learning about all sorts of ghastly conditions in children that were rare in general practice. I do not recall doing much in the Emergency Department where probably the most important thing to learn is how to tell if a child is ill or not. This can be much harder with children than it is with adults, but it is an essential skill.

Exams passed I headed to final year in 1968.

CHAPTER THREE
FINAL YEAR – WHY THE COUNTRY?

Although my life at university had been difficult and at times I had lurched from crisis to crisis, I was looking forward to the challenge.

My future role in medicine was unclear but there were lots of things pushing me towards living and working in the country. My earliest memories and experiences were very positive about rural Australia. My father worked for Robern Dried Fruit Company the forerunner of Angus Park, so frequently he visited the Barossa Valley and the Riverland and once he had a share in a dairy at Mt Compass.

Two of my uncles were commercial travellers in the country and another uncle and my cousins had friends in Elliston, as did my mother in her youth. Last but not least my fourth uncle was from a farm and was a graduate in Agricultural Science. Occasionally we visited his sister on a farm at Meadows south of Adelaide.

My paternal grandfather would tell me bedtime stories in which both of us roamed the Adelaide Hills in a horse drawn caravan. This had a big influence on me. In my childhood and early teen years Australia was said to "ride on the sheep's back". Wool and other primary industries were incredibly important to our economy. Farmers were admired, were prominent in politics and business and everyone seemingly loved going to the Royal Adelaide Show.

At school we learnt about Sturt, Stuart, Eyre and other explorers who were regarded as heroes. I read books by of Patterson, Steel Rudd, Ion Idriess, Simpson Newland, Rolf Boldrewood, Jeannie Gunn and others that praised the self-sacrifice, hard work, toughness, skill and determination of country people.

Perhaps no one has described the inborn love of the country and the frustrations of the city better than "Banjo" Patterson in his poem "Clancy of The Overflow" when he writes "For the drovers life has pleasures that the townsfolk never know". He tells how he is "Sitting in my dinghy little office"---- "And I somehow rather fancy that I'd like to change with Clancy". Incidentally "Clancy" and "Banjo" got their names from horses they had owned.

This was written in 1889. I had similar feelings in 1967 and the hordes of people travelling and camping in Australia to this day suggest some deep yearning within us. Whether it is genetic or psychological to want to spend time outdoors in this "wide, brown land" I do not know. Perhaps it is both like so many other things that we do.

And of course there were movies. I am sure many of us were deeply affected by the cowboys of the silver screen from the United States and to a lesser extent Australia. Relations between girls and boys undoubtedly owed a lot to these movies and no one said it better than Tarzan. "Me Tarzan you Jane"

Country music in my child hood such as "Don't Fence Me In" (that Dad used to sing), "Blue Eyes Crying in The Rain" and similar modern songs moved me then and now. Isolated lonely places and lost loves are a reality.

With all this background swirling around, I became friendly with many boarders at PAC.

A particular friend was Dick Bagshaw and from the age of 16-24 I visited his home in the South East of South Australia many times. He, his mother and father, their friends and neighbours influenced my life more than anyone other than my parents.

I became part of their world and was proud to be so.

As well as innumerable social visits I worked for six months or so on nearby farms mainly for a man named John Paltridge who also influenced me a great deal.

I remember John's mischievous little boys, Jimmie and Laurie and sadly I met them as grown men at their dad's funeral in 2008. Jimmy remembers me being a very good cricketer and drinking lots of beer. He does not recall me working 12 hours a day with and for his dad.

In 2010 our son was appointed manager of what had become Jim's farm.

Country people were kind and generous to me and I could not help but be impressed by the toughness, courage, patience, strength and versatility needed to be a farmer or a farmer's wife then and now.

We did of course have a lot of fun playing cricket and other things. One night at Bill Dawes' place I was answering a call of nature in his back garden looking at the stars and feeling very relaxed. This changed when he sneaked up behind me and fired a Mauser pistol. It took a week before I could pass urine again.

Another memory was about "Bikey" Tor. We had a party in a cottage at Ian Longmire's property and I was in a chair gazing into the fire dreaming of what might lie ahead that night. "Bikey" chopped down the door with a chain saw, walked in and said "Hi! Nice to see ya'all" –a real BBQ stopper.

Another party trick was to open a long neck bottle of beer in an FJ Holden driving along. There is a gap in the Holden steering column where the gear stick moves whilst changing gears. The top of a beer bottle can be held there and changing from second gear to third removes the lid.

At Christmas time in 1966 I had my first experience as a stock owner when I somehow acquired seven merino wethers in full wool. They were big animals and needed to be shorn and I had a FJ Holden sedan to transport them.

A variation on a joke about elephants and Volkswagens comes to mind.

Question. How do you get seven full wool merino sheep into an FJ Holden car?

Answer. Two in the front, three in the back and two in the

boot on the way to shearing and four in the back and three in the boot on the way home.

The shearers looked at me strangely during this operation.

Somehow three sheep disappeared and Dick could no longer feed the others. So with two in the boot and two in the back seat I was off to Mum and Dad's house in North Glenelg en route to Uncle Lloyd's spare block at Port Noarlunga

Mum and Dad were looking after my Labrador in their small back yard. I put the sheep into the back yard and they immediately ran around the side of the house. The Labrador couldn't believe his eyes so went to investigate. This panicked the sheep so they ran out onto the lawn. Numbers one, two and three knocked the dog over but he was ready for number four and grabbed it.

I took the sheep to Port Noarlunga and made a yard for them. Uncle Lloyd lived on the top of quite a steep hill that is the boundary between Port Noarlunga and Christies Beach. The sheep escaped and ran down the hill to the middle of Port Noarlunga with aunty Con after them. They finished up at the local abattoir.

More sensibly Dick Bagshaw and I once watered a mob of sheep that were in the "long paddock". Australian roads are traditionally three chains wide. A chain was a surveying tool 22 yards (about 20 metres) long that was used to measure and survey land and indeed cricket pitches. Even with a modern strip of bitumen there was still ample room to drive stock and many farmers survived by doing this in times of drought.

The stock had to be moved a certain distance each day but often the drovers took side roads and other little tricks to slow their journey..

Our drover had a horse drawn caravan just like the one grandpa told me stories about. It was so small that he had to roll back his mattress to sit on the driver's seat. Late every afternoon he would erect a fence and send his dogs "wayback" to get the sheep and put them in the yard. The 2000 sheep with some lambs were strung out for two kilometres on the roadside verge - they were far too smart to walk on the road.

About the same time we would turn up with about 2000l of water in a tanker on a trailer. We would unload and assemble troughs and give the sheep a drink. We did it for about a month but eventually it was too far to travel.

There were a lot of silly, dangerous and a few illegal things that happened but I learnt to handle sheep and cattle, work in shearing sheds, build fences, how to fall off a galloping horse and roll over and miss a rock with my head, drive different vehicles, cart hay, shoot rifles, crack a stock whip and be part of the rural world.

So back to university I went to prepare for the future whatever that should hold.

THE REAL DEAL

The time for games was over and in 1968 I was on the last lap of the medical course and favouring rural practice. There was no 'Eureka" moment but a few things fell into place that made this rather vague dream turn into solid reality.

Firstly, in May I met Leonore Sullivan who became the love of my life then and now as we approach our golden wedding anniversary. It was very obvious that we liked each other and not very long before there was an understanding that somehow, somewhere, sometime we would do something together. Leonore's mother was born on Mount Leonard cattle station to the east of Birdsville and Leonore had always been keen on a rural life.

Next influence was one of my surgeon teachers, Sinclair Smith who had been a General Practitioner at Broken Hill for seven years before doing surgery. He was a great teacher and a mentor to me. I do not think I knew that the compulsory year of intern training could be done at Broken Hill until he told me. He arranged for me to contact Vince Barron the Medical Superintendent at Broken Hill and in due course my mate Peter McEvoy and I were interviewed and offered jobs that we both accepted, at the Broken Hill and District Hospital.

Three ticks so that was it. Off to Broken Hill in 1969 was the plan and the fourth tick really nailed it

Though still a student I was lucky to get a job at The Queen Elizabeth Hospital as an intern and did full surgical and medical terms and even time in casualty.

This was of inestimable value as I developed reasonable examination and procedural skills that enabled me to cope with the situation that developed at Broken Hill.

There were many new and exciting things that happened not the least of which was that as a doctor (even a make believe one) the nurses treated me differently to a mere student. Instead of grovelling and pleading to find out where the Coopers beer and stout were kept I just had to ask.

Seriously the nurses were terrific and if any young doctor who ignores the knowledge of nurses is very foolish but more of that later.

There were three cases I remember very clearly for different reasons

The first was being called at night to see a man in a state of delirium tremens from alcohol. He was a sad and pitiful sight, made worse by the fact that he was a cousin of my father and had given me a slug gun 15 years before. There was an explanation but whatever that was it didn't matter. It was sad and a shock

One of the tasks I tried to do well was to ensure that patients and/or their families knew what were going on. There was a patient who had been admitted with a high temperature. I suppose he was otherwise unwell but there was no apparent cause for this high temperature .This can be a sign of hidden malignancy or other nasty things so needs to be investigated.

We found out that he had TB which was good news because it could be fixed. I told his wife this in a pleasant way and I will never forget her reaction. She almost shrunk in front of me.

She was about 60 and for her generation TB was, like cancer today, often a death sentence and particularly in the "Golden Years" from 15-25 years of age.

It was also known as "Consumption" for good reason. It could spread anywhere in the body and cause horrible masses of "caseation" tissue. We saw these things in pathology museums and some were the size of a fist. Oh by the way "caseation" means "cheese like" so it is easy to understand her grief which I am pleased to say I allayed.

The last case was much more dramatic. I was called to examine a teenage girl who was unconscious from a car accident.

When I arrived Rod Hall the surgical registrar was showing a group of fourth year students how to examine an unconscious patient.

I leant against the wall trying to look like a real doctor. When the registrar and students left I went to her bedside to write the registrar's findings in her medical record.

For some reason, maybe to practis9e my technique, I decided to examine her. A few minutes later I shone a light at her pupils and the right one was fixed and dilated.

This is a super emergency as it means there is pressure on the brain that must be relieved by making a hole in the skull.

Rod Hall came in a hurry when I called him and he organised a neurosurgeon and an operation as soon as possible.

Some years later that neurosurgeon remembered my involvement and complimented me, a sentiment that was much appreciated.

The girl must have been told of my actions because when I went to see her she asked me if I did ordinary doctor things and I said I did.

She then asked me if I knew about periods. I did and my diagnosis was confirmed when she sent me a nice picture a few months later of her baby.

I was still working as an intern when our final exams were held.

One exam was called "lumps and bumps" There were a dozen or so patients sitting in a room and students were directed by the examiners to particular patients.

My examiner was my boss who directed me to examine the eye movement of one of our in-patients. I tried to whisper that I knew the patient but he repeated his instructions in a firmer voice.

I went to the patient and said hello and reported back, in proper doctor talk, that the patient could not move one eye to look to the side. I was asked the cause and my answer was what the patient had told me a week before that "A bloody German sniper shot me in the eye at Ypres in WW1" Go past go collect $200.

A similar thing had happened the year before when I was asked to examine someone's ears in an exam. I introduced myself and he yelled "I can't hear you I got 'oles in both me ear drums"---how sweet it was.

I also picked the long case in our medicine oral exam and the main question in the surgical paper and prepared for them so my luck had changed.

I passed my exams and went off to Broken Hill. Leonore went to Perth to do some further study but that is another story.

CHAPTER FOUR
BROKEN HILL

INTRODUCTION TO TWO-UP

My friend and colleague Peter McEvoy and I moved to Broken Hill in January 1969 and settled into a flat.

Feeling hungry one night we asked a policeman where we could get something to eat. He directed us to the two-up school down a lane where a guy with no neck and a shaved head was guarding the gate in an iron fence.

He let us in to a little cafe where there was a selection of food for hungry gamblers – whether losers or winners. Sausages and mash were 25 cents and steak a dollar.

Through the cafe was "The Game" in a room with a three by three metre "ring" with a border of a 20cm high brass rail. Behind this were one or two rows of occupied seats with many more men standing behind them.

The game is simple. A person who wants to be the spinner i.e. to toss two pennies into the air from a piece of wood called a kip held in his hand enters the ring and makes a bet which is covered by the man running the game. He must throw two heads three times a row to win. A $10 bet would result in a return of $80. He then has the choice to walk away or to try to throw more heads. Throwing tails means he loses. One head and one tail are tossed again.

Before he tosses the coins the on-lookers are asked if they want to make side bets. They do this by waving money around calling heads or tails and the people running the game grab the money and match it with someone wanting to bet the opposite. They put the total bets on the floor. They are pretty clever remembering who has bet what from the 30-40 people who may have bet and it certainly is not quiet.

When the side bets are finished the ring master calls "All set on the side" and if there is no response calls "Come in spinner" and the coins are tossed. The side bets are settled after each toss.

This of course was illegal but had the reputation of being the safest place in town. If someone wanted to leave with a heap of money guards would block the door for five minutes. I saw a jaw X-ray once of a man who had started a fight and was publically beaten up and then sent courtesy of the school to a specialist in Adelaide for attention.

Later in the year my parents visited and I took my father to "The Game" and he said it had not changed since the 1930s.

So we had an introduction to perhaps the most infamous place in Broken Hill.

LEARNING TO BE A DOCTOR IN A DIFFERENT WORLD
There were two specialist physicians, two surgeons, a radiologist and pathologist, a couple of doctors waiting to go

into general practice and six junior doctors including Peter and myself as interns and four more experienced guys.

There were also a number of visiting specialists mostly from Adelaide.

In a teaching hospital interns do menial work such as writing forms, sorting out tests, taking blood and so but in Broken Hill we had much more responsibility.

Our rosters were for Medicine, Surgery, Anaesthetics, Obstetrics, Emergency and Paediatrics - plus we took part in the after-hours roster.

As a student or a doctor in a teaching hospital it is unusual to know any patients or to see them outside the hospital, but in Broken Hill I first experienced this. It became a part of my life: dealing with people at work that my wife or I would then meet in the street, the shops, the pub or playing sport, at schools or elsewhere. Sometimes it can be annoying but I would not have had it any other way.

But there were times in Broken Hill when I was out of my comfort zone. Once was with a mate, Tony White, at a sheep station late at night.

We arrived at a party in full swing and it was not long before there was some drama. There was a 44-gallon drum of water placed horizontally over a fire connected to another drum of water about three metres above it by a pipe. There was a second pipe from the top drum carrying water to a tap about a half metre off the ground.

Not surprisingly the laws of physics caused the water in

the top tank to get very hot.

Some silly bugger climbed up to the header tank and tipped hot water on himself. The cry went up "Where's a doctor?" Like everyone else I looked around for a few seconds until the realisation struck me that it was me. The station had a Royal Flying Doctor Kit so I gave the man an injection of morphine and the RFDS picked him up.

I had a similar reaction when someone was looking for a doctor in the Emergency Department to go to an accident. Oh hell that is me.

Off I went in an ambulance to where a semi-trailer had tipped over trapping the driver in the cabin. There were all sorts of people and vehicles around the place. I nervously approached the truck and knelt down and asked "What is the trouble?" The answer, in a firm non shocked manner, was "I have me bloody thumb jammed between the steering wheel and the roof and cannot move."

I thought I should do something as there was an air of expectation so after obtaining a verbal informed consent (!) I lay on my back and wriggled into the cabin with my right arm extended parallel to the ground poking hither and thither with my syringe of morphine. When the driver and I reached a consensus about a fair and reasonable location I pushed the plunger and soon after he was extricated whilst I extricated about a 1000 bindiis/three corner jacks from my backside.

And there was the day I was nearly killed.

I was given an underground tour of a mine and noticed a

gap where the cage, a type of lift, stopped to allow miners to get in and out.

I walked over and had a look over the edge into the Stygian darkness of the shaft, saw nothing and stepped back to hear a faint whooshing sound as the cage descended pretty much free falling. It certainly would have been the end of me if I had looked for a few seconds longer.

As the weeks went by we settled into what was a marvellous working environment and we were exposed to a variety of significant clinical situations and pitfalls.

I was fussy with neurological examinations after my experience at TQEH and I saw several patients who were unconscious with no tendon reflexes except from their forearms and no response to pain and who yet woke up instantly some time later. No one has ever been able to explain this but they were all alcohol related.

One guy had a history of Depression and alcohol abuse and a doctor started slapping him to wake him up. He woke up all right, threw one punch that landed and knocked the doctor back into an instrument cupboard and then happily went to sleep again.

There was a lot of trauma, frequently alcohol related. There were many pubs in Broken Hill and nearby flagrantly breaking the law with the hours they opened.

I well remember putting my hand on the head on a family man who was driving towards home and had been hit by some idiot at high speed. His head felt like a crushed egg shell.

There was another dramatic case with a better result fortunately.

A keen gun collector showed his wife an old rifle he had bought. She looked at the price on the tag tied to the trigger and fired the rifle into her own chest at point blank range. I was called to help and remember the surgeon cupping his hands and throwing blood out of her chest. Somehow she survived despite multiple cardiac arrests. All of us saved her life responding to those arrests. We had RFDS planes but they were not big enough to allow much in the way of treatment when airborne like they are today, so patients had to be stabilised and then transferred.

Not long after this I was on call and a message came through that there was a gunshot wound on the way. We prided ourselves on not calling out second on-call doctor if we could help it, but this was worrying so there were two of us in the ED, two drips set up ready to run and all sorts of other stuff were "locked and loaded".

I was getting more anxious by the minute and wandered out to the waiting room where a 14-15-year-old boy was sitting.

I asked him what was up and he pointed to his knee and said "I have got a slug gun pellet in me leg."

I have mentioned how helpful nurses were and I particularly remember Sister McMillan who was in charge of the Paediatric ward and Sister Harding in the Medical ward.

As a medical student paediatrics is interesting but is only

for three months and covers all sorts of "Birds of Paradise" conditions. By this I mean if you look out your window you are likely see sparrows and sea gulls not "Birds of Paradise." Of course we have to know about leukaemia and its variants, brain cancer etc in children but what we most need to know is how to tell that a child is sick. This and obstetrics are where nurses are so valuable and can impart so much wisdom to young doctors if they will listen.

Sister Harding was a slim, busy, no nonsense woman. One of the most unpleasant tasks an intern cops is manual faecal removal. This occurs when old faeces can get hard and jammed in the rectum. If enemas fail these faeces must be removed piecemeal by an invading finger and this finger was usually on the end of a nurse's arm in Broken Hill.

One day on a ward round we found a patient like this and I said something like "He will need a manual removal." Sister Harding locked her eyes on mine and pointed clearly meaning "Your job sunshine."

I did not and still do not have a strong stomach for poo poos. I had a choice. Maybe I could refuse but it would not have been smart, no not smart at all. So I put on a gown three masks and two pairs of gloves and started the procedure but was gagging and dry retching into my mask.

She gave me an unmistakeable look and tossed her head all of which added up to "OK get out of here, I'll fix it." And I did and she did.

Peter and I were content, getting to know each other and

our colleagues and learning the things no one teaches you in medical school. We were well served by the other junior doctors, who were more senior to us medically speaking, in this learning process. Obstetrics was a pleasure. In metropolitan teaching hospitals only second year graduates would be employed, but here there were with only the GP Obstetrician and us to share the work.

Obstetrics can be terrifying but mostly babies and mums do what they are supposed to do, but one patient had a terrible time when she went home.

There is a story about a young man about to be a dad who asks an older workmate when sexual relations can be resumed after a baby is born. The answer was "Depends whether she is in a ward or a single room." I thought that was very much a tongue in cheek comment and had no bearing in reality.

I soon came to realise that indeed "Many a true word is spoken in jest." Sometimes to save tearing and severe damage to the vagina and further a controlled cut is made in a vagina during delivery to allow the baby to be born. This is called an "episiotomy" being about 3cm in the vagina and the same in the skin. This is then repaired. It looks awful but the tissues heal very quickly.

One patient was sent home in this condition and came back bleeding heavily. Her husband had intercourse with her and the stitches hurt him so he cut them out with a carving knife.

It does not take a lot of imagination to guess what the rest of their life was like.

Soon after this Peter and I had to go to Adelaide to attend the monthly meeting of the University of Adelaide's Council to confer our degrees so that we could be registered as medical practitioners in NSW.

Mum, Dad and Nana were there and a photograph of Nana and me I was published in the "The News." She was glowing with pride and rightly so as she had played such a big part in my life.

Mum and Dad took me to dinner and I found I had a taste for martinis. During dinner Mum noticed a picture of Leonore in my wallet and said "She is a lovely girl." I agreed and thought why is she in bloody Perth and I am here?

Without further ado I asked if I might use the reception desk telephone and rang Leonore in Perth, proposed marriage and was accepted with Leonore saying that she would come home as soon as practical.

Next day Peter and I returned to Broken Hill.

Soon after tragedy struck when Peter and a female friend had an accident when on a dark night they drove into the side of an ore train crossing the main Adelaide to Broken Hill road on its way to or from Port Pirie. She was killed and Peter died some weeks later in Adelaide.

This was an utter tragedy and saddened us all. I remember being very moved by his brother Bob who was an army officer, in full dress uniform, saluting Peter at the grave side.

It somehow symbolised the whole sorry saga and waste of two lovely people who would never have the life that so many of us have had. Two other doctors left so then there were only three of us to do the work of six.

MY WORLD CHANGED

Leonore and I were married at Saint Pauls Retreat in Adelaide on June 28 1969 only a short time after Peter was killed. I was nearly 26 and Leonore just 23 years old.

We sorted out any Catholic-Protestant difficulties that existed in previous generations without any fanfare and with the total support of our families.

We spent our honeymoon at Anglesea in Victoria. A time blighted somewhat by me losing Leonore's 21st birthday gift, an Oroton purse which held $100 of her holiday pay.

On our return to Broken Hill we moved into a brand new house in the hospital grounds.

Soon we had a little baby to care for, a female black Labrador puppy named Medea.

Work was tough. Every week day we worked from 0830 to 1800 and every third night were on-call. The day then started again at 0830.

Because we needed two of us about the place it also meant we each worked two weekends out of three so in six months I only had eight weekends off and Leonore worked some of those at the hospital.

Yes it was difficult but we were assisted as much as

possible by the nurses and others. Peter Heysen averaged 100 patients per day in the Emergency Department (ED) in the winter time and in the spring-summer roster I saw 80.

It is not quite as bad as it sounds for two reasons. One there was a health scheme of sorts where members paid two dollars a week or similar and could get free treatment and that extended to panadol. I remember a patient waiting seven hours to see me and all he wanted was some panadol, not that he was sick at all.

Secondly we were super well organised working from two offices with two nurses next to us. One would write prescriptions, the other blood tests and X-rays. The medical record was completed by the doctor.

When writing this I reflected deeply on just how lucky I was at the time. Of course I was excited about being married and all that entailed and kept busy with the work load. I can't imagine how I would have coped with Peter gone if Leonore was not there.

For the first but certainly not the last by far Leonore was a sanctuary at a stormy time for me.

SOME PATIENTS I REMEMBER

There were no vets in Broken Hill so we were often asked to see sick animals. We were not supposed to do this. The boss banned us for doing so but when his rabbit got sick I was only too happy to help and was rewarded with a lottery ticket from the Easter Bunny.

We were often required to do medical examinations for people who were suspected of drunk driving.

One young man brought in by the police for assessment and was polite, coherent, clean and tidy and admitted to drinking eight cans of beer.

I was puzzled to not find anything in his gait, neurological testing or anything else to say he was affected by alcohol. Later I had to appear in court as a witness at his hearing and was asked all sorts of questions. One was "Did you shine a light in his eyes?" "Yes I did". "What light?" "There are six penlights, four auriscopes, two angle-poise lights etc. It was one of those."

Next week in the paper the magistrate was quoted as saying I was an unreliable witness.

We were the first generation of medical students to study psychology in pre-clinical years prior to the usual psychiatry in final year. As graduates we were confident in diagnosing Anxiety and Depression as primary conditions rather than excluding organic causes for illness and leaving patients with a diagnosis of "brain rot."

We also had much more effective medications to use such as benzodiazepines (Valium etc.) and tricyclic antidepressants (Tofranil. Tryptanol etc.) to use for anxiety states and depressive disorders respectively. These drugs had only been around for 10 years so we grew up with them.

I did have time to see patients with complex conditions, do tests and follow up appointments in my time in ED because of the arrangements mentioned.

One was a woman in her mid-thirties who had severe migraines when menstruating. I spent some time with her and found out that some ghastly thing happened to her when she was 14-15 and her parents were tortured or killed when she was menstruating. We discussed the supposition that she was able to concentrate on the migraines, rather than the mental agony of her past.

The next time she had a period she had no migraine and I was so pleased for her and a bit chuffed with myself as well.

The next one she tried to kill herself. I had removed the crutch that she had used to cope with this unbearable experience.

I often think about this when I hear or read about friends helping people in emotional turmoil. Support and encouragement is desirable and safe. Interference and direction may not be.

Ernestine Hill wrote "The great Australian loneliness" in the 1930s after spending five years in the Australian Outback and I saw a living breathing example of this.

There is a "Dingo Fence" that wriggles its way from Dalby in Queensland 5600 km to the coast near Fowler's Bay in SA. This was built from 1880-85 to keep dingoes, an apex predator of ruthless efficiency, separate from defenceless sheep.

It requires maintenance obviously and people live a lonely life indeed patrolling it. It is not far north of Broken Hill and one day a man who patrolled this fence brought his child to see me.

The 9-10-year-old boy could not talk except in grunts and other sounds that his father could understand. He was examined by me and others and thought to have normal speech organs and the intelligence to speak but the processes were not functioning. Dad was taciturn and the little boy spent all day every with dad riding a horse up and down the fence.

My great grandfather worked and died in Broken Hill, Grandpa and Dad worked there for a time, Leonore's uncle spent his life there and we spent the formative years of my career and our marriage there so we owe it and love it a lot.

Last but very much not least there were two surgical registrars in my time at the Broken Hill, one was Peter Reid, GP surgeon from Broome, who I followed when he returned to that evocative place when my time was up in Broken Hill.

The second was Phil Houghton a Kiwi who just happened to be the first person since Captain Cook to circumnavigate New Zealand, in a sailing boat, a few years before and to write a best-selling book, "Land from the Masthead," about his journey.

Last but not least a Dr John Kerr, a doctor from Scotland came to work with us and boy was he welcome. His wife Jane was a physio and they lived next to us and we became good mates and later visited them at a place called Auchtermuchty in Scotland where he returned to work.

I did not realise that New Year's Eve or Hogmanay was the main event of the festival season for Scots but John ensured that we soon found out.

That New Year's Eve was the coldest and wettest New Year's Eve ever in Broken Hill and John was so pleased. He ran around all excited that Australia was such a wonderful place it even put on this great weather for them.

Interesting people abound in Broken Hill – always have and always will.

CHAPTER FIVE
BROOME

PERTH TO BROOME

I was pleased and excited to get a job as District Medical Officer in Broome.

As I mentioned before I had read a great deal about northern Australia and this fuelled the expectation that Broome would be picturesque, interesting, exciting and challenging for a young doctor.

After leaving Broken Hill Leonore and I stayed with my parents for a few days at Glenelg near Adelaide's airport. Soon we were in one of the planes we had hungrily watched climbing into the sunset heading for Perth.

The only sad thing was that I did not think I would see my Nana again and sadly I was correct. I had been so close to her all my life.

The day after we arrived in Perth we made an appointment with John Rowe, the head of rural medical services. He welcomed us warmly and ticked the boxes required for Leonore and me to work in Western Australia. He handed us an order book, the keys to a new Holden station wagon and told us to be in Broome in six days.

Leonore and I had known each other less than two years, had graduated married and on our way to live in one of the most exciting and beautiful parts of Australia. This was a major event in our lives and a forerunner of our lives to come.

We drove to Carnarvon and stayed for two days, then Exmouth and a short cut to Onslow where we stayed overnight. The short cut was long, sandy, hot and lonely. The beer in Onslow was one of the three best I have ever had. The next stop was Port Hedland in the grip of iron mining mania. We stayed a very pleasant two nights at the Walkabout Motel.

We had our Labrador puppy with us and she hid under our bed. It was very hot and we had the air conditioning running, the curtains drawn and we ordered gin and tonics,

The drinks were delivered by a young man who was about to put the tray on the bedside table. The puppy was curious and wriggled from her hiding place and knocked the drinks flying which scared her so she shot back under the bed.

The waiter must have been unflappable or perhaps having come from the blazing light of a forty degree day into a darkened room he did not see the lighting fast black dog and he put the tray down on the dog's head, silly fellow.

It was all was sorted out and he returned with replacement drinks.

Next morning rested, fed and watered we started the last leg of our journey to Broome.

It was 612km of dirt road from Port Hedland to Broome and there was nothing, repeat nothing, in between until the

Sandfire Roadhouse was built at the halfway point a year or two later. Spare fuel, water and food had to be carried.

We had a flat tyre repaired in Exmouth and had another flat about half way to Broome. Unfortunately we had left the jack in Exmouth.

Soon two guys came along driving a clapped out 10 to 12-year-old Holden. The two men were European. One was smooth, obsequious and spoke good English. The other was surly, unsmiling and silent. I was concerned enough about these guys to have a loaded rifle handy.

The first guy ran around unsuccessfully trying to use their jack and luckily some people in a Land Rover stopped. Their jack fitted and soon we were on our way.

Just before we took off our would-be rescuers asked us to follow them to Broome to see that they were ok.

I was uneasy about these two and they clearly did not want me to pass them as they were doing 100-120 kph, hogging the centre of the road and throwing masses of fine dust into the air. We did eventually pass them and as planned met Doctor Peter Reid in the bar of the Continental Hotel in Broome.

The two Europeans eventually turned up and asked me for a loan that they would re pay when in Darwin. When I explained that I had little money they suggested that a tyre or two from the Government car would do, but I would not come at that either so we parted - I did buy them a beer. They had tried to help.

When writing the above it dawned on me that, two years before, I had traded a carton of beer for a jerry can of fuel with an army truck driver at the Parachilna pub in the Flinders Ranges. He reckoned he could get much better fuel consumption than the army calculated so he should be allowed to share the benefits of the fuel he saved by being such a good driver.

PARADISE AKA BROOME

Broome is on the narrow Dampier Peninsula with Roebuck Bay to the east and the Indian Ocean to the west.

The dominant colours outside the green town with its white buildings were green-blue sea and the red sand known as pindan. The town was full of palm trees, flame trees, mangoes, frangipanis and many other tropical plants.

Broome had changed little since the height of the pearling industry before World War 2. There was Chinatown in the north, state housing in the south and the old town in the middle with the bungalows hidden by lattice with their large, colourful and cool gardens. Many of these were or had been owned by pearl masters. In bygone days these men were said to wear several changes of white suits a day and to have them laundered in Singapore.

The hospital and other government buildings were also in the central area. One of these was the post office, a magnificent building said to have been prefabricated for erection in the South African "Kimberley" but had found a home in Broome.

The hospital was in two joined parts, an old wooden tropical building with shutters and verandas and a new brick building, all painted white of course. There were an outpatient/emergency area, wards, operating theatre and delivery suite with a radiographer, a laboratory service and experienced staff.

We lived in a pleasant house in the hospital grounds with a nice garden that was maintained by the local guests of her majesty.

I soon met a Dr Landers the medical officer on board the HMAS "Moresby" a survey ship of the Royal Australian Navy that was operating form Broome. Interestingly that they had found Matthew Flinders' charts to be faultless.

We visited the ship and were privileged to be invited into the ward room, where even the Captain had to be invited by the junior officers. It was a wonderful night and finished with a game of wriggling through portholes. This silly little game had some validity in the real world of risk and danger. If a ship was sinking that may be the only way out and if you were too big...

The officers recounted the story of one of their band of brothers who was on the Australian destroyer HMAS "Voyager" when it was cut in half by the aircraft carrier HMAS "Melbourne" in 1964 and 81 people died. He was too big to get out and gave his life to push as many as he could through the portholes. Gee it's amazing how a story like that quietens a party.

One of the nice things about Broome was buying 20kg cartons of steak from the meatworks very cheaply. One night Leonore and I drove the hospital Land Rover to a nearby beach for tea. I managed to get it bogged well and truly with both differentials stuck on rocks. We decided to stay the night and had a little fire which burnt down to a bed of coals about the size of a lap top. We gently cooked two rump steaks on the coals and the often tough Kimberley steak melted in our mouths.

We invited some of the guys from the 'Moresby" to our place one night and while standing around a fire in the backyard yarning and having a few beers I told them my new way of cooking steak.

Of course everyone was suddenly hungry so steaks on the coals seemed a hell of a good idea. They were probably half the size of a laptop and this time the fire was more like the size of a car bonnet. Some steaks survived and were eaten but most were unsalvageable. Next morning our Labrador was sniffing around and happily ate the ruined steaks. All her life afterwards she would carefully search through a dead campfire.

In 1970 the multiple celebrations by the various national groups were joined into "The Festival of the Pearl" or "Shinju Matsuri".

The local dentist and I carried the drum in front of a ceremonial dragon that led the first parade.

We had certainly had settled in.

DOCTOR LIVINGSTONE IN A LAND ROVER

One of the first patients I had was Dr Reid who had cracked his pelvis in a car accident. He was a cranky bugger at any time but I did what he told me to do medically and he recovered. What a scary introduction to my first real job.

It became even odder one afternoon when I was home in the garden.

A man about 20 came through the gate. He was dusty, slim and was wearing jeans, a blue singlet, high heeled scruffy boots and a hat that had seen better days.

He said: "G'day doc me 'orse is crook, would you 'ave a look at 'im 'cos the vet's not 'ere".

I asked a few questions and it sounded like the horse might have a chest infection. I went to the hospital and picked up a stethoscope and followed the young man to the cattle yards.

There were three or four men sitting on the top rail of a yard wearing cowboy hats and riding boots with the heels hooked onto rails with roll your own cigarettes stuck to their lower lips.

They were looking at the sickest horse I have ever seen. He could barely stand up. His legs were splayed out, his head hanging down and he was breathing fast. I listened to his chest and heard a sound we call "creps" or nowadays "crackles" and this occurs in pneumonia.

I asked the audience if horses get pneumonia. Looks passed between these guys and one said "Yep". I was feeling chuffed and was about to give the horse some penicillin when a Holden station wagon pulled up in a cloud of dust and out jumped the local vet.

He was a rude bugger and barely acknowledged me but I was most impressed by what happened He roped the horse in some special way, pulled the rope and the horse fell over. Someone sat on the horse and the vet put a thing that looked like a rabbit trap in its mouth and twisted something to open the jaws and the horse's mouth and locked it. He then put his whole arm through the gap and dragged out handfuls of what looked like fibres of puss. I asked him the problem. He muttered "Lung abscess". I reckoned that was near enough to my diagnosis and left.

Soon after the "horsecapade" I was told to go to Cape Leveque north of Broome to vaccinate the lighthouse keeper and his family against small pox because some Indonesian fishermen had landed.

My boyhood dreams were coming true and I felt like Dr Livingstone albeit in a Land Rover.

We also called in to the nearby Cygnet Bay Pearl farm to see if any vaccinations were needed. We met the owners, Lyndon and Bruce Brown. It happened to be Bruce's wife Alison's 21st birthday and we were invited to join them and were entertained royally.

It was a beautiful night, warm with a full moon and we ate

oysters picked from the mangroves, turtle, blue bone groper and dugong.

We enjoyed the food and a drink of something and listened to a Robert Boyd play Blue Hawaii on an electronic organ. He was an interesting person, a jeweller by trade, travelling minstrel by choice and school friend of Lyndon.

This trip my wife and I shared made the difficulties I had at university and the insane work circumstances at Broken Hill melt away. We realised that we had a future full of love and hope and dreams as Kris Kristofferson might have said and indeed we have had.

Dr Livingstone's Land Rover now felt like a Range Rover.

SOCIAL LIFE AND A TENNIS VICTORY

The social life was excellent as there were so many people there for a short time. We joined the tennis club and met two very good players. One was Ann Watts who had played with Margaret Smith as a junior and had a large right wrist to show for it, and Morrie Dowsing who had beaten Lew Hoad in his youth. Some experts considered Hoad to be the best player of his generation or even one of the ten best players ever.

We made our own fun and one unforgettable evening the tennis group organised a silver service meal at Gantheume Point, over-looking the sea, near the famous fossilised dinosaur footprints.

After one tennis game we went to the pub and I was grizzling about playing women 20-30 years older than me. I was not much of a tennis player but I could play a few winning serves and shots at the net. I was reasonably agile and being tall I hit the ball hard on occasions.

The problem was that when I did that some ladies would jump out of the way and say I wasn't being fair. They of course ran me ragged hitting the ball out of my reach all the time and if I did not make the most of my opportunities I would never score at all.

I was rabbiting on and a bloke must have heard me say I was good out of context. He interrupted and bet $20 that he could beat me and I heard the Swan Lager say "Ok town court at 1700 tomorrow".

We both kept our words. $20 was worth maybe $200 today. As we walked onto the court in front of crowd of 10-12 people, I might add, the guy whispered out of the corner of his mouth "10 bucks". I hesitated about his offer for about a tenth of a second and agreed.

The game started. It must have been about the worst game ever played by two fit healthy young men in Broome. We were utterly pathetic, not even good enough to be laughable.

I was so tense and worn out running after these pathetic shots and returning equally poor shots and started getting bloody cramp in my leg. Oh the shame of it all.

We had to change ends and the guy said "Bloody hell mate I'm buggered you win" so I graciously agreed and I suspect we drank the $10. 100% success in a professional tennis career is pretty special.

A NIGHTMARE COMES TRUE

Someone once said: "If it sounds too good to be true it probably is."

Work, play, the climate and the place itself lulled me into a false sense of security and a nightmare, I once had, came true,

Four years before in 1966 as a fourth year student after a boozy night I attended a post mortem one Sunday morning at the Royal Adelaide Hospital.

Not really being keen on the post mortem I read all the notices on the walls and one, "Extracts from the Medical Act" was on a piece of fly specked card 20 x15 cm. Some words jumped off the page and buried them in my now alert brain.

ANY MEDICAL PRACTITIONER MAY BE COMPELLED BY A CORONER AT ANY TIME TO DO A POST MORTEM.

I felt disbelief, horror and fear at the time but life moved on.

This however was cut and four years later pasted from cyberspace to Broome.

A female taxi driver was returning a male passenger to his ship and drove off the jetty. He survived she did not.

Next day the search for her body started. This was deadly serious stuff. A giant groper, measuring 6 foot 8 inches and 680 pounds or vice versa, when it was later caught, lived under the jetty.

Many divers are more scared of big gropers than sharks. They have such a big mouth that they can just bite people in half or maybe eat them whole should they decide to do so.

The commercial divers would not dive so the police did and recovered her body. The oil rig supply boat, either "The Tasman Tide" or "Tasman Dawn" that found the taxi, was converted to a fishing boat in Port Lincoln and I can see it from my window as I write this.

I was and still am disgusted at the ghoulish behaviour of dozens of onlookers who parked their cars on both sides of the jetty interfering with emergency vehicles, having picnics and showing their kids the drama.

I went to the hospital and contacted the duty pathologist in Perth and asked him to come and do a post mortem as this was obviously a Coroner's case, it could even have been murder. He refused to come to Broome.

So it was up to me.

I went to the morgue and examined the body and found no obvious injuries. Although I was nervous I had attended maybe 20 post mortems so I did know what incisions to make and samples to send to Perth.

The Police Officer that attended as required was not there long before he sort of fainted and fell out through the door.

Later he attended his wife's confinement but the required forceps application had him falling out through another door.

Later I received a report, the details of which escape me, but essentially she died of something that I did not have to worry about.

Enough of this unpleasant stuff.

MISSIONS WORK

Every two weeks I did medical clinics at aboriginal missions run by the Catholic Church alternating between Beagle Bay and Lombardina in the north and La Grange to the south of Broome.

The missions' staffing was complex, with nurses, teachers, farm managers and others. There were clergy, religious and non religious people in the mix.

The missions all had livestock and vegetable gardens and provided good food and health care to their communities. The older children and adults were taught skills that they could use at the missions or elsewhere.

The children were clean, healthy, with clear shiny skin and abundant energy. They had routine blood tests and any parasites or anaemia were treated and examinations for head lice, skin sores and ear checks were made by nurses or the doctor on his monthly visits.

Many children had chronic ear infections with pus constantly running from their ears. Most of the severe ones had perforated ear drums. Sometimes 50% of the ear drum was a hole. The effect on hearing, learning and so on was obvious.

The nurse at La Grange used to syringe the ears of these children with water which was against normal practice but a visiting ear surgeon was most impressed that the ears were so clean he could repair the holes straight away with skin grafts.

These were fascinating places and I was told that Beagle Bay even paid its way ignoring the capital costs.

Times however changed and the church ceased to run these missions. Beagle Bay was managed by the church from 1890-2000, Lombardina 1911-1975 and La Grange 1924-1985.

I would interpret these latter dates as when the Aboriginal Corporations took over.

In the early 1900s a mother superior aged 25 and five or six trainee nuns aged 15 went to the Beagle Bay mission.

I worked with and was a friend and fishing mate of Phillip Cox in Broome. He remembered his grandfather telling him that he saw the nuns walking ashore through the surf, from a lugger, like "great white birds" because they wore and continued to wear habits and veils all their lives. This was a wonderful description because these French Sisters of Charity were and still are called "Butterfly Nuns" within the Catholic Church.

One of the great privileges I have had as a doctor was to care for the Mother Superior aged 95 and the sole surviving nun 85 who lived at the convent in Broome. Unfortunately they were unable to tell me much in the way of stories from their early days.

COWBOYS AND ROCKET TRACKS

On a trip to La Grange I was asked to call at Anna Plains to check the manager's wife who was pregnant.

This cattle station was owned by an American TV personality Art Linkletter whose show was telecast in Australia. He was a major developer of farm land in Esperance in the 1950s as well and died in 2010 aged 97.

Anna Plains is 250 km south of Broome and is nearly a million acres which really should be 1473 square miles (none of this decimal currency stuff for sheep and cattle stations thank you).

My wife and I drove onto the station track for a short distance and were stunned to see a shut gate belonging to the Commonwealth Government with "NO ADMISSION" , "STOP",

"TRESPASSERS WILL BE SHOT" (just kidding).

Scared we drove through the gate half expecting a guard to leap out of the bushes.

We then came across a most unexpected structure. In all its glory it was a 5000 feet (1524m) long bitumen airstrip (capable of landing any aircraft in the world I found out later) and a lot of buildings one of which someone told me had the longest bar in Australia.

This was Talgarno and was built as part of the British Australian Blue Streak project in the 1960s. The project was intended to protect Britain by producing an intercontinental ballistic missile (ICBM) capable of carrying an atomic warhead.

When that was abandoned it was hoped that the ELDO. (European Launcher Development Organisation) consortium at Woomera would use Talgarno to monitor the Blue Streak rockets that were to carry satellites into an equatorial orbit. That did not happen either. So it sat around "mothballed" for perhaps 20 years

Next stop was the homestead where we met Bruce Gray and his wife.

Bruce was a larger than life character who had been the manager at "Fossil Downs" near Fitzroy Crossing (bought in 2016/17 by Gina Rhinehart). He had the distinction of always sleeping in a swag on the floor and never in a bed. I guess he had a crook back.

It was a great time to be there as the stockmen (aka "ringers") were getting ready to go away for about six weeks mustering the 18,000 cattle on the place

There must have been about a dozen of them, many of whom were aboriginal and they were picking out the 10 or so horses they would take with them. Many also collected their mail and were opening their parcels from RM Williams ready to pack their swags each of which would be the owner's "house" for the next six weeks.

It was a very special experience indeed to see this preparation for mustering which, apart from the motor vehicles, had not changed since cattle were first run on large properties.

On Anna Plains and most if not all cattle stations salt

/corned beef is a staple and much nicer than any I have ever had from a butcher. Perhaps it is because butchers prepare theirs in brine whereas on this station at least the meat is salted (with a bit of sodium nitrite to keep the colour) and laid on stainless steel trays in a cool room for a certain time.

This was quite a weekend.

MORE NEW STUFF

Much was new to me in Broome and checking the crews of ships from overseas for smallpox was one of them. Smallpox was decreasing in the world and was declared eradicated in 1980 but it was still a risk in 1970.

There was an oilrig operating further off shore from its base than any other rig in the world and was so close to Indonesia that the crew had to go through the small pox checking process. I went to the rig once in a Wessex helicopter that was the second biggest in the world and could carry a platoon of soldiers with their gear.

On this trip there was only the pilot and I. Just after lift off from the rig he told me to hang on and opened throttles for the two jet engines to three quarters power and went vertical and fast. I swear I saw the edge of the earth. Before landing the pilot did a full sweep around Broome and I took many great pictures that I sent home to our parents.

Another customer was The "Centaur" a cruise ship that ran between Perth, Broome and Singapore and on the return voyage had to be checked for smallpox. The need for this was shown by the flying of a yellow triangular flag that could only be taken down when the health officer i.e. me said so.

Only two weeks before writing this I saw a TV documentary about Venice. The Venetians were the first to use a humane way of isolating actual or potential victims of the Black Death (Bubonic Plague) in a place where they were kept for 40 days. In Italian, "Quarantine" means 40 days.

So off I was doing something else new. I checked the vaccination records and the forearms of the crew where the blisters of small pox first appear in an infected person. When this was done the Captain and I would have a chat and a cuppa. The Captain was a portly English gentleman in an impeccable white uniform who could have stepped out of or into such a role in an English film.

One day things were radically different. We had sat down to organise the vaccination checks when a guy in a customs uniform and hard hat entered the cabin and said 'Good morning Captain, I am so and so, from the Australian Customs flashing his ID. Please instruct the crew to stand to in their cabins with their lockers open".

The Captain picked up the telephone and passed these orders to the purser and the Customs guy left. We talked about this for a short time and there was a knock at the door. A steward came in with a tray of tea, coffee and cakes.

The Captain was surprised and asked the steward why was he there with his tray. The term "looked like a stunned mullet" is an excellent description of the Captain's face when the steward answered, "Sir you ordered a tray of morning tea from the purser". Talk about misunderstanding. Such a degree of misunderstanding of an order would seem to be a serious and indeed dangerous thing to happen on a ship.

We all wore Seiko watches that a rather large enterprising Chinese man would arrange for us in Broome. It was said that when the customs guys boarded the ship they walked amongst the crew who stood with both arms festooned with watches presumably under their shirts. Rumour had it that many watches also went out the portholes but the customs were after bigger fish to fry.

Not long before this some other serious customs officers appeared from goodness knows where in a helicopter and boarded a ship that had been modified to drill for oil. Someone got a cutting torch, cut a hole in the funnel and pulled out a bag of drugs.

That night I was having a beer with Bruce Williams the Superintendent of Police and talking about this. I expressed my amazement about how clever they were finding the drugs.

He gave me a kindly and patient look and said "Peter, thieves fall out". He was a lovely bloke and he and his wife Gladys had a drink with all and sundry every night at the pub, a side of policing that has faded away, more is the pity.

SOME EXPERIENCES WITH THE POLICE

Another aspect of medical practice I became aware of in Broome was the close links between doctors, nurses and police. We share tragedies, laughter and life experiences at work and in our social, sporting, family and personal lives in small communities.

I have always had a positive view of police and nothing happened in my youth to change that despite being on the wrong side of police officers on occasions.

The first dealing I had with police in a work context was when acting as an intern at The Queen Elizabeth Hospital in Adelaide. I was picked up speeding and in explanation said I had been called to the emergency department.

The officer said that they would follow me so off I went with the police in close pursuit.

I was actually rostered to that department at the time so I thought there was a fair chance I would know someone and so I hatched my plan. Drive in and park next to the emergency entrance (imagine doing that today) jump out of the car and crash through the door a bit like a cowboy in a saloon. Seemed like a plan.

I stopped the car, leaped out and almost hit the police car that had pulled up alongside. I apologised to the two smiling young men and one said "Just as well we had a good time at a party with some nurses from here last weekend-see you later mate"

Later I was recounting this story and was told that a very senior specialist tried this trick about being called to the hospital and that is why he was speeding to have the policeman ask if he was called to the hospital why was he actually driving away from it!.

I also told Charlie Akkermans, an eye specialist, this story and boy did he top it. He was studying in Sydney and was sent to "harvest" a cornea for grafting. In other words a donor had died and Charlie had to remove the person's eye, put it in a jar with some special fluid and get it to the Eye Hospital quickly. He was speeding and picked up by a policeman.

The rough, tough Sydney copper must have thought he carried an eye around in a jar to trick coppers and actually followed him into the relevant department and watched him put the eye in the refrigerator. I do not recall whether he was pinched or not.

Anyway back to Broome where I had to get a driving licence on arrival so went to the Police Station where a policeman filled out the form for me because "How on earth would you know the one way streets in Perth sign here please?" Great public relations.

Yet another thing I had not done was to use the authority doctors have to admit someone to a Psychiatric Unit. There are a lot of different words around this but essentially it means that if a person is danger to themselves or others for reasons of impaired mental health then a doctor can require the police to transport that person to an appropriate mental health unit. Often the police initiate this process. Gee that was a mouthful!

A little aboriginal man had done something relevant so I filled out the appropriate forms and someone arranged for a rather large police officer and me to board a plane and sit with this man between us. He sat with a blanket over his head all the way. I had a syringe of something in my pocket but all went well and we delivered him to wherever it was in Perth.

I do not remember why but we had some time to kill in Perth and saw the movies 'Ned Kelly" with Mick Jagger, "Midnight Cowboy", maybe "Paint your Wagon" and "Easy Rider". The last film was about Peter Fonda and Dennis Hopper looking for America on their motor bikes.

They ran up against a small town sheriff who hated them and their free spirits and put them in gaol because there was some dope use and sexual hi jinx. They were kicked out of town and on their way they were literally blown away with shotguns by white trash vigilantes. It was awful, powerful and a hell of a shock.

I was certainly no lover of hippies but stunned and saddened by the ending. The policeman with me really meant it when he said "Pity that didn't happen to more of the bastards" that I thought was not a nice mindset for a police officer.

So I was a bit each way with the Broome Police but then I met 'Thirsty" Carlton or TC as he was known.

One night Peter Reid came to our place for tea. His car had been pinched that afternoon. Our dinner was a bush turkey that must have been the unluckiest turkey in history. Leonore had a few shots at a beer can. Maybe the turkey was attracted to the shiny tin but it flew into a bullet that hit its head and of course killed it. Now we were in a quandary because these are protected but I believe that if I kill something, fish, fowl, rabbit or kangaroo it should be eaten.

The turkey was in pride of place on the table when TC knocked on the door. I thought that we were in big trouble but he was there to tell Peter Reid that his unharmed car had been found.

I was standing in the doorway and TC said "Aren't you going to let me in for a beer" and I moved aside of course. His eyes lit up when he saw the bird and said "Bloody nice aren't they" and grabbed a beer.

I saw him here and there after that. We were both friends with a Gerry Faulkner who ran the laboratory at the hospital. Gerry and his wife Fran had two little girls and her third child turned out to be a boy. Clearly it was a perfectly good enough reason for a party.

Leonore was in Perth so I took our Labrador pup around to Gerry's place. When I left I probably drove a bit quicker than I should as there was no one around. When I got home I had forgotten the dog so back I went to Gerry's and home again.

The next day an irate lady reported to the police that a lunatic was driving around town back and forwards and disturbing the peace. The police officer asked whether she got the licence number to which she answered "Yes it was 123456". The police officer happened to be TC who wrote all this down and thanked the lady for the report.

My white Holden station wagon had a few bits and pieces on it different to all the others in Broome and a few days later the lady returned to the Police Station and again TC was on duty and opened the book and with pencil poised waited.

She told him that she had seen the errant car but made a mistake as the number was 123465. TC shut his book and patiently explained to the lady that too much time had elapsed to allow her to make another complaint – or something.

BROOME POSTSCRIPT

One way aboriginals fight is with boomerangs about a metre long with an asymmetrical bend i.e. there is a long straight section and a shorter end fashioned to have a bend of about 30 degrees. They are hard and sharp. I saw a man practicing with one at Cygnet Bay and it reminded me of someone relaxing with a seven iron and a few golf balls.

He stuck a long stick in the ground and took his boomerang about 50 metres distant and threw it at the stick, but not directly. If one imagines a clock face he was at six and the stick at twelve o'clock. He threw the stick in the direction of two o'clock. When it hit the ground it was moving very fast and spinning end over end and turning towards the stick. It finished 30-40 metres past the stick target. It missed the stick but would have caused serious injuries to a group of people had they been near the stick.

Soon after we left Broome the passions of those in a love

triangle at LaGrange had reached flash point. The participants were a young girl, an older man to whom she was promised and her young lover.

A duel with fighting boomerangs was arranged and was attended by most of the community. One of the boomerangs was thrown at an angle as described and hit an over enthusiastic spectator and badly damaged his eye.

An eye that is badly injured like this can cause a severe inflammation in the good eye that is likely to cause blindness. The treatment is to remove the injured eye or else the person may well become blind in both eyes.

Peter Reid was a pretty good surgeon so with some direction I am sure he coped admirably and the prompt action would have prevented damage to the uninjured eye.

CHAPTER SIX
PORT HEDLAND

INTRODUCTION

I was transferred by the Medical Department to Port Hedland after six wonderful months in Broome. I was sorry but on reflection, although it had been an exciting and novel experience in Broome, we had been to all the attractions, caught fish, experienced the ambience and to stay longer would only have been to repeat things whereas Port Hedland was a new experience.

Compared to Broome with its magnificent sandy beaches, cobalt blue sea, lawns and palm trees Port Hedland was certainly different. We had a crummy transportable house in a poor area with sand and weeds for a garden but we managed.

Port Hedland was dusty naturally but made worse by the pall of iron ore dust. Hundreds of thousands of tons of salt and iron ore were stored at the harbour area where there was a bewildering array of steel structures, conveyor belts, railway trucks, cranes, trucks, ships of course, other paraphernalia and personnel that would complete the transfer of iron ore from the inland mines into the waiting ships.

The Port Hedland infrastructure dealt with the ore from the then BHP owned Mount Newman operation. Across the harbour was a smaller operation at Finucane Island with an iron ore loading facility for the Mt Goldsworthy mine. In those days there were 30 million tons shipped out per year of which 23 million was from BHP. It is now little more than a million tons each year.

The work at the hospital was interesting and the staff capable, pleasant and in adequate numbers. Two people whose paths I crossed were Kingsley Faulkner and Ian Mitchell who both became surgeons in Perth and may have retired by now.

The hospital had operating theatres, a well-equipped Emergency Department, Delivery Suite, Radiography Department and Laboratory so we were able to do most things we needed to do.

Port Hedland also was the site of a Royal Flying Doctor Service (RFDS) Base so a transfer to Perth was an alternative way to manage patients and of course the RFDS brought patients into Port Hedland from surrounding areas such as Mt Goldsworthy, Marble Bar and the cattle stations.

We all shared on call status for obstetric, anaesthetic and emergency duties and also aero medical work with the RFDS.

The work was, as expected, with injuries, venereal disease and lots of babies and older children. Skin infections were rife in children and occurred almost always when they had been living in Port Hedland for six weeks when their immunity was overcome by new and more bugs and an hostile climate A lot of people chasing the iron ore dollar lived in caravans so that may have contributed.

People were well paid and I met a man who had been a foreman at the Brighton Cement works near where I had lived in Adelaide. He had been paid $3000 a year. In Port Hedland he was paid $10,000 dollars a year plus a subsidised house and transport to and from work.

My salary was a bit less than that but I was given a car and I paid about $20 a fortnight for rent and every so often got a cheque for travelling expenses from the WA government to defray this rent.

EXPERIENCES WITH PATIENTS – SOME VERY DIFFERENT
One of the highlights of Port Hedland was becoming lifelong friends with Lyn Phippard a nurse who I worked with and her husband Ian.

Ian came to see me with severe tonsillitis so as we often did in those days I sent him off to a nurse for an injection of penicillin.

For weeks later a female nurse friend of his and Lyn was noticeably cold and even rude to him so one day he asked her why and she really had a go at him for being such a bastard to his lovely wife.

He was speechless and calmed her down eventually and basically said "What the hell are you talking about"? Her comment was "I saw you in line with all the other buggers getting shots of penicillin for gonorrhoea. You do not deserve Lyn!"

When Lyn and Ian read this it will be the first time they will know it was a complete coincidence not the set up I have been telling them for 46 years.

There were two separate female patients that were unusual. One was a sultry sexy looking girl about 20 scantily clothed, in a singlet and brief shorts, which was not unusual in such a hot climate.

She complained of an abscess under her right arm so I asked her to sit on the examination couch which she did.

I stood up, walked over to her and gently lifted her arm with my left hand to look at her armpit. While doing this I rested my right hand on her right shoulder.

She looked at me in a knowing way, turned her head and gently kissed the back of my right hand.

I jumped back into my chair without touching the floor muttering and mumbling about incising the abscess or giving her antibiotics or something and probably wrote her a prescription. Not before or since have I experienced anything like that.

Some weeks later a demure school teacher came in for a smear test that I performed and then sat down at the desk to do the paper work.

I must be careful in my choice of words. She did not appear in any sense to be flirting and asked if male doctors found these examinations sexually interesting. We had a short discussion to my reply in the negative as it is not an uncommon question actually.

Anyway she tootled off and my eyes nearly popped out when I saw that she had left her panties behind.

A few days later she was showing some kids around the hospital and saw me in the corridor, went red in the face and said "Did I------?". My answer was "Yes". I have always regretted that I did not ask her how she found out that she was "going commando".

On the subject of females and indeed males Lyn was on duty in the emergency department one night and rang me about a young male and female who wanted some help to remove a potato that they had "mislaid" whilst playing hide the spud.

Lyn was more than happy to find and deliver the said spud.

Now for a change of gender.

I have a copy of a letter written by a patient from a ship delivered on 29th March 1971.

It reads in letters typed on an old typewriter with a worn ribbon

"Dear Doctor

Me Mr.------------------------who cannot speak very good English that's why brought this written to let you know from which disease I am suffering. I am passing urine every 3 minute and my organ is burning $$## at the end like hell--------and so on".

A clear history indeed of a common social disease.

I have not mentioned the conditions of work in the open cut iron ore mines. The ore was very high grade of about 50% which was why it was profitable to mine, rail and ship it as far as Japan. Iron ore was $7.35 a tonne let us assume. I was told that the profit was the 5 cents.

I was also told that the high grade meant that two iron ore rocks could be welded together.

The weather was fiercely hot in summer and once someone told me they could not pick up wooden handled tools. It was tough anywhere outdoors and particularly so in the crucible of an open cut iron ore mine.

Water and salt tablets were consumed in huge amounts but every now and then people would need to be admitted with what used to be called "Stokers Cramp" from salt deficiency and given some intravenous salt solution.

A patient I admitted for exactly this treatment asked to leave hospital relatively soon after admission for a most unusual reason.

He had bet $100 (about $2000 today) on Beer Street to win the 1970 Caulfield Cup and coupled it with many of the Melbourne Cup entrants to win the double.

Beer Street won the Caulfield Cup and my patient had 20 or so horses running in the Melbourne Cup that he had coupled with Beer Street.

The bookmaker in Melbourne who held the bet faced some huge pay outs so he contacted my patient and asked him to go to Melbourne and he would reduce the odds on his bets and re-arrange them so that he had bets on all the horses in the race and couldn't lose.

The smallest collect he could get was $5000. I was earning $150 or so a week and a Holden car was $3000 so $5000 had to be worth somewhere near $100,000 today.

As it happened Bagdad Note won the Melbourne Cup and the man won $5000 the smallest win but the horse was not in his original bet.

I suppose the above stories have some degree of entertainment value and earn a wry smile but the next one just should not happen and is one of the worst and most sickening things I have seen.

An Aboriginal boy about 10 came to see me one day and I asked him what was the trouble. He said "I got a fly in me eye" and sure enough that is exactly what it looked like.

It was however far from being that simple. The lad had brown eyes and the "fly" was a piece of the iris or coloured part of his eye poking through a hole in his cornea. The cause was severe conjunctivitis from gonorrhoeal infection caught from washing in a communal bucket. There were two or three other babies admitted with this but they did not progress further than having pussy eyes that we fixed up.

The mini epidemic was cured by putting holes in the bucket and using it as a shower. We sent the lad to Perth and I do not know what happened as I left Port Hedland soon after.

GOLDSWORTHY

Soon after we arrived in Port Hedland I was asked to fly to the mining town of Goldsworthy with its few hundred people and do clinics once a week that soon became twice. There was a small medical centre with a male and two female nurses and they were very good.

The RFDS provided twin engine Beechcraft Baron Aircraft to ferry me back and forth to Goldsworthy that was 100km or so away from Port Hedland.

This worked out really well for me. I saw as many as 35-40 patients a day mostly women and children. Some pregnant women had seen seven or eight doctors during the course of their pregnancy so they appreciated a more stable medical service. I consulted there for more than eighteen months and enjoyed every minute.

Very early in the Goldsworthy consulting I saw a Canadian woman who was pregnant. I asked if she had any other children and she said that she had one little boy who was two or three and naturally I asked her obstetric history. It was absolutely awful story for mother and child. I felt myself going into denial that this lady was even there let alone pregnant and wanting me to manage her pregnancy.

She had been living in Guyana in South America and became ill with renal failure and was flown home to Canada. She and her baby had all sorts of complications and I was goggled eyed. Anyway we reached an agreement that I would look after her but she would go to Perth if I said so.

I watched her very closely and actually checked her urine that wasn't done in South America and she had an uneventful delivery of a daughter on 11th April 1971. Leonore and I became great friends with the family as did Ian and Lyn and we did many things together in SA and WA mostly involving fishing.

I used to have a cuppa with she and her husband them after lunch when I visited Goldsworthy. One day he and I we were idly perusing a Playboy magazine as one did for well written interesting articles.

She asked me if I had ever seen women with breasts like the Playboy pictures and I said I had not. Somehow we got around to talking about beautiful women and she told me about a South American friend who had done well in the Miss Universe or some such competition and later married Michael Caine.

About 10 years ago I read his autobiography "What's it all about?" and that confirmed their marriage.

He describes that when he first met her he was drinking two or three bottles of Vodka a day and that it was a bit hard to keep count but within a short time he only drank wine at dinner sometimes. A lovely story compared to what might have been.

My visits to Goldsworthy whether for work or pleasure were usually simple and uncomplicated but every now and then we were reminded again that the people one meets in the outback can be different.

Our first child Kirstin Ruth Marie was born uneventfully at Port Hedland on 2nd December 1971. I was in Goldsworthy that day and on our return announced her birth over the aircraft radio operated by Flight Service to the aviation world.

We arranged to spend Christmas day with our friends in Goldsworthy and rang to let them know when we left Port Hedland with our baby as we had no air conditioner in the car and of course it would have been around 40 degrees C.

For some reason Leonore was driving. When we reached the Goldsworthy turnoff there was a car stopped on the side of the road with two young men standing alongside it looking worried.

I told Leonore to stop but keep the engine running and leave the car in gear with her foot on the clutch. They were polite, well spoken tidily dressed lads and had run out of fuel. I had 20l of fuel that I considered giving them but as I mentioned elsewhere there was nothing between Port Hedland and Broome so all that the fuel would do was get them 20l distance further into trouble, so I told them to follow me into Goldsworthy. By this time our friend had reacted to our slight delay and was leading a pall of dust towards us so we headed off.

We met at his place and dropped mother, baby and dog and my mate and I went to the wet canteen to see TC my copper mate ex Broome and ex Fitzroy Crossing.

I told him about the boys and how sad it was that they were in the middle of nowhere on Christmas Day, a long way from their families, blah blah. TC reacted like a Labrador dog hearing the refrigerator door open-all business like and ready to go. "What was the number of the car", "What were they wearing", "Height weight etc."

I said something like "C'mon mate they are nice young fellas stop carrying on like a copper". I had no sooner said that than a guy rushed into the canteen yelling "Where's the copper some bastard has drained me petrol tank". TC looked at me with a little smile and raised one eyebrow.

We had a few beers and eventually he wandered over to a HF radio or the telephone and rang the Broome Police Station where they were inevitably heading.

Oh by the way it was the third car they had pinched since Perth.

While on the subject of different people, male nurse Ted from the Goldsworthy Medical Centre ran into a couple.

He was a pleasant English gentleman and devoted scout and often drove the ambulance to Port Hedland hospital from Goldsworthy via the Port Hedland –Broome Highway.

Once on a return journey he picked up two young women hitch-hikers. When he reached the Goldsworthy turnoff he stopped to let them out but that did not suit them at all. They suggested that he take them to Broome and they would take it in turn to share the driving and to entertain him in the back of the ambulance. I thought that they must have had a guitar or something.

Later my education went up a notch when someone told

me this was known as a ride for a ride and quite a common way of girls getting around.

Also getting around at the time was a penicillin resistant strain of gonorrhoea called "Vietnam Rose". Probably they travelled together.

ON A DARK AND STORMY BLOODY NIGHT

One of the RFDS pilots was a Dick Coxon and we hit it off really well and became firm friends for many years until he died in 2008. He taught me a lot about Western Australia and flying.

I made about 200 flights in those Barons to Goldsworthy and other places and for a time had lessons for a pilot's licence but was due to go solo when our daughter was born. Another time I was to fly solo I needed to deliver a baby. Then we went to Woomera so I gave up my dreams of being a pilot.

Most of the flights with Dick and the other pilots were uneventful but once we were relaxing at our place in Port Hedland looking south at the thunder storms in the Hammersley Ranges. There were five or six repeated bolts of lightning taking up an arc of about 30 degrees.

Next thing we knew we were heading right smack bang into it to pick up someone from an accident and take them to Perth.

Many times I have heard and read the pilots' axiom of reading your instruments not follow your senses. Dick was busy working out things and I held the steering wheel of the plane. I seem to remember that there are two instruments I was watching. One shows the wings of the plane relative to the ground and the other the ground relative to the plane or something like that and I was gently turning the plane so that the wings were heading towards vertical but I did not feel a thing was wrong. Dick soon righted it and we flew on.

To state the blindingly bloody obvious to get a plane onto the flat bit of land past the pointy hard bits called giant rocks in a dark and stormy night demands skill and concentration to create a path that turns and descends to put your plane into a landing position.

Ok Dick did all that and was lined up to land when the bloody light showing that the landing gear was down and locked did not go on.

Dick had to put power on and climb away from the hard bits.

The air strip lights were car headlights on the side of the strip. We had to get down again so people could have a look to see if the wheels were down. They were and we landed safely. There was a little something that interfered with the indicator light but we were not to know so I took up a crash position.

When we got to Perth and to a pub it was daylight. We had run out of cigarettes and I bought six packets. God knows why.

Funny things one remembers. I was interested in the instruments, flight planning and so on. We put the flight plan in and there was a huge map with Australia in the middle,

Indonesia at the top and the Antarctic at the bottom. I was gobsmacked as I had never seen anything like it before. A few years later it was on everyone's TVs.

One of the things pilots have to do is identify landmarks and what time they plan to reach them so that if they do not call in at the appropriate times search responses are cranked up.

Dick was very cool in the air. South of Port Hedland he radioed his call sign and said "Abeam Strelley" (a sheep station). I asked where the hell it was. His response was to look at his watch and say "It must be there somewhere" in other words if the flight plan said he was supposed to be somewhere at a certain time then that is where he would be –simple.

SHIPS AND THINGS

Port Hedland was and is a major port in Australia. How quickly it was growing became very obvious from the time we arrived until we left about 18 months later.

When I started driving along the Esplanade to and from work there would be several ships at the anchorage waiting to come into port to load. I soon realised that they had, say, 40-60,000 tons capacity. Then a bigger one would appear of 100,000 tons and soon they were all 100,000 tons and getting bigger. The biggest in my time was the Fukakawa Maru at 160,000 tons. I believe that they are now 200-240, 000 tons but the progression from 160 to250,000 tons took a long while compared to what I saw. Interestingly the crew numbers went from 30-40 or more to 20 odd in my time - from 1970 to 1972.

These ships had to be checked by customs and have smallpox checks as explained in the Broome chapter most of which were done by the Senior Medical Officer, but I also did some.

It certainly was interesting. I walked across the top of an engine and the cylinders must have been close to two metres across. The holds were truly huge. 100,000 tons is a load 5000 big semi-trailers would carry.

We were well treated and I remember one occasion when I was walking along a passage with the customs guy a few meters behind me and a Japanese guy appeared in front of me and pushed something into my abdomen that was a bottle of Johnny Walker Black. I would have had on a shirt and shorts so how I hid it I do not know.

I used to wear thongs (the shoe kind!) all the time which was stupid when I had to climb the gangplanks that were nearly vertical when these behemoths were empty and I was quite scared climbing them.

If it was five o'clock or later I would be offered a drink that usually came in the form of a high ball glass full of Johnny Walker Black. This temporarily cured my fear of heights going down the gangplank of course.

There were a couple of strange things happen. One was an Australian radio operator, from a Greek ship, who had some pretty dodgy, possibly, maybe, perhaps, cardio vascular symptoms. As he was heading off in a ship, I owed him a decent diagnosis so admitted him for tests and monitoring.

The Greek skipper went ballistic. He was a prickly little guy, cocky (reminded me of the actor Gilbert Rolland whom some really old readers might remember) and very macho as ships' captains can be.

But I was the captain here and said that the radio operator had to leave hospital as they needed two radio operators by law. In an attempt to be helpful, I suggested that if they had one surely someone else could keep an eye on things and answer the radio "Alpha Bravo Charlie reading you loud and clear stuff". He spat "Morse code they have to know Morse code". I think the captain was correct in that he wanted to get paid off the ship but I stood my ground reluctantly.

The next day I was home in the garden and the captain appeared having been on the phone to Greece. He was no longer swarthy. He was white and shrunken and pleaded with me to discharge the guy which I did as his observations were fine.

The other situation was different. The customs people and doctor usually boarded the ships in port but for some reason the powers that be decided to trial a small helicopter to land on the ship while anchored and drop off the customs people and the pilot.

The first day they tried this there was an ill and bedridden crewman so I went along to see him instead of him having to wait a further 15 hours or so.

I went to his cabin and with the aid of a Japanese guy who translated and obtained a good history of pneumonia and this was confirmed by examination of his chest. In a small area there was a specific sound audible with a stethoscope that occurs in pneumonia. He did not have a high temperature nor was he breathing fast He seemed quite comfortable and was taking appropriate medication.

We would have needed two trips to take the customs guy, me and the patient to shore as the helicopter was quite small and more importantly he seemed happy and secure with his countrymen.

As promised. I returned to the ship next morning and was taken to his cabin to find it empty and whoever took me to the cabin said that no one had been there sick or otherwise.

What had happened to him I just do not know. I am as sure as I can be that he would not have died from his complaint. Perhaps he worsened and was moved and like the Greek skipper they had to have him on board.

Last of all a ship had hit a buoy marking the channel. These were cone shaped with three or four vertical steel members running from a circular steel tank three or four metres in diameter (this acted as a float and was anchored to the bottom with chain) to meet at the light on top of the structure.

The ship had damaged one or more of the vertical braces so it was brought alongside the wharf to be lifted ashore by a crane and repaired.

The tidal range is several metres and it moves quickly in and out. The wharves are high so there was quite a distance between the end of the crane arm and the top of the buoy therefore a possibility of a lot of leverage if things were not arranged just right and they were not. The tide was moving out so the buoy started to as well and overcame the holding capability of the crane which tumbled over the side into the water. The crane driver dived out of the crane and was unharmed.

Last of our adventures was a cyclone that we thought was fun. Our nursing friends from the house opposite came to our house. We filled the bath with water, got torch batteries, food and most importantly beer and had a pleasant time.

I do not recall being scared in any other storms I had experienced in my life that, at worst, felt like they might dislodge a shed roof, or maybe a scrap of wood or iron might get blown away or a tree up rooted when the wind gusted.

In that cyclone there was a feeling of enormous, remorseless and invincible power and a feeling that if anything let go everything would.

There was some minor flooding and a few cars were sandblasted on their windward side and one caravan was tipped over. A few years later there was a much bigger one and the hospital was severely damaged.

On the subject of cyclones I was stunned to learn that 'Tracy" in late 1974 was a category four. God only knows how destructive a category five would be.

We had some wonderful times at Port Hedland, made good and long term friendships with the Phippards with who we keep in close contact, and also with Dick and Cathy Stedman and Dick Coxon who are unfortunately no longer with us. I also keep in touch with Tiffany Stedman who I had delivered as mentioned on April 11th 1971.

Port Hedland though was a tough place to live in many ways and not somewhere we wanted to spend a long time so when the opportunity to leave came we took it. Our little baby girl was making us homesick for civilisation.

CHAPTER SEVEN
WOOMERA

INTRODUCTION

We flew to Adelaide from Perth on holidays and on the way I read an advertisement seeking a general practitioner for Woomera.

My wife liked the idea and in a day or two later we were interviewed by Dr Allen Green, the Commonwealth Director of Health in Adelaide. We visited Woomera and were offered and accepted the position.

We returned to Port Hedland and collected our two Labrador dogs, other belongings and returned to Adelaide and then Woomera in early May 1972

The British were on the bones of their backsides after the war. But they became the early drivers of the atomic bomb, before the war, because they realised sooner than most the need for these weapons and had the physicists to do it.

Geographic, security and financial necessity resulted in the work being done in the USA and despite all sorts of agreements the Americans took over the project and even excluded Britain from any post war co-operation.

Russia first exploded a nuclear bomb in 1949. At the end

of World War 2 they had captured many of the German scientists and facilities where an atom bomb was or perhaps soon would have been built.

The Russians also had a covey of spies in Britain such as physicists Nunn May and Fuchs who even worked in the Manhattan Project that, with British expertise initially, detonated the prototype of the bombs that destroyed Hiroshima and Nagasaki in 1945.

Despite their parlous economy, it was the fear of a war with Russia and the USA casting them adrift that drove Britain to develop their own weapons. Woomera and later Maralinga were built to test these weapons by the British and Australian Governments.

In 2015 or 2016 I read a chilling interview about those days with the pilot of a British V Bomber. These were the aircraft that would have attacked Russia with nuclear weapons in the event of war. He was briefed to not bother coming home because once hostilities had commenced there would be nowhere left in Britain for him to go.

At the time of redrafting this section 1n 2017 or 2018 Elizabeth Tynan, the author of "Atomic Thunder," was interviewed on the ABC. She was critical of the poor safety practices and slap-happy way the British cleaned up the test site at Maralinga. The comments of the pilot quoted above help to understand why. I read that book and highly recommend it to anyone who wants to get to know more about these times.

While I am on about books "Fire across the Desert" by Peter Morton (no not me, he is an historian from Flinders University in Adelaide) is the definitive history of Woomera.

Britain demonstrated V bombers in Australia in the 1950s and Dad must have spoken to an ex RAAF mate and we went to the Mallala airstrip north of Adelaide to see this plane. Mum, Dad and I sat in wooden chairs on the tarmac with the VIPs.

The aircraft flew low and was silent but boy oh boy it made a thunderous roar when it reached us and the pilot poured on power to climb almost vertically. I can remember seeing the fear on people's faces. There were no jets in civilian use then so this would have been the first time that most of the people had heard a jet plane's noise

Woomera was a closed town with Commonwealth Police guarding all the gates at all hours. Only pass holders were allowed in or out except for emergencies.

The population was about 5,000 while short range missiles were still being tested but then went into decline. And although Woomera provided support for the United States Air Force (USAF) base Narrungar its importance was waning.

The USA had operated a tracking station on a trailer from 1957 until the NASA Deep Space station was established at Island Lagoon 25km south of Woomera. It operated from 1960 until 1972.

Together with other stations in Australia, which formed

an arc that stretched from and included Canberra and Carnarvon, Island Lagoon played a major role in the preliminary satellite launch programs which had led to the moon landing in 1969.

My job specifications were unusual. I was a Commonwealth Medical Officer (CMO) and performed medical examinations for all sorts of things, managed Workers Claims and cared for in-patients. For this I received a salary.

There was also was a limited right of private practice as a general practitioner when seeing patients who were not admitted to hospital.

There were three or four doctors in my time from 1972-75, one being a specialist surgeon. The Senior Medical Officer was Arthur Morphett, a truly lovely person and doctor whom I knew from school and university.

The work was variable and enjoyable with a mixture of nationalities and for the first time for me included private patients. The patients were younger than those found in the waiting rooms of most general practices because only employed people and their families could live at Woomera

I did minor surgery in outpatients, one caesarean section under supervision, tubal ligations and assisted our chaps and visiting surgeons. I was keen on doing or helping with surgery but I feared and disliked giving anaesthetics as it was like being a pilot with long periods of boredom interrupted by moments of sheer terror.

Giving anaesthetics was not the only clinical situation that could provoke that state of affairs though. One Saturday afternoon I was called to the hospital to find a patient sitting on the casualty operating table.

He was drunk, having a severe asthmatic attack and one leg was moving sideways because of a fractured tibia and fibula. An unusual clinical situation it may be safely said and one where there were so many ways it could go "pear shaped".

He was given Ventolin for asthma and his leg straightened under intravenous Valium and admitted with huge relief from all concerned.

Another patient with an unusual illness was a lady around 35-40 who was brought to hospital lying on her back, not moving, speaking or responding to our voices or mild painful stimuli with her eyes closed and quite calm in appearance. Detailed neurological and general examinations were normal. She was from the USA.

Somehow we reached the diagnosis of a catatonic state although stupor and hysteria were just as likely. She was closely observed in this state for a few days and then literally opened her eyes and got out of bed and soon went home.

Most Americans really loved the wide open spaces but some spouses found being so far from home and family very stressful. This was her way of turning off for a short time to recharge her batteries.

The next drama was the death of a woman and injury to

her husband and child in a car accident. I took her husband to Adelaide on a RFDS plane and returned the next day.

Oh no. Not another post mortem. Fortunately the multiple fractures revealed by X-rays were accepted as a cause of death by the coroner. I arranged her funeral and sorted out her son's problems AND I sorted out the 22 $50 notes and three plastic bags about the size of a cigarette packet full of opals found on her husband. A thank you note, carton of beer or paying my bill would have been nice but none of them happened.

Despite the rarity of the above clinical situations the weirdest happened soon after I arrived. An Eastern European man was in a minor car accident and came to the hospital to be checked out. Woomera was a prohibited area and this was possibly an attempted illegal entry.

He was interviewed in Security Officer Brian MacDonald's office in my presence with Brian asking all sorts of questions. A bottle of Canadian Club whiskey appeared and the three of us had a few tots to loosen our tongues particularly his. I do not recall any espionage being discovered but years later Brian was still angry that he wasn't reimbursed for the whiskey.

Another memorable event involved a Canberra Bomber that was on a training exercise to Alice Springs and back when on approach to land discovered that the left landing wheel had not locked down.

Although Woomera had fire engines a larger one was

always sent from Salisbury when operations like this were on. Just as well civilian flights did not have any accidents!

The bomber flew around for a while to use fuel and allow us to get ready down below. The ambulance with me aboard, the big Salisbury fire engine with a water cannon on the cabin roof and the Woomera unit waited in a taxi way and as soon as the plane went past roared out onto the runway where foam had been laid.

The pilot was fantastic and somehow he kept the left wing off the ground until he came almost to a halt and tipped the wing into the foam.

The big fire truck beat us to the scene and was busy squirting foam from the cannon all over everything. Our fire crew would not be denied and drove up to the plane the crew leaped out, ran towards the plane pulling the fire hose, stopped, pointed the fire hose and pulled the trigger but nothing happened.

The fireman looked at the nozzle, shrugged his shoulders and looked quizzically at their fire truck to see foam spewing out under the truck. He then chucked his hose on the ground and went to watch the big guy doing its stuff. And yes I have pictures of it all.

The pilot and his offsider were admitted to hospital. They had done the bit where the pilot told the navigator to eject and getting the reply "I will stay with you skipper" but they were clearly anxious about it all and were talking a lot. Our surgeon asked if they would like a drink and their eyes lit up.

When the matron was asked to get some tea or coffee their faces fell only to look much happier when I added "Please bring the hospital brandy as well". Imagine that today.

One last interesting thing happened in those early days and that was to me! Woomera had open, public, illegal gambling with six or more bookmakers lined up along a veranda with betting paraphernalia such as bags, boards and so on describing the horses and the odds-on race days.

Pay nights had a different way for punters to invest and that was Crown and Anchor or other dice games. These games were held in a toilet block. There was a trestle set up across four toilet cubicles with the doors open and the game organisers plying their trade from the cubicles, flogging nice cold beer to the punters and running the dice games..

I was a loser and wandered off home at 10-11 o'clock. I was stunned when the guy who ran the game later knocked on our door and sheepishly gave me back my money.

He had been sprung by Brian MacDonald, my Canadian Club drinking mate from security, using crooked dice and advised of a path to redemption that he followed.

All too soon my friend Arthur returned to his substantive position as a CMO in Adelaide at the end of 1972. He later became a Pathologist so the position of Senior Medical Officer (SMO) was available.

I wrote a nice letter to Dr Green, the Commonwealth Director of Health in Adelaide, asking to be made the SMO now please as Arthur has left.

He was a scary sort of man at first experience and whether he rang or wrote left me in no uncertain terms that a job application did require a tad more information. Naturally I complied and was appointed to the position.

Dr Green introduced me to the structure and functions of the Commonwealth Health Department in practice and in theory. He was also a practicing Dermatologist, a branch of medicine I liked and he was helpful with that as well.

Ed. Arthur has retired now and looking forward to reading this book he recently told me.

A NEW WORLD

Woomera had been run on military lines with a high ranking military officer as Range Superintendent but this changed with the arrival of Frank Lucarotti as Area Administrator. Frank had been an RAF officer in World War 2 so the powers that be had a bit each way.

Woomera was a testing site and part of the Weapons Research Establishment at Salisbury in Adelaide. I suppose I was answerable to the Area Administrator and the Commonwealth director of Health in South Australia for medical matters.

One of the things that persisted from the military days and worked well in my opinion was the system of messes. There were the Senior and ELDO, (more later about those initials), Staff and Junior Staff messes equivalent to Officers, Staff (meaning Warrant Officers and Sergeants) and Junior Mess for

Other Ranks in the services.

Entry was determined by position in the workforce and was rigid. I think that I was the only person to belong to both the Senior and ELDO messes for a short time.

In my new position I was in charge of the hospital i.e. a Department Head and that meant a lot to me financially and socially.

I received a significant rise in salary probably from $7-8000 to $14-15000 as I now was a certain level of Medical Superintendent.

Allen Green I mentioned organised a week in Adelaide for me to check out the Repatriation Department and Hospital and other areas including a Caravan Park and rubbish dump.

Every Monday I attended a meeting of about six Department Heads. These people were all very senior public servants and I picked up a lot of knowledge just seeing how they operated.

Jeff Heinrich; the father of Chris, the catapult driver from TQEH when we did obstetrics, was the second in charge of WRE and a frequent visitor to Woomera and he gave me some good tips on public service administration.

I had access to all sorts of people. At the mess one evening there was a guest from Canberra. I recognised his name at the time but cannot recall it. He had written a report on Indonesia's threat or otherwise that became Australia's policy position. He actually explained some of it to me. Later I thought about working in Botswana and wrote to him. He replied with a detailed written brief about that country.

Soon after this appointment I decided to study Medical Administration and thoroughly enjoyed it. I really liked the subjects as they were so utterly different to anything I had done at school or university. They included organisational dynamics, motivational theories, legal subjects particularly about negligence and the "average man", accountancy, statistics, epidemiology, political science and so on.

I could discuss these subjects with many people and that was an enriching experience. One of the Americans who managed a company tied up with the USAF had been to courses run by the doyen of management consultants Peter Drucker and gave me one of his text books with "Perception is Reality" written in it.

That is a fact and a concept that I have used and thought about thousands of times and has underpinned my life and work in many ways.

WOOMERA WAS DIFFERENT

Frank Lucarotti, the Area Administrator had been a railway engineer in India, Africa and the Pilbara in Western Australia immediately before moving to Woomera. I had reason to be glad that he had that overseas experience in the railways because the companies in India and Africa sent new people "up country" for a look see.

Applying this to Woomera he sent me out with the Range Overseer, Tony Jay, on his yearly range inspection. That was something rare and special because it was a prohibited area and only WRE people could travel those fabled roads that the famous Len Beadell had built in the 1950s and 1960s.

This was incredibly exciting and interesting. Tony Jay was a pilot in World War 2 and was in charge of Australia's heavy bombers with the rank I assume of Air Vice Marshall.

He came from a well-known sporting and medical family in Adelaide and I had played football with his nephew Michael. Before he was posted during the war he was presented with a set of matching "cut throat" razors by none other than Sir James Holden whose company built the first Holden car known as the 48-215 in 1948.

Where ever he went the Japanese arrived quickly. So quickly that on one occasion he did not even have time to pick up his razors when he fled.

He was unwell after the war and spent some time in hospital and very early in the life of Woomera went there as the third Range Overseer.

He also piloted the first aeroplane to land on the Emu clay pan where the first Atom Bomb test took place on the Australian mainland. Earlier testing was done at the Monte Bello islands hear Onslow in Western Australia.

Tony's job was liaison with sheep and cattle station owners or managers in the vast prohibited area in the north west of South Australia.

There was an arboretum at Woomera where house holders could get plants to make their yards more attractive than the fenced flat, rocky, sandy saltbush surrounds of Woomera known as "donga".

Tony took thousands of the plants to stations on his rounds and that is the reason for some beautiful gardens today,

The trip was a serious venture. There were four people in two long wheel base Land Rovers with long range tanks and high frequency radios which we were required to use at certain times to let Woomera know where we were. These contacts were called "scheds" pronounced "skeds".

We headed down the line of range in a north westerly direction to the Stuart Highway and then north to Coober Pedy and camped on Mabel Creek station about 40km west. The next day we passed through the dog fence.

This fence is 5500km long and runs from the centre of Queensland to the west coast of South Australia near Fowlers Bay. From Sydney to Perth is just over 4000km. The fence is designed to keep dingoes away from sheep.

West of the fence there is an area the about a million square miles with nothing except some aboriginal settlements and geologists' camps. The line of range is north-west or 270 degrees and crosses the coast of Australia about a third of the way from Broome to Port Hedland as mentioned in the chapter on Broome.

Immediately after the gate in the dog fence there were tracks of a cow and calf and a dingo heading west. Those tracks (and us) followed a set of wheel ruts over the sand hills at an angle for 240 km to the Emu clay pan.

There was an old drum of petrol and with Tony's approval I fired a .303 bullet into it. I was most disappointed when all that happened was a leaking .303 inch hole.

We camped at Emu and the next day headed due south to Maralinga, 250km away.

En route we stopped at a place Len Beadell found when he was making all the roads in this India-sized piece of the Australian Outback. .

The area was maybe 2-3 acres with a flat central area and layers of shale of increasing height maybe two metres high in all. It had the appearance of a little stadium with seats about one third of the way around the flat area. On the flat parts were structures made up of two or three or more pieces of shale 40-50 cm by 10-15 cm leaning against each other with another piece of shale across the top. There may have been 20-30 built seemingly at random on the different levels.

No one has been able to explain them. There was no road before Beadell so a joke would seem unlikely and aboriginal people have denied any knowledge.

I took my sons there 10 years or so later and sadly there had been a lot of damage.

25 years after I was there I was the Port Lincoln prison doctor and asked a young Aboriginal man about this place and he seemed to know about it. I had patients waiting so I asked him to come back the next week, but when he did he denied any knowledge or even the previous conversation. So

maybe it is not ignorance but silence.

Tony had taken people from the CSIRO there and they found, with great difficulty, a match box full of charcoal for carbon dating. One of the scientists carried it back to Melbourne and was walking to work from the Flinders Street railway station through perhaps the busiest piece of bitumen in Australia when he dropped and lost the precious charcoal.

Back to the track and yes the three sets of animal footprints were still visible, but they disappeared 50km from Maralinga where there was a bitumen road built to take gear to the test site.

What was left of the township was monitored by two caretakers who lived in the old hospital.

They offered us the use of a shower which was great and I asked if there were any restrictions. The man's reply was "We have 100,000 gallons (450,000l) of distilled water, so you'll be ok"

The next day we drove alongside the Trans Australian Railway and turned off to Fowler's Bay and later Ceduna where we camped in the bush and cooked a crayfish we had bought from a guy in the Thevenard hotel. The next day I woke to a frosty morning and peeped out of my swag to smell eucalyptus and see the still red coals sending wisps of smoke into the mist. Gum trees seemed to be hiding in the mist like ghosts but were slowly being revealed by the glow of the morning sun. After breakfast we headed for home

I had been camping before but this was a defining moment

that helped stimulate my love of camping and the bush that has lasted to the present day. In fact we a going on a trip to similar country I have described in July 2018.

PEOPLE I MET

Soon after this trip Leonore and I were invited to dinner at the home of Frank Lucarotti and his wife Soo Lim who cooked her usually magnificent multi course Chinese meal.

There was another guest, Jim, from Southern Africa and he was to take up a position as a Native Patrol Officer in the Woomera Prohibited Area. Being now an instant expert on travelling in that part of the world I was blathering on about swags and camp ovens on and so on.

Frank stopped me in my tracks when he said "Peter, Jim was a white hunter so he knows quite a lot about camping". I was so embarrassed but no one seemed to take offence and Jim was a great story teller. I remember two. Jim was in charge of the animals in the film "Hatari" which starred John Wayne. I asked him if everyone's dream cowboy was the real deal and he confirmed that he was doing his own stunts etc.

The second one was that Ernest Hemingway had challenged a Spanish bullfighter to fight a buffalo in the wild and Hemingway's son met Jim to make it all happen. Hemingway senior would not fly and during the delay in waiting for a ship he killed himself.

"Jungle Jim" was a great dinner guest that is for sure.

Gough Whitlam was elected as Prime Minister of Australia

on December 2nd 1972. We happened to be staying at the Boston Hotel in Port Lincoln- that I can see as I write this.

Whitlam was a controversial character and I well remember the election campaign where he criticised the US bases in Exmouth, Pine Gap and Narrungar. The USA was open about the role of such bases in the USA and would also have been so in Australia, but we would not let them. For example, from time to time an Australian would be in charge of Narrungar on rotation but that was never mentioned by the Australian authorities.

Whitlam polarised people but I recall his election night with some pleasure as the birth of our daughter Sarah on August 24 1973 confirmed.

The attorney general in the Whitlam Government was the pleasant and elegant Kip or Kep Enderby who called into my office one day to say hello with the head of WRE a stern-faced Dr Don Woods.

Whilst I was sitting at attention Mr Enderby was trying to put me at ease and picked up a couple of rubber stamps that I had been given with BULLSHIT" AND "PISS OFF" written on the handles. He laughed and said "I suppose you use these for your government correspondence". As he said that he looked at the underside of the stamp and said.

"My goodness they do say that."

Dr Woods remained unsmiling.

Sir Mark Oliphant in his capacity of South Australian Governor visited the hospital and while having a looking around told us that he had been a patient in the intensive care ward at the Royal Adelaide Hospital two weeks before with heart trouble. He certainly got the nurses and my attention.

Later that night there was a dinner for him with Heads of Departments and spouses and the USAF commander. He asked if there were any media people present and there were not.

He made a speech that was quite controversial and newsworthy. I have never seen any reference to the content of that speech - so I have kept his trust.

Another interesting person was the Deputy Secretary or equivalent of the US Department of Defense (USA spelling). In that world he was number three to the President.

He was talking to me at the airport about computer models of injuries as a form of triage and also administration. He said he had wanted major alterations to his department but could not sack individuals - so he had had to sack the whole department and then tell favoured individuals to stay.

Lastly he described how vulnerable to small arms fire fast moving aircraft with sharp leading edges to their wings were. He said they had lost 2000 in that way.

I met many politicians, military "brass", senior public servants and the USAF Commander Colonel Burley Vandergriff whom I met at his welcome party.

At the end of the night I found myself leaning on the bar talking with him and I asked if he and his wife Loretta would like to come home for a drink and he agreed.

We became really good friends and socialised a lot and this certainly helped when there was any official business with the USAF.

In particular I joined the poker school that became the "Thursday Night Garden and Social Club" held at our house and I have an engraved watch to prove it.

It was a win or lose $50-100 in a night game and this was serious money in 1972. I had played ordinary draw poker for ages but this was seven card stud with high and low winners, jokers wild and aces high or low – fair dinkum. I was very careful and won the early games most nights. Then, when I thought I had the measure of the game, I usually lost.

The guy who previously was in charge of equipment at the range had once lived at our place. One of the unofficial sheds we had was three by three metres with 32 power points and a table and refrigerator from the Island Lagoon Tracking station that an observant reader will remember closed down in 1972 - just at the time we wanted to furnish our poker shack.

It was a well- known event in the town and every Thursday afternoon six or seven secretaries would go to Westpac bank and withdraw money. Friday morning the same secretaries would either slink in to get more money or bounce in to deposit cash.

A lighter side of my administration role was the role of health officer. One Friday afternoon, just before knock off time, I received a phone call from someone who had seen a rat in a missile container from the Philippines.

Predictably the caller suggested it could wait until Monday. I suggested that was not a good idea so the Area Administrator and I went on a mission wielding rat killers, otherwise known as brooms, and killed the rat. I sent it to a laboratory in Adelaide and was pleased to find it had nothing nasty in or on it.

Many of the people employed at Woomera and Narrungar had served in other, warm, wars including World War 2 and Vietnam; some of them at the sharp end of such conflicts.

At the bar of the Senior Mess one evening I introduced two of my patients to each other and told them that they both had been in Changi prison in Singapore. One man said "Yes but I did not stay".

He later told me he walked to Burma and fought with "Wingate's Chindits", a guerrilla force led by British General Ord Wingate.

Our neighbours Stan and Rita Gilliver were surrogate grandparents to our daughters and joined with us in the USA, Australian and British gang that got together to play charades. Stan had us in fits playing this game since he could not get the gist of it at all.

He was a chubby, jolly, kind and strong man who ran the power station in Woomera. One day I was chatting to him over the fence and he described a recent trip to Melbourne where some kids almost pushed him over on an escalator. I said "It's a wonder you did not clip them in the ear". He said

"I would not do that".

I was puzzled and asked him why not. His answer was that during the war in the islands he used to go ashore, armed only with a knife, to remove the sentries/observers before the troops landed

Our other neighbour Kirill Bolonkin operated the Jindivicks, the pilotless target aircraft. Everyone could do something and most of it was very special.

I knew respected, liked and worked with many nurses and because of the nature of Woomera also socialised with them.

Two however really won my heart. One was Clare Surman who, with her husband Vic, had been in Woomera since day one in 1948. She had been the acting (not a midwife) matron forever. She was a lovely lady kind, unflappable and most competent.

She held my hand in so many ways as a clinical and administrative doctor and I did her a few favours as well. She and Vic retired to Sydney and they both reached their nineties. I spoke to her a few years ago and she still sounded well and truly "with it".

The second person was Shirley Hawter who had a hell of a life in many ways. I forget where she was born but she married and lived on a sheep station east of Geraldton in Western Australia

She had one or two daughters and a son. The son's name was "Romey" and he had cerebral palsy and died after many years with her nursing him as a mum not a nurse.

Her marriage ended and she studied general nursing and midwifery and became a double certificate nurse quite late in life.

She used this tragedy in her life to be an amazing and caring nurse and a happy fulfilled person. Apart from her being such a nice lady and great nurse she loved our daughter Kirstin who was six months old when we arrived in 1972 and Sarah who was born in 1973.

Shirley freely admitted to being frustrated by her own daughter/s not producing grandchildren but certainly compensated for it by the wonderful stuffed toys she made for us. One was March Hare, a metre high. We still have him sitting on a chair in our house. Shirley was also instrumental in lots of funny things being given to me when I left Woomera.

Once she worked at the Lake Hart launcher site when live firing was being counted down and she thought it would be a good idea to have a cuppa and a piece of toast. Yes you've guessed it. The toast burnt, set off the alarms and the launch was aborted.

Maybe 10 years later I knocked on her door in Perth but she did not recognize me. I was so sad.

A WONDERFUL HOLIDAY – THANKS WOOMERA PEOPLE

By mid-1974 things were working out very well for Leonore and me.

We had two gorgeous little girls and I was enjoying a very good job and liked the people I worked with and the town itself. The Senior Mess was a passing parade of interesting people including a guy who had wrestled the best- known professional wrestler in the world at the time - a Chief Little Wolf and so on.

We decided to take the overseas holiday that we had dreamed of since we were married and planned it to be from the end of November for three months. My parents, God bless them, offered to care for our three-year-old and nearly one-and-a-half-year-old daughters.

We had become good mates with George Wells a bachelor bank manager of Westpac. He was a guiding light when I established my private practice and he helped to set up our overseas trip. He even baby sat our house while we were away.

Kirstin used to delight in going to see Mr Wells and "helping" with pens and papers while Leonore was doing our banking. Kirstin was fascinated by the toilet and would politely ask George to take her. He would get flustered, go red and immediately call for one of the female staff. He also was scared of her getting into the red ink.

There were many other people who helped us including John Drennan an ex British Army guy who lived near Leonore's parents in Adelaide and commuted to Woomera. He arranged for us to be looked after in Hong Kong for a few days and told me where to get shoes in London. I followed his advice and still have some.

The "Thursday Night Garden and Social Club" came to the

fore with Don McLaughlin arranging to meet us in Brussels, Ken Davis in Florida, Richard and Leigh Macy in New Orleans and Burley in Las Vegas. Burley had also organised a USAF Colonel to look after us in Hawaii on the way home.

We of course made some arrangements with mates and my mother's relatives in the United Kingdom and also by ourselves with George Wells' help.

A special favour was done by John Doyle Snr, a friend of Leonore's family who was a big wheel in the SA Railways who contacted the Mexican Railway authorities and arranged for me to meet their head doctor in Mexico City. The logic of this was that I was responsible for the medical part of the railway disaster plan for so many kilometres either side of Woomera.

I had $A3000 to change for $US4000 (that is not a mistake). George told me to wait a week or so and Nixon devalued the currency. I then was able to get $US4500. George's advice was worth about $US5000 today.

The early part of the trip went like clockwork and we did all the touristy things in London and drove to Wales where we met some of Mum's family. A special person was Nana's stepsister. She lived in a bed sitter in a dark and dismal part of Wales. She was a tiny little lady and very excited to see us.

She lit a coal fire and told us how she had gone down the street to get two slices of Welsh ham for us. Boy our family had come a long way in seventy odd years. I thought how lucky I was that my grandparents had taken the courageous step of migrating.

The next step was Brussels where Don McLaughlin discovered a mistake with our tickets. Never mind, we went off on the train for a couple of weeks and then back to Brussels and picked up our tickets he had sorted and headed for London and Miami.

Ken and Sally Davis duly picked us up and we shared a motor home around Florida and Alabama and saw all the tourist sites and sights. Ken took me bass fishing and I chucked a lure into a tree accidentally and when it fell into the water a fish jumped on. He was not impressed - I think the term is pissed off.

We then stayed in New Orleans, and what a night we had with Richard and Leigh Macy. Next day we were poured onto a flight to Mexico City to keep our appointment with the head Doctor for the railways.

We were dressed in casual gear and two or three doctors in suits and white coats were waiting for us on the steps of an enormous Spanish Hospital building with 5000 beds. We were ushered into a beautiful room where there were about a dozen doctors also waiting to meet us who slowly dispersed after I told them Woomera Hospital had 30 beds.

It was logical that Mexico's railways played such a big part in the health system because of the poor or non-existent roads and isolated villages. Doctors and patients travelled to and from the central hospital by train.

Next stop was to see Bob and Jean Braddon in the San Bernardino Valley in California. They had really loved their time in Woomera where Bob was with the USAF. They lived on a two-acre ranch they named "Gum Tree Station" and there were two sheep "Adelaide" and "Augusta". It was heartwarming to realise how much they had loved Australia.

I just thought about an amusing difference in some words when used by Americans and Australians. 'Fanny" was someone's "bum" and "to root" was "to barrack". We were very conservative in the 1970s as far as rude words in mixed company went. So Leonore and I were a bit like kids saying rude words and giggling inside.

After a lovely couple of days we went to Las Vegas to meet Burley and Loretta and to experience a place that was as wondrous as I imagined - and we even won a few dollars.

We were fortunate to see Bobby Gentry who I remember singing "Ode to Billy Joe" and "Mississippi Delta", both songs about as country and western as you can get. She was amazing and sang everything, except country songs, from rock and roll to semi classical works. She wore a slinky full-length gown and looked stunning.

We stayed at Nellis USAF base and it looked as if there were more big passenger jets on the tarmac than there were in the whole of Australia.

Hawaii was the next stop and we again were treated royally by a colonel who also was an ophthalmologist and had worked with monkeys to check the effect of nuclear weapons on their eyes.

The only thing wrong on the whole trip was some clear air

turbulence that the 747 struck over the Pacific. I actually looked out the window and saw stars so I took off my seat belt and lay down with my head on Leonore's lap. Suddenly the jet fell and we pulled g-forces. My legs floated towards the cabin top. I grabbed the seat and held Leonore down as she who was floating up towards me. I have a vivid memory of a girl in the seat in front floating upward in a sleeping position. She woke up and yelled on the way down to her seat.

We returned to Adelaide and picked up our children and two Labradors. I did not realise the task I had set Mum and Dad who were both 63 at the time. It was such a wonderful thing they did for us and Leonore's parents helped as well.

We had to buy a trailer to carry the mountain of gear we had brought home plus the Christmas and other presents that the girls had acquired. I remember thinking we had no room to carry spare water other than our five litres of drinking water on our way home.

Between Port Augusta and Woomera on a hot afternoon the car boiled so I stopped, let it cool and filled the radiator with our raspberry cordial and ice, with the engine running of course. About 10-20 minutes later it boiled again so I pulled up alongside a Highways Department truck and asked if I could get some water and of course the driver said "Yes".

I took off the radiator cap quickly with my hand wrapped in a towel as wasting water did not matter and to the utter amazement of the driver and me a geyser of, not only red water, but ice came out of the radiator.

No one has ever been able to explain to me how that could happen.

I must admit that I chuckled to myself imagining these guys telling the story in the pub that night.

GOODBYE WOOMERA AND THANKS FOR THE MEMORIES

After we arrived home from our trip we thought about our future. I had nearly finished my administrative studies and decided to look for a full-time job in that field.

Woomera was winding down although Narrungar was still operating but there was only one of my American friends left and I had experienced the very essence of Woomera and the outback life.

I have mentioned many people but almost all of them were figures in a passing parade, and indeed what a parade it was, but more importantly there were a number of people that became part of our lives for decades.

Burley Vandergriff visited us once in Australia and we saw them three times in the USA and I will mention this in more detail in a later section. As recently as 1998 Burley and Loretta came from their home in Colorado to see us in San Francisco when I was on my way to be a guest speaker at a conference in Saskatoon.

We had a magic time on Fisherman's Wharf watching the "Blue Angels" the USAF aerobatics team performing over the Golden Gate Bridge and Alcatraz Prison. Burley used to fly similar planes and so he added another dimension to the experience.

I worked with a nurse, Sue Smith, and we became friendly with her and her husband Rod. One of the reasons we returned from our trip when we did was for me to deliver her baby Emily. That baby is now a mother of two and lives in Shepparton in Victoria as does our son whom I also delivered. They are good friends and both have Labrador dogs. Leonore and I now have our seventh Labrador, although what that has to do with anything I really do not know!

We saw Rod and Sue maybe every couple of years in various places where we lived and their home in Perth and always enjoyed their company.

In 2002 we had planned to attend a wedding and stay with them in Perth but had to cancel because we were moving to Darwin to live and work.

Sue always thinks before she speaks and has a quiet voice. When I told her we were going to Darwin there was a long silence and then she replied---------"Peter-------we ------are----going ------to ----Darwin".

Needless to say we had a wonderful three years there and did all sorts of things together in and around Darwin and more recently visited their home in Rockingham Western Australia and frequently talk on the telephone or internet.

Back to Woomera. Soon after we originally arrived I was walking near the shopping centre and noticed a rather nice looking woman walking towards me who much to my surprise removed her sunglasses in the elegant way ladies do and said "Good morning aren't you Peter Morton"?

She was Judy Dutton, a friend of Julie Bagshaw, Dick's sister, whom I had met when I was at school. She was married to Robin Dutton whose dad was a British Army Colonel who had been in charge of the ELDO project.

These initials stood for the European Launcher Development Organisation. Britain tried to develop a missile launcher based on the Blue Streak rocket but, as I've mentioned, this was not successful.

ELDO in 1960 wanted to use the Blue Streak to launch satellites. This was only three years after the Russians successfully launched the world's first satellite named 'Sputnik"

From 1964 to 1970 there were 10 launches but no satellite was put into orbit. A cynic might say no bloody wonder. Britain provided the Blue Streak, France was responsible for stage 2, Germany stage 3, Italy the satellite, The Netherlands and Belgium tracking and telemetry and Australia got a guernsey because it provided the launcher.

In due course I delivered Judy and Robin's baby, Jeffery, and I'm proud to be his godfather. We still keep in touch with them.

Last but not least are Brian and Pam Murray who managed Parakylia station about 100km north- west of the Woomera village. To the station they had to drive through the range head and into the range itself.

Brian's nick name is "Boomer". This is a name usually

given to big kangaroos but in the case of Brian it was because he is a loud, jovial, gregarious and warm-hearted man. He is also big and strong.

We played cricket together and Leonore and I visited the station many times. Woomera was about making your own fun and I set up a group we called "B.O.S.S.O.W.U.S.PA which of course means Barbecue on a Spit Society of Woomera United States and Parakylia.

We became good mates and in due course Pam and Brian became wonderful god parents to our son Peter. Brian had a big influence on him taking up a career as a farmer.

Once we were at the station, on a back track between the opal mining towns of Andamooka and Coober Pedy, and a bus drove in and pulled up by the petrol pump. The driver got out wearing a pair of mini shorts followed by four women dressed in rather nice but over done dresses. Yep, it was the fore runner of *Priscilla-Queen of the Desert*

The driver filled the bus with petrol and clicked his fingers at one of the women who reached into her bosom and pulled out a roll of cash some of which he peeled off handed to Brian.

Another day some other unusual visitors called in. One was a middle-aged man in a Land Rover pulling an old mobile army kitchen with the cooking equipment removed. The other was a rather skinny unhealthy looking teenage boy driving a similar vehicle pulling a tandem trailer.

They were buying old vehicle batteries for scrap, a useful source of beer money for station managers.

The boy could not lift a truck battery. The only accommodation was the defunct kitchen with a single dirty mattress.

Most of the time we were in Woomera there was a drought. In 1974 there was so little feed that many sheep died walking to water and had to be dragged out of the troughs.

The property was 1300 square miles and there were 20,000 sheep so it was tough for Brian and his one workman.

We were privileged to see at first hand the cycle that has bedevilled, destroyed and sometimes made people rich on sheep and cattle stations.

We saw starving sheep, then heavy rains when Lake Eyre filled for the first time in decades. We saw sheep getting flyblown bellies because of the high grass and lastly several hundred square miles of Parakylia being burnt when lightning ignited the grass. All this happened in twelve months.

Soon after the rain I drove on a track where sheep had died of starvation. It was so lush I could not avoid running over Sturt Peas.

Parakylia was for sale and Brian and I thought about buying it. I even went to Westpac in Adelaide and was interviewed by a senior person. I made my pitch for a loan and when I finished I was about to get up and say "Thanks for your time" and "Goodbye". The man looked up and said, "The money is yours". I sat glued to my seat and mumbled something. Then he said "But it will be a personal loan" and that rapidly unglued me and I promised to think about it and left.

I was earning $25,000 a year at the most and as mentioned Woomera was winding down. $165,000 was needed and the drought was still going on. My biggest fear was that bankruptcy would have the effect of deregistering me.

The 20,000 sheep were valued at $2 each and within six months or so, after it rained they were worth $25 each. There were 5000 lambs that had not been counted. What might have been-------------?

Sometime in 1972 I was sitting on the edge of a swimming pool at the homestead with six-month-old Kirstin right next to me. Brian exploded from his seat and threw himself towards the pool and grabbed Kirstin's foot a metre under water. She had sunk like a stone and was OK but his quick action probably saved her life.

We had a lot of good times with Pam and Brian and nearly 10 years later after we moved to Port Lincoln we bought a 1000acre farm between the four of us north of Coffin Bay. We reckoned it was the smallest sheep station in Australia. It was not a great financial benefit but it was good for Brian to get away from Parakylia. We also had a share in a 28-foot-long boat as we both liked fishing and Port Lincoln and Coffin Bay ticked all the boxes.

The farm was a great place for me to work hard physically – a welcome break from the hassle of being a general practitioner and it showed our son Peter a path in life that he has successfully followed.

Brian retired from the station 20 years ago and he is still working on his and Pam's vineyard near Clare, a place of hot summers and frigid winters. As I write, he is a few days from his 81st birthday. He is a tough bloke no doubt about that.

Pam is well settled in Clare and works at the cellar door of Mitchell's winery. Like us they have grandchildren that keep them busy. Their third daughter and her family live near to, and are friendly with, our son Peter and his wife Patricia at Naracoorte.

The name of the vineyard is 'Witzend" which reflects Brian's impish sense of humour and positive outlook on life.

Brian Macdonald I have already mentioned. We became great friends and shared many conversations about life and the problems we have had at various times for decades.

Brian and his wife Margaret had three children and while they were all under three years old Brian did a degree in Politics mostly by distance learning. His lowest mark was a high credit.

He had a passion for scholarship of many kinds and was a very clear thinker and writer. He died a year or two ago and was still studying and writing about Hadrian's Wall. I miss his wise words in his unchanging Canadian drawl very much.

George Wells the banker who was so good to Leonore and me is no longer with us. As a young man he nearly became a Jesuit priest. Then he left the church because he fell in love with a woman. She was killed in a car accident whilst he was waiting at the altar of a church to marry her. I do not think I have heard a sadder story. How he was such a caring, kind, happy and helpful person after that I do not know.

So our time at Woomera ended. Our lives had been enriched and our experience and my professional knowledge broadened in so many lasting ways.

I had seen an advertisement for a Medical Superintendent in Warrnambool, was interviewed in April 1975 and moved there in May.

CHAPTER EIGHT
WARRNAMBOOL

INTRODUCTION

Warrnambool is now the biggest city in Western Victoria, the fabled wool growing country. In the 1950s and 1960s it was rivalled by Hamilton but with the lessening value of wool over the decades by the time we moved to Warrnambool the population was about 20,000 compared to Hamilton's 10,000. At the time of writing it is 34000 and 9600 respectively.

Warrnambool was not dependent on wool. The area was settled by Irish people from the goldfields of Victoria who were farmers who grew potatoes rather the graziers who grew wool. It was interesting to see how many short and dark people were in Warrnambool compared even to Mortlake only about 50 km north where people were taller and fairer.

The Irish of course brought their religion and customs. There is a Killarney, Port Fairy, Koroit and other places with Irish names. Koroit actually has houses with the front doors opening onto the footpath.

Warrnambool also developed a range of industries beyond potato growing. There are some sheep and lambs and many dairy and beef farms. There is a large cheese industry, the famous Fletcher Jones trouser makers, a woollen mill and Nestles where the first instant coffee in the world was produced for the American troops in the Pacific theatre during World War Two.

A university, schools, many government offices and of course tourism and other businesses have made Warrnambool a thriving, powerful and wealthy community.

WHAT A DIFFERENCE TO OTHER HOSPITALS.

Hospitals have been likened to Cathedrals in the middle ages. They were centres of civic pride, wealth, architecture, science, teaching, culture, political power and scholarship. They were also built on the highest hill reflecting the above but to be fair maybe there was a military reason as well.

Much of what happened in Cathedrals happened in hospitals in Australia and in Warrnambool. There were still gifts of eggs in vast quantities, a practice dating from the days when the evening meals were cooked by nurses.

The board of management was loaded with talent. Some I recall were a lawyer who soon became a senator, the General Manager of Nestles who every now and then went trouble shooting elsewhere in the world, the accountant at Fletcher Jones, the manager of the woollen mill, the works manager from the council, two doctors and a dentist (chairman).

The CEO was an ex dairy farmer and a lovely bloke who was easily the best boss I have ever had.

These people were really close to the Hospital and Charities Commission (H&CC) and politicians. Having J.M.Fraser as the local federal member did not hurt, I suppose.

Perhaps an example will paint a picture. The kitchen was old and the board thought it should be replaced so the new Medical Superintendent (and the first one employed full time) was asked to assess the fitness of the kitchen to serve food.

It was old and worn and a report was prepared by yours truly to the effect that it was not fit for serving food and that we should have a new kitchen and the report was duly submitted to the H&CC who replied "Fair enough but we do not have any money left this year."

Like a gunslinger the CEO replied "How about we lend you a million dollars and you can pay it back later" and the H&CC said "OK".

I was and still am gobsmacked by that. There were donations to the hospital but the main way they raised this cash was by putting their quarterly allocation of funds (or whenever it was) from the H&CC on the money market until their bills had to be paid and banking the interest.

There was always a can-do attitude that believe me is a rarity in hospitals. I suggested a party to the CEO to welcome new junior doctors attended by board members and Visiting Medical Officers (VMOs). "Good idea. Frank, the head of catering, will get the apprentices to make something special and organise the beer and wine".

Perhaps their foresight was the biggest attribute. They always knew at what stage the development of the hospital was, even if it was years ahead on the master plan. Lunches with the architect at the A-league restaurant, Two Faces, in Melbourne aided that process of course.

They also were smart enough to see the increasing feminisation of the work force and built flats where married doctors could live. We never had any problems recruiting staff and this undoubtedly helped.

The hospital washed the linen and nappies for junior doctors. They also sought out people who needed help. For example managing the linen for a severely handicapped adult is difficult but Warrnambool's central linen service would pick up, wash and return the linen for someone in that situation.

It is probably fair to say that most regional hospital by whatever name have centralised services i.e. they make patients come to them and this is certainly understandable when considering X rays, major operations and so on, but Warrnambool did and still does try to provide regional services in the region where and when it can.

WHAT DID I DO?

First and foremost, I was made very welcome at the hospital and asked to address either two or three of the annual general meetings of satellite hospitals where people asked a lot of questions about Woomera amongst other things.

Allan Matthews, my boss, also volunteered my services to chair an appeal by a disgruntled teacher at the local TAFE who had not been promoted or something similar. It seemed to me that he had not kept up to date with his subject. It was interesting to look into a different professional world and was all grist to the mill.

My main job was to look after medical services in the hospital. The VMOs were a relatively stable group. At the time they all worked in an honorary capacity whether GPS or specialists but this did not last long as the Federal Government through the Medicare system started paying fees to VMOs. There was quite a blossoming of nice new cars in the doctors' car park soon after.

The main work I did was the recruitment and appointment of junior staff: interns and residents. All applicants were interviewed by me and then a computerised system linking medical student and hospital preferences decided who went where in Victoria.

There were not any formal jobs in the hospital beyond two years after graduation. A Don Howie went off to study orthopaedic surgery and indeed became a professor of such. The others as I recall went into general practice in Warrnambool, the general district or elsewhere. This was a wonderful mechanism for providing country doctors.

There were three or four GPs about my age working in the town when we arrived and four I can think of, from my time, who joined practices in Warrnambool trained and spent their careers there.

It certainly was a good way of doing business.

I was also responsible for pathology, the dental clinic, pharmacy and radiology but there was little that ever went wrong with any of these areas. However sometimes we needed to recruit people for these positions and I was involved in that process.

I had oversight of allied health services and in particular was involved with the Day Centre which was relatively new. There were physiotherapy, occupational therapy, social work, speech therapy, district nursing and a geriatric departments and my role was to help old and young with rehabilitation for various conditions. The aged predominated.

Home modifications were also done by the handy man, Tom Sawyer, who was also good at making devices to wind fishing line off and onto reels.

I mentioned before that outreach services meant exactly that and many hidden problems were detected when the homes of patients were visited.

Richard Ziegeler was a young occupational therapist and very talented. His grandfather made many of the town hall clocks in the area so he had some mechanical genes in his DNA.

He made a device to check the hand function of a patient. There are three nerves to the hand: radius, ulnar and median.

He had a log cabin tobacco tin with 8-10 nail holes in the

top and a few nails the size of the holes in the tin.

How did it work?

1 If a patient can unscrew the lid that shows that touch, coordination, sensation, vision and a degree of strength are OK.

2 Putting the nails through the holes shows touch, sensation, fine movement, hand eye coordination are all OK

WHAT ELSE DID I DO?

I did rounds at our two aged care inpatient units and attended Board and other meetings often over a lovely three course lunch. Oh yes there were always sandwiches and cheese in the doctors' lounge.

I also did some clinical sessions for a new organisation working to assess the successful development of children in kindergartens. This was a standard procedure at the child's kindergarten with mum and or dad present. This was much less threatening than a doctor's surgery---I had a child as a patient once and the mother told him/her that she would get the doctor to give him/her a needle unless the behaviour improved. No further comment

Each child had to do a series of tests such as putting so many blocks on top of each other, drawing a circle, triangle and square and other similar things.

The logic behind this is that we learn 70% of all we are going to learn between 0 and 5 years 25% between 5 and 18 years and 5% after 18 and yet educational expenditure is the reverse of that.

I may have the numbers wrong but the general principle has been recognised by the Jesuits for centuries.

In our little way we were trying to assess if children were "good to go" to school or would be better to repeat kindergarten. If they could not draw at four then they may well not be able to write at six and so on.

But kindergarten was not free whereas school was. One child was really poor at these tests but mum was a teacher and reckoned it was all a lot of nonsense.

I enjoyed the work it was fun to work with children outside the surgery environment, but I have no idea what the long-term results were. I did fly the hospital flag in the community and that was important.

On the subject of flag flying I did three short term locums for doctors who were ill or had family problems to deal with. They were from single doctor practices in Cobden, McArthur and Edenhope. Bill the guy from Cobden gave me $100 and I bought an Abu 2500 fishing reel that is battered and worn but I am still using it to catch whiting.

The main thing I did outside Warrnambool was to attend meetings of the Medical Superintendents of Victoria. This organisation turned into the Royal Australian College of Medical Administration in 1967 and many are still in that group.

They were articulate, bright and took me under their collective wing and some were actually lecturers in subjects I was studying to become a Fellow of that College. I was very privileged indeed.

Last but not least the monthly meetings were held in the boardrooms of the big Melbourne Hospitals with leather and wood furnishings and pictures of distinguished forebears on the walls. This was a great privilege with the power and wealth of Victoria seemingly oozing from every pore of these rooms and people.

To add to the panache I flew from Warrnambool to Melbourne via BIZ JET. This was an airline started by an executive of Ansett to service the Pilbara with a small jet from Melbourne at the time of the 1960-70s mineral boom. The boom had run its race by the time I used their piston engine plane.

We flew into Essendon and I was chauffeured by the owner of the airline into Melbourne in a Cadillac – old but still the real deal.

Waiting to be picked up in the cold windy canyon of down town Melbourne was not so good. I bought a big black woollen coat that I might have worn six to eight times since I left Warrnambool.

I mentioned earlier that I had a frightening experience returning from our overseas trip when a 747 hit clear air turbulence.

It was not a lot of fun flying in and out of Warrnambool as it was often rough with poor visibility. I can read an altimeter and whether BIZ JET or another airline they often landed well under the regulated height permitted for instrument landings. One trip was scarily rough with no visibility and the pilot, who was flying on instruments, had an engine failure which makes the plane fly on one engine which is very frightening until it is under control. The bloody pilot forgot to turn the fuel on for one engine.

On the subject of aeroplanes and bad weather the local flying instructor took his wife to Melbourne one morning to stay for a few days and the daughter of one of our senior doctors hitched a ride with them.

The plane flew straight into the ground at the Warrnambool airfield on return from Melbourne. The wings were flat on the ground and the fuselage crushed into an area the size of a small room. Obviously the pilot was killed but no one knew whether the girl was on board or not as her parents had not been able to contact her.

We took the remains back to the morgue and Joe Brooks an obstetrician/gynaecologist and I dealt with it. I must say that it was not easy to do so but we managed to convince ourselves that there was only one person in the plane.

When I got home I recall that I had a bottle of cognac that had belonged to my mate Peter McEvoy who was killed in Broken Hill that I intended to give to his brother.

I didn't think Peter or brother Bob would mind if I had a snifter or two so I did. I gave it to Bob in due course probably more that 20 years after Peter was killed, in an office on Greenhill Road after he had retired from the army.

In a much lighter vein but still on the subject of trauma there were another two episodes. One cold and stormy night a prisoner escaped from somewhere and was thought to be in the Ballarat area.

There were the usual warnings not to approach etc on TV. At the time I said to my wife how sorry I felt for the man as he could die in that weather. I have no idea why but I said "Maybe be he could turn up in Warrnambool".

Next morning something told me to walk through the Emergency Department rather than the normal way I entered the hospital. There was the escapee lying on a bed with a wounded leg. I asked the attendant policeman what had happened and he said 'I shot him". I said "With what?". He pulled what I thought was a 38 calibre revolver and pulled a silver bullet out of the chamber and said "With that".

Another day I was staring into the space that happened to be my open door when I saw a woman I knew to be Jan Shaw. She had been a physiotherapy student and a member of the group dissecting the body next to my group's body at the Adelaide Medical School.

She was holding a two-year-old little boy with a cut foot that I sewed up for him.

She invited us to dinner at their property near Stawell where we met her husband and became quite friendly. We have a picture of Nick, their son and our daughter Sarah in a bath together at the time. Wheels turned, time moved on and all that stuff. Nick and Sarah have been married now for 13 years and have two little boys.

OUTSIDE OF WORK

Our two little girls went from three and a half to eight and from two to six while we lived in Warrnambool and we had two Labrador dogs, mother and son. We spent a lot of time at the beaches nearby walking and fishing with the girls and the dogs and of course with the activities tied up with having children at kindergarten and school.

We visited all the local spots like Koroit, the gorgeous Port Fairy and really enjoyed the old volcano at Tower Hill. The volcanic geology of Western Victoria and South Australia from Warrnambool to Mount Gambier is quite interesting and responsible for the rich soil.

I played squash and improved my game a lot and also golf which did not improve. Having been raised in the almost river less SA we were very excited by the rivers that were east and west of Warrnambool the Hopkins and Merri respectively and others near and far including the Glenelg near the SA border.

I bought a 12 foot tinny that I only sold in 2017 and with a mate or the family we would poke around the rivers and sometimes get some bream. One day I found some fishing line tangled in the rocks near the jetty and just for fun put some bait on it and pulled in a little cod of some kind.

I took it home to give to the dog perhaps but my neighbour spotted it and he suggested we take his crayfish pot and try our luck.

There is a large breakwater in Warrnambool which is understandable as the next stop is Antarctica. Just how many days it is safe to go on the ocean side of the breakwater in a small boat I do not know but this day it was OK and we got a monster crayfish. With its flattened tail it may have been one and a half times longer than my small lap top is wide.

I organised a trip to Kangaroo Island where we had a red letter day catching snapper. I went to Mornington Island in the Gulf of Carpentaria with a chap who had his own twin engine Beechcraft Baron. That was a heck of a trip and for only an hour flying north were we over green land the other six or seven hours was over pastoral land.

I also organised a trip to Karratha and Broome in WA for an old friend of mine, Tim Malseed who came from Portland, and a doctor I worked with in Warrnambool. That was super special.

I was sometimes able to take Leonore and the girls to a meeting or conference at weekends and had a wonderful trip in Bendigo and Castlemaine. I recall and the Grampians were popular for a day trip or longer.

Of course Melbourne was on the list for football. My Dad and I saw the Collingwood Carlton Grand Final in 1979 and Mike Brady sung "Up there Cazaly". It was spine tingling stuff

One weekend we were booked into the Windsor as it was walking distance from some exams I was sitting. Our older daughter Kirstin was carsick so en route Leonore undressed her and carried her into the hotel. I sorted out things at the desk and went upstairs to see Kirstin, stark naked, running down the passage pushing the elderly Windsor Hotel porter's trolley. All he could do was point and in a strangled sort of voice saying "The child the child". Later I saw him putting on a little pantomime for the staff and they all seemed to think it was funny.

The good news was that they were mixed up because they had two Drs Peter Morton staying there so we had to have a suite.

We also visited my mate in the South East and it was not a major hassle to go to Adelaide

We made friends with many of the staff and doctors and I even had a game of footy and baseball. They really were a nice bunch of people.

I have mentioned many of the things we did as it was a nice place to live and I enjoyed the job in Warrnambool and the extra activities in Melbourne and other places.

Quite central to my life at this time was studying. It became obvious, as I have mentioned before, that post graduate qualifications were necessary and I did most of the studying for Fellowships of the Royal Australian Colleges of Medical Administration and General Practice and a Bachelor of Health Administration while in Warrnambool.

I was not a good student at university but with a lovely wife and two gorgeous girls I was at peace and did not find it hard to study at all. I got a lot of credits and even the odd distinction.

QUALITY SURVEYING AND DISASTER PLANNING

The 1970s was when the concept of measuring the quality of care and management in hospitals took root. The "Australian Council on Health Care Standards" (ACHS) was founded in 1974 (the H initially stood for Hospital) and developed a set of standards for hospitals to measure themselves against. If a Hospital passed it was considered to be accredited with the ACHS.

The Warrnambool Hospital was in the second group of hospitals to do this. Maybe that is why they wanted a full time Medical Superintendent! I found the subject most interesting and the implementation of this study of whether we met or did not meet the standards became largely my responsibility. I have mentioned before that there was a can-do attitude at the hospital and it really shone through when the Hospital sought accreditation.

The standards came in a folder about five cm thick and all the typing, organisation of meetings, document reviews etc. were done by or through my secretary or me. Meetings were often held at lunchtimes with the hospital supplying lunch.

Everyone cooperated and despite some very anxious moments at the time of assessment we passed with flying colours.

I was interested in this aspect of Medical Administration and later became a surveyor for the ACHS and the equivalent body preparing, trialling and surveying standards in general practice.

During this process disaster planning both internally and externally was reviewed and many changes made.

This involved me spending a few days at Mount Macedon at a counter disaster course. This included consideration of who has the authority to evacuate people, call out troops and so on and was most interesting. Apart from classified military stuff I think that was about as high level as there is.

I remember one Englishman who was in the Australian Federal Police who was very quiet but later was featured in the news taking a gun from someone at an airport.

The Glanville train disaster and Cyclone Tracy were in everyone's memories and were used as case studies. General Stretton who was in charge of the disaster response in Darwin after Tracy was one of the speakers. I will not forget his comment that when he first arrived and left the airport they did not know where the road was there was so much damage.

I am not sure but I think some of the disaster planning I was involved with, as part of accreditation, was used in one of the all too frequent fires in Western Victoria.

FINALE

We enjoyed every bit of the time we spent in Warrnambool at work and play. It broadened my knowledge of how the health system worked and who made things happen.

I can only reiterate that Warrnambool Hospital from the Board, through management, the professional and other staff was a can-do place and created not only a fine clinical unit but a model for dealing with one of the great concerns in medicine: the recruitment and retention of rural doctors.

After four years I felt it was time for a change. There was an administrative ladder in Victoria that by tradition people climbed. A few years later a contemporary colleague of mine was Medical Superintendent of the Royal Melbourne Hospital so it is reasonable to assume that in time I would do such a job.

Little things count in life's decisions. I remember that I thought one of the attractions of administration was the lack of afterhours work but when I mixed with the super stars of Medical Administration they seemed to talk about working Saturday mornings and other times. It was naive of me to think that would not happen.

Then I thought about living in Melbourne and driving through 20-30 stop lights to get to work because I would have been unable to afford to live in the richer suburbs.

I was thinking that this was not a package that we wanted. I am not lazy but driving two hours or more per day with a nine or ten-hour day in between plus night time meetings seemed to lose any attraction it might have had.

I have mentioned before how lucky I have been and it happened again. An advertisement for a GP in Port Lincoln appeared somewhere so we did a 180degree turn around. I applied for the job, was interviewed in Port Lincoln and accepted the job in a place that had good memories for me as a child and for both Leonore and me as adults.

We left Warrnambool in late October 1979.

Penultimate story as they say. In 2015 I did a locum Medical Superintendent's job at Portland Hospital that is heavily involved with Warrnambool where the Medical Superintendent was Peter Obrien.

I also met Darryl Pedler who also had that job in the past and in 2015 was working for the local university. The odds on this happening must be huge but the three of us all had that position and had been GPs on Eyre Peninsula.

Last of all. On January 11th 1979 Leonore had a little boy. Guess who delivered him? Me. We had sat in the car, with Leonore in labour, looking over the sea listening to Bobby Darrin singing "Artificial Flowers" an achingly sad song. We were a bit late getting to the hospital and the doctor did not get there in time so I did the honours. Good timing or bad who knows?

CHAPTER NINE
PORT LINCOLN

INTRODUCTION

The more we thought about our decision to leave Warrnambool and move to Port Lincoln the happier we were. We had lived in five places in 10 years and thought that Port Lincoln would be ideal for us to make a permanent home. It is about a seven-hour drive from Adelaide and relatively isolated but far closer to our families than some other places we had lived.

There were several daily flights to Adelaide taking 45 minutes and I later found I could get up at seven o'clock and be in the Adelaide CBD by nine o'clock

The climate is mild and the coastal scenery is equal to any in Australia and Port Lincoln itself is built on the shores of Boston Bay which is many times bigger than Sydney Harbour and was named in 1802, like most landmarks in the area, by Matthew Flinders after places in his native Lincolnshire.

I am embarrassed to admit that I did not know until recently that those doughty souls who sailed to the New World and settled Boston in Massachusetts were also from Lincolnshire. Port Lincoln is a place for people who like the sea, fishing, sport, camping and other outdoor activities and did not like living in big cities.

We had a very positive approach to Port Lincoln from previous experience and were ready and willing to make it our home. We both knew people from school, nursing, and medical studies who already lived there, so we were warmly welcomed.

Soon after we arrived I was asked to play for the Wayback B grade cricket team by Bill Holland, the club's president, who appeared at our house with a tray of King George Whiting. I was theirs.

Undoubtedly they thought this was an excellent investment as I made 100 in my first game. I played in four of Wayback B grade premierships and in my last game went out in a blaze of glory making 85 not out after I had gone in to bat at 3 for 15. The first ball I received I hit to a fielder about five metres away who dropped the simplest catch I have ever seen. I must confess that I don't recall doing much in between those two innings but it was fun.

In all seriousness sport was tribal. My mate, "The Duke" Whitehead, a super footballer, played for Waybacks and told me that the club president instructed players to deal with him when he opened his car repair business and I certainly benefited as many Wayback people came to see me at the clinic so it was a nice relationship. I made a lot of friends but Kevin Enright stands out. He, like me, played a few games for the Sturt Football Club in Adelaide. He had a shack at Coffin

Bay and taught me the gentle art of catching King George Whiting. He and his wife Marilyn were fantastic to Leonore and me and made a real fuss of Mum and Dad in the years to come and our children always got on well together.

Ken MacKenzie also an ex Sturt player was another. I delivered his and Liz's daughter, Sally, who sadly I met at Ken's funeral in 2015 in Perth. She reminded me that I had given her the star from a Christmas tree at Coffin Bay when she was little and said that she still puts it on her tree every year. Money can't buy that.

Things were looking good for us so when we saw a house we liked for sale, we decided to investigate. It was old, large with big garden and on the esplanade with a view of Boston Bay to kill for. I knew the owner from university days when he lived at Lincoln College in Adelaide and this seemed a positive omen. A telephone call was pleasant, brief and we did a deal. He implied that he was pleased I had come along and made a sensible offer. Mum and Dad visited soon after and as we drove past from the airport I casually said we had bought it and they were thrilled. The house was really something in those days and was even marked on the British Admiralty charts to guide ships into harbour.

We were truly ecstatic but it certainly upset one of the practice partners and more so his wife, who ignored Leonore in the super market, as they were the people who had been offering to buy. Quite inadvertently I had made a better offer.

That was one factor but the other was that I had dared to

buy a house when I had not paid to become a partner but obviously wanted to stay in Port Lincoln. I had signed an agreement not to practice in Port Lincoln for three years if they did not offer me a partnership.

I had no ulterior motive and simply wanted to buy a house for our family to live in for the foreseeable future. It was certainly not a ploy to be a partner but I can see how a person with a devious mind might think that way. The other complicating factor was that restraint of trade laws may have allowed me so set up practice if I so wished.

Soon after this unpleasant interlude I became a partner and there was a skerrick of humour about this. I went to Westpac to borrow money for the house and practice and explained I wanted to borrow all the money for the practice and use what cash we had towards the house. The bank manager said "No the bank likes a 50:50 borrowing." I repeated my request firmly and he reluctantly agreed.

This was just before our son Tim's baptism in Adelaide and that night the social butterflies amongst us had dinner at the rather flash Decca's restaurant in North Adelaide. At the end of the meal I grabbed cash from everyone and wrote a cheque. Somehow I made a mistake or two or even three and corrected and initialled the corrections. The next week Tim's godmother, who organised the dinner, was rung by the restaurant and told the cheque had bounced. Fortunately they thought it was funny and evidence that we had had a good time. If they hadn't we might have had police knocking on our door or heaven forbid turning up at the clinic. My name was printed on the cheque and a telephone call would have resolved it. Surprise, surprise, the miserable bastard who had bounced the cheque had retired the day before so he laughed last.

Tom Hardy, the new manager, calmed me down and I stayed a Westpac customer. A few weeks later I had some cash I wanted to invest on the money market but it wasn't the required amount. Tom said "I'll put in the rest" and he did. Westpac and I have lived happily ever since. At the time of writing Westpac found that a card of ours had been hacked of $6-700 and replaced it. Good people to do business with.

Quite seriously having personal contact with Westpac staff over the years has been a real boon and has made our life and financial affairs a lot smoother than I imagine they are for many older people or those living in the city.

The population of Port Lincoln was about 10,000 in 1980 and The Investigator Clinic with nine doctors in a partnership was the only general medical practice in town. There was one physician and one surgeon resident in the town and a number of visiting specialists. There were good radiography and laboratory facilities. We all gave anaesthetics and delivered babies. With only nine doctors and allowing for holidays, study leave and the need to always have two doctors available we had to be on-call two week-ends out of three and a night during the week. It certainly wasn't as bad as single doctor practices but it was bad enough. At the time of writing the population is about 20,000 and there are 33 doctors.

I had reasonable experience in a general practice environment but nothing like the sustained demands by patients and partners in the private practice in Port Lincoln. I found out recently that one girl in reception discouraged people from seeing me. I was hauled before the partners again and told there had been complaints that I had told people that there was nothing wrong with them, was rude and grumpy and so on. The rooms were small and I am a big person and someone suggested that I shouldn't wear a dark leather jacket! It was all very vague but I was told to improve or else I would cease to be a partner.

I was surprised about the competition between doctors for patients and it reinforced an inkling I have that doctors need their patients as much or even more than vice versa. Patients did not like my reluctance to prescribe antibiotics and my caution with powerful pain killers.

Understandably people who have been waiting for hours with a sore throat and the like expect antibiotics and they were often visibly annoyed when I did not prescribe them. I have never told anyone that there was nothing wrong with them and every now and then a mother would say, 'I am pleased he doesn't need antibiotics," and I would gird my loins once more for the battle.

My personality maybe was a factor. I have never been a person who was super popular and yet I was best man at three weddings and that is not common.

A garrulous old bugger Reg Ween was a patient and he told me every visit to put a sheep's head in the hole where tomatoes are planted, but also after every visit he would give a big smile and say, "A lot of people don't like you but I reckon you are a great doctor."

To finish this homily Hippocrates urged doctors to 'Do no harm". I sometimes overused antibiotics I am sure for clinical conditions but not to make myself popular or earn more money. We were taught in the mid-1960s not to abuse antibiotics and anyone only has to read or watch the news today to know that there is a crisis in antibiotic and analgesic abuse. I do not think I have been the best doctor around but I have been aware of Hippocrates' comments and tried to follow them.

I did whatever I could to stay in the practice and succeeded somehow. Patients and doctors tend to reach a balance of mutual suitability and that included me.

I must finish this by saying that Dick Schoeman, Michael Lusk, Len Long and Chris Kennedy were helpful to me in this difficult time and if I have missed anyone I am sorry.

PETER'S BIRTH, SOME STABILITY, ASSOCIATESHIP AND NZ TRIP

So from about the middle of 1980 things stabilised for me and a lot of good things happened for us from 1980-1985. By far the most important thing was the birth of our son Peter at the Port Lincoln Hospital in January 1981. The delivery was uneventful medically but very special in another sense. Leonore's late sister, Susan, was a Dominican nun and with another nun mate and a wonderful person, Collette, came to Port Lincoln to help at this time. Susan attended the delivery and I will never forget the look of love, joy and wonder on her face as Peter was born to join Tim who was two five days later.

Our daughters Kirstin nine and Sarah seven became very involved with these little boys. Kirstin was already besotted with Tim and when Leonore came home I put Peter in Sarah's arms and said something like, "Kirstin has Tim and now you have Peter to look after" and she looked so proud.

Those two little girls grew into the role of big sisters perfectly and were an incredible help for Leonore because I was so often late home or doing something else. They played a huge role in the boys' lives when they were growing up and still do. The four children now have 10 children of their own between them and wonderful spouses. We are so proud of all of them and I am sure this was set in place when they were all so young.

Sometimes we went to Adelaide and shared Christmas with our families but in the main my parents came to Port Lincoln or Coffin Bay for the festive season. They developed a wonderful and lasting relationship with the girls and later the boys. We also had a lot of fun fishing at Coffin Bay and often Kevin and Marilyn Enright had us for tea where Mum enjoyed the beer battered whiting Kevin did so well.

We were also fortunate in being given prawns and tuna by our next door neighbour Anton Blaslov and crayfish by John Taylor in Port Lincoln. One year John turned up with 13 crayfish for us as long as Leonore would cook them and give him one. Now that was special.

I continued playing cricket as I mentioned for four years and firmed up several friendships with team mates particularly Peter Hubbard who was the manager of the local meatworks. He was previously a stock agent and knew some of my cricketing mates in the south east so we got on very well. His father-in-law was Max Mortimer who had predated Peter by many decades as the manager of the local meatworks. Their address was Box 1 Port Lincoln. When Max retired the company gave the mail box to him and he passed it to Peter who gave it to me when he left Port Lincoln.

I had always wanted to have a farm and this dream became true. We had remained friends with Brian and Pam Murray from Parakylia Station near Woomera and together we bought a property, we called Ramsend, 65 km from Port Lincoln north of Coffin Bay near Mount Greenly. Brian and Pam used to come down from Woomera to help us with fencing, burning of scrub and other jobs. The fences were cyclone with wooden strainer posts and steel droppers hammered in every 10 metres. I asked Brian to make me a dropper knocker, a steel tube, one end closed, 10cm in diameter and 50-60 cm long with two handles on the side. This was put over a steel star picket, lifted and slammed down until it was the desired depth.

Brian turned up with a 16 pound, i.e. seven kg, sledge hammer that had a 15 cm long handle. I asked what the hell I was to do with that. He said, "Hey boy ya just grab the dropper in the left hand and knock it in with the hammer that's what we do on the station- 'ere I'll show you". This he did and hit the dropper a few times to no avail - limestone will do it every time. He did some fencing the next day and told me it was the hardest day of work he had ever done.

We soon bought some cattle. "Ninety calves from the Territory" were to arrive on a given day and I thought it would be great to get some nice little calves. The bloody things were all half grown and a Brahman jumped fences and disappeared for a time. Kevin helped me unload and walk them to Ramsend.

Our girls asked if they could have a calf of their own and pointed it out. I thought it was their caring nature but when I asked what they were going to call it the answer was 'Chops" so their intent was clear. We did have a lot of fun and some hard labour certainly is a good stress reliever and the beers with the barbecue helped.

Bruce and Carli Pontifex, who I knew from school and the south east respectively, joined us one day and very soon the pregnancies of both the girls were revealed. At the appropriate time two baby boys were born who went to school together in Port Lincoln and Adelaide and in their mid-thirties are still good mates.

About 18 months later we were having another picnic at Ramsend with the Hubbards and Peter somehow finished up bottom first in a rabbit hole with his hands and feet framing his face. Poor Tim was crying out, "My brother, my brother." We eventually stopped laughing long enough to pull him out.

That day Tim played in the dirt and was absolutely, small boy filthy and cute. After taking a photo we washed him in the cattle trough headed for home and a bath. It was his birthday so another picture was taken with sparkling clean and combed hair, in his pyjamas and in front of his birthday cake. We put the two pictures in a frame and gave it to my parents who kept it on their refrigerator as did we. Tim of course often looked at it.

A few months later, Tim was having his morning cuddle with Leonore and me and as usual wriggling in between us. This is the Oedipus complex where little boys see their father as threats to the bond they have with their mother. Of course I teased him by cuddling Leonore even more. I thought it was about time to sort this out as he was getting a little distressed so I gave him the Daddy and Mummy love Tim and Daddy put a seed in Mummy's tummy blah blah and that's where you came from story.

Quick as a flash he shook his head, looked sad and said "I don't like that" in a heartfelt fashion. I gently asked where he thought he came from. His answer was "I came from the trough at Ramsend" ---------Gold!

We kept the Ramsend partnership going for a few years

but Brian and Pam's girls were at boarding school in Adelaide and they needed a unit there so we amicably bought them out. Pam and Brian are Peter's godparents and have been and still are fantastic to Peter and his family.

The only way that we were able to manage Ramsend was with the help given to us by Noel and Ruth Linsell who farmed nearby. They became guides, advisors, friends and mentors. They helped us yarding, loading, unloading, marking calves, drenching, fixed our windmill, organised our shearing later, put in a crop or two, helped us plant a two km by ten metre shelter belt of trees, carted stock and many more things. At the time of writing Noel is fixing the motor of a spray unit for me. They are still looking after us.

As well as cricket I also played golf most Wednesday afternoons. There were a lot of professional and business people who did the same. I played at Glenelg with Dad sometimes when I was in Adelaide and later joined the Royal Adelaide Golf Club as a country member. But golf needs more time than I was willing or able to devote to it. Four things limited me to Wednesday afternoons; weekends on call, the girls' sport, Ramsend and the shack we bought at Coffin Bay and a large garden at home. So golf lost out and I regret that but it just wasn't a priority.

Obviously Port Lincoln is a country town with all that means professionally for a doctor. As well as owning a farm I became more and more involved with people who were or had been involved with the rural sector in Port Lincoln or other parts of Eyre Peninsula.

I have mentioned Noel and Ruth Linsell who were farmers as was Noel's brother, Richard. Kevin Enright worked at the local prison but for decades had been a stock agent, Peter Hubbard likewise before managing the meat works and Ken MacKenzie was a jackeroo at East Bungaree station near Clare before joining Elder Smith's.

I made further connections with rural people through a patient of mine, Eddie Mickan, a retired farmer from Cummins who invited me to have a beer at the Great Northern Hotel one day after work. This was a great pub and for many years I would go there on my way home once or twice a week.

It was the pub for teachers, farmers, stock agents, some accountants and lawyers, shearers and many other business men and I knew Graham Ween and Ashley Harvey from schooldays. It was a very pleasant place.

A Frank Lillecrap from a well-known pastoral family sold us Ramsend and he and his wife Maeve became good friends of ours. He told Brian and me a fascinating story. When he was 14 years old he was droving a mob of sheep near Orrorroo and had camped for the night. A bloke, none other than Reg Williams, rode into his camp on a bicycle on his way to Adelaide to make boots and other leather goods. Frank told us that he later bought the first pair of boots made by the man universally known as RMW. If any readers see or have seen the "RM Williams Way" sign in Orrorroo that only came about from my telling the RM Williams historian Frank's story many years later.

Jack May the manager of Elders who was also a patient, a customer of the "Northern" and good mate. A couple of times he organised a trip for me with his son Chris on a prawn boat he skippered in Exmouth Gulf in Western Australia. There were a few nurses who bobbed in and out on occasions. I knew all of them and still see them around the place.

I recently found a card about the size of a laptop given to me by Pam Sampson, wife of Jack, owners of the Northern that has at least 20 signatures wishing me good health when I had an emergency appendix removal in 1982 or 1983. The late Gary Turnbull, a loveable rascal and builder who did a lot of work on our house wrote that "It must of been all those prawns you keep winning in the raffle jamming up your gut", or similar. I went there for many years but the breath analyser and the installation of pokers machines fixed that. Being a doctor in a small town is like being in a fish bowl but I always felt very relaxed at the Northern.

Another enjoyable thing we did in the 1980s was to become Amway distributors. People did and do sneer at people who take on these sort of businesses and why they do that when people are trying to improve themselves I do not know.

I was in a pub one night and a rather attractive woman introduced herself to me. She was Rosemary Moody (nee Glynn) who with Jenny and Mary Glynn her cousins as a teenager, I used to hang around with after school at the notorious milk bar 'Sigalis's' in Rundle Street Adelaide

She and her husband Andrew got us involved in Amway. Andrew had been a farmer but then sold insurance. They had assembled a team of some very smart farmers such as Oran and Helen Shardlow, Lyle and Kay Grund, Maurice and Lyn Siviour, Graham and Thelma Giddings and Glenda and John Baker and we enjoyed the company of such ambitious and hard-working people and still are friends with the Shardlows and Siviours

None of the above people came from Port Lincoln so again I was gaining a broader picture of Eyre Peninsula than just Port Lincoln.

An even bigger stimulus to this attitude literally and figuratively was that I stood as a candidate for the Federal seat of Grey, the second biggest electorate in the world, the biggest being Kalgoorlie. This was a challenging and interesting venture but I must say that I am glad I did not succeed, although the contacts I made certainly helped in the years to come.

I forgot to mention that, pretty much from day one at The Investigator Clinic and being the new boy, I was the visiting medical officer at the Port Lincoln Prison. This went from an hour or so once a week to twice a week over the years. Initially the prisoners were aboriginal people from Port Lincoln and elsewhere on Eyre Peninsula and paedophiles who were there for the good of their health and a few long term prisoners who worked in the kitchen. In total there were

40 or so prisoners and one or two nurses. Later when the Liberals had a short spell in government they doubled the number of prisoners so we got more general prisoners including corrupt police and a killer or two. When I first visited I used to get depressed at the prisoners' lot and their long-term hopelessness. I tried to treat them with sympathy but firmness. The nurses were much the same and they were highly regarded by the prisoners and by me.

One prisoner did or said something inappropriate to a nurse one day and another inmate heard or saw him and informed the nurse that the bloke would not be bothering her again and he didn't. There were some funny things that happened. I asked an aboriginal guy from the real bush why he was in prison and he said "I was playing cowboys and Indians with coppers" (with real guns), I asked him which one was his mob. He answered "Oh we were the Indians, boss".

Once I was raising money for the hospital and as it was a prison farm the prisoners collected manure for us. We sold cow manure for $4, pure Hereford manure for $5 and bovine organic growth stimulant for $6 a bag.

It was all in the marketing!!

Some things changed and a psychiatrist started visiting from Adelaide to see special needs prisoners who were essentially aboriginal schizophrenics well beyond my capacity to look after.

The other new service was to provide methadone to prisoners - for dubious reasons in some cases. I had looked after a prisoner who self-harmed for years to get narcotics, but they were never prescribed. Off he went to Yatala in Adelaide and some nice caring young doctor blithely put him on Methadone. He and others on this drug resulted in about six nurses instead of two being employed so they could visit seven days a week to administer this stuff.

Some people are allergic to morphine, pethidine and other narcotic drugs. When we were medical students we were told that a drug called physeptone could be used but it was highly addictive and should be used very carefully. Readers may be surprised to know the other name for this drug is our old mate Methadone.

Any way I tried my best and learnt some more about human nature and the depths and heights humans can reach. One prisoner committed a heinous crime with a child. Just before I stopped working there he told me he had met his victim's mother and it was the hardest thing he had ever done. He looked at me and said "She forgave me".

A celebrity prisoner turned up at the prison and as they all did had to see me for a medical. He was quite polite and told me how he knew Dad and what a great bloke he was.

Most if not all of the prisoners were kind to the farm animals and someone once said "Animals have never hurt or harmed them, people have done that" and boy oh boy does that say it in spades.

I worked there from 1979 to 2002 and may have been the longest serving prison medical officer in South Australia. At the time of reviewing this section in late 2017 I was told that more than 80% of prisoners at the Port Lincoln prison are dyslexic, no wonder they have problems in the outside world.

There were two other aspects of work that happened in 1984 and 1985.

One was that I became part time Medical Superintendent at the Hospital and secondly after a lot of arguments we became associates, meaning no longer partners. In a partnership all income and expenses are divided equally but associates have certain complex expense sharing and keep what is left over from their earnings. There was some logic in it because there was a widening gap between the high and low earners. No one ever showed me any figures so I do not know the details. For a mess of potage for some we went from having six weeks holiday, two weeks study leave a year and long service leave every five years to two to three weeks leave a year.

I actually started a consultancy in occupational safety in the mid-1980s for a few years and for 10 years I don't think I had any complaints about me.

The outstanding personal pleasure we had was a trip with the family to New Zealand when the children were 13, 11, 5 and 3. This was a great experience and took a lot of thinking and talking about.

The girls were lovely. I started giving them pocket money and they saved half of it and bought treasures while they were away. Kirstin was 13 on the last night we were there and of course the airlines charged her as an adult for that leg.

There was an upside. We had a family dinner at our motel for her birthday and a lady diner was so impressed with her niceness and behaviour she gave her ten dollars.

We had planned a trip on a game boat in the Bay of Islands which was a great experience and exciting. The boat, *Lady Lynn*, was a slow 40 feet displacement boat on which we spent two nights. The skipper was Eldon Jepson, a retired farmer who was great and even cooked us roast lamb. I found out later that no one else would take a couple with four kids but our children were an absolute credit to us.

We were unsuccessful in catching or even seeing a marlin but I did catch a Mako shark, a recognised game fish and a much better fighter than other sharks. It may even leap out of the water. Our three-year-old was sitting on the cabin roof while I was wrestling with the Mako. Understandably it was threshing around quite a lot and Peter, who had an unusually deep voice said, "I think you should stop playing with that shark." We landed the Mako and headed for home. After we had tied up at the jetty the secretary from the game fishing club presented me with a 'pin' which was silver with a flag on it as mine was the first game fish of the season.

I arranged to meet the secretary in the clubhouse for a drink later and I was standing at the bar waiting to be served when a man sitting on what was obviously "his" stool at the end of the bar spoke to me. He said "Bloody Australians. Bowl underarm in a cricket match, won't let Think Big run in the

Melbourne Cup and catch all our fish." To say I was gobsmacked would be some understatement. I replied "No one in Australia liked Greg Chappell making his brother Trevor bowl underarm, I don't know anything about horse racing and your fishing is bloody fantastic." I was almost as surprised at his next action as the previous comment. He looked at me slowly smiled and said "Have a beer" and slid a full glass of beer along the bar to me like in a western movie.

Before we leave the beautiful Bay of Islands: a year or so after this trip Leonore and I went back there to fish in a tournament and as we were the only Australians we were granted the status of "The Australian Team". Leonore caught a small yellow-fin tuna that we were happy to eat.

The very pleasant tournament organiser for many years was a small lady who had never actually competed until her mates made her. The tournament rules were that it was lines up at 4pm/1600hrs unless an angler was hooked up and that is exactly what happened to her, she hooked a massive Striped Marlin at 3-30pm or thereabouts.

We all had tea and drinks at the club and waited and waited some more and she turned up at 11pm having landed what was a world record or close to it fish of 3-400 pounds or thereabouts. This was an extraordinary effort as she was too short to put her feet against the transom from the game chair and that is essential for anyone to gain leverage on a fish. Naturally she won the tournament and made her acceptance speech. In particular she thanked the young boat skipper who helped her to compensate for her lack of reach. She explained how the skipper stood facing her and leant against the transom for seven hours while she had her feet against his thighs, tummy muscles or private parts. The room exploded with laughter.

1985-1990 HOSPITAL WORK AND ACCREDITATION

On return from New Zealand I resumed my duties as Medical Superintendent of the Port Lincoln Hospital and I enjoyed this very much. Among other things I had to check the fee for service charges of my partners and later other practices. That was clearly an area that could be fraught with difficulty. I am proud to say only twice in what turned out to be nearly 20 years in the job did I have to speak to anyone about over charging

In my administrative capacity I worked two half days a week and attended board and other meetings sometimes in Adelaide or elsewhere. I checked the doctors' charges as mentioned and the quality of the medical records. There were other things like interviewing staff, delineating clinical privileges and so on. I was interested in quality in hospitals from my time in Warrnambool and could see a need for it at Port Lincoln. I became a surveyor with the Australian Council on Health/Hospital Standards (ACHS) and did some surveys in country hospitals.

It seemed to me that it was given that our hospital should seek accreditation with the ACHS but I was wrong. The Chief

Executive Officer (CEO) and the Director of Nursing (DON) were against it but the good news was that the Chairman of the Board Pamela Francis, a TAFE teacher, was for it as were many of the senior nurses and that made it happen.

I was involved as were the medical staff association, my secretary Barb Joseph, Win Modystach the Deputy DON and the senior nurses, and once the Board had made up its mind the CEO and DON of course participated and we duly were surveyed and accredited.

Four years later we did this again and it was a similar experience, but after that there were one or two people fully employed and it was a vastly more complicated exercise. A very important part of the standards was preparation for internal and external disasters - in other words disaster plans. These are often prepared by bureaucrats following the example of big institutions.

For example there may be a list of responsibilities for dozens of people but that is unreal in a small to medium hospital. There will always be senior nurses, specialist doctors, GP and GP anaesthetist, pathologist and radiographer and an engineer of some sort on call. Leading lights theoretically like the CEO and deputy, DMS, DON and deputy cannot be regarded as available as they may well be away at work or play.

It takes a lot of effort to simplify disaster plans and ensure that everyone knows what to do including the nurse on her first day. There was also of course the hospital's role in integrating with other services particularly the ambulance people and police

A useful definition or explanation of a disaster is an event that overwhelms the capacity of an organisation so other steps need to be taken such as decanting recuperating patients to nearby hospitals, calling in extra staff, flying in specialised medical teams and so on.

I became very interested in this and went on a very pleasant tour of Eyre Peninsula hospitals courtesy of the RFDS with Gary Phillips, a specialist anaesthetist, to check out their anaesthetic and emergency equipment. This ultimately resulted in Thomas Packs being provided for the small hospitals. These back packs are carried by air borne paramedics and the like and are works of art given the amount and quality of kit that they hold. Later we also managed to get places for many Eyre Peninsula doctors at Early Management of Severe Trauma (EMST) courses that are all about what to in the first or golden hour when people often die after severe injuries. Perhaps the comment that "By then every patient should have or have had a tube or finger in every orifice" explains it better than I can with a lot more words.

The development of this course came from extraordinary circumstances. In1976 James Styner an American orthopaedic surgeon was flying his plane with his wife and four children as passengers from California to Nebraska and crashed.

His wife was killed and the children and he badly injured. Three of the children were unconscious but he and the other child got them out of the plane in sub zero temperatures and somehow he flagged down a vehicle and got them to a hospital that was woefully disorganised.

In particular he was concerned "That no one seemed to bother about protecting their necks." This heroic man developed the course that just about everyone nowadays who deals with trauma is required to do and maintain currency.

This trip with Gary Phillips and meetings with other services also led to the Eyre Peninsula Disaster Plan being developed in more detail. There are nine small hospitals with the closest distance between them being about 40km. Eyre Peninsula at that time had eight hospitals with one to three doctors.

In an emergency, usually a car or farm accident, the nearest doctor would go to the scene if indicated and arrange for the injured to go back to the hospital he came from. That is Ok if it was a simple injury but a more complicated incident, and in particular if more than one person is seriously injured, there are obvious and serious gaps in that approach.

We developed the concept that the nearest doctor would go to the site and arrange for people with serious injuries to go to the nearest hospital, <u>other than</u> <u>the one he/she had just left.</u> We designed a colour coded map to demonstrate all this. I believe that 10 or more years later when there were catastrophic fires in Lower Eyre Peninsula this plan was activated.

I mentioned previously that we were now associates rather than partners and while that reduced the income of many of us there was more freedom and doctors were able to develop specific interests. Mine was occupational health and safety and for a time I had a small consulting practice in that field. Someone approached me to become involved with some trials preceding the establishment of Workcover in South Australia.

These trials were modelled on the Allan Bruce five-x-five plans he had developed for the Australian military.

The results and responses to work caused injuries is or can be an exhaustive subject but some things seem to be true:

1 Almost all work injuries mend in six weeks.

2 It is beneficial to return injured people to meaningful work as soon as possible with alteration to their workplace if necessary.

2 Psycho-social factors are always likely to be in play with work caused injuries and they start to become the major reason for most injured workers remaining off work after six or more weeks.

3 At 12 months post injury 90% of the reasons for people being off work are for psycho-social reasons and 10% for physical reasons such as major/multiple trauma in the original injury.

This has been one of the most important things I have learnt in my career.

The plan was simple really once everyone in an organisation understood the concept.

I was employed to go to one or another of three government departments to do routine medicals, to review injured people and liaise with their treating doctor and to be on their side with the organisation in the review process and of course to recommend and supervise the modification of their workplace or role. As well, I was involved in rehabilitation activities and work hardening and in recommending ways that the organisation could help deal with social and psychological problems - sometimes simply taking the non driving spouse of an injured worker shopping.

But it was not all about work and I recall two stories about our daughters and our Series 3 Ex Police Land Rover Station wagon that I could make backfire at will. I had known the girls' science teacher Tina in the past. She was and indeed still is a pretty, vivacious, slim, blonde and highly intelligent lady. *Top Gun* was the rage in those days, so when I drove the kids to school I wore my hard hat and Ray Ban lookalike sunglasses. If I saw Tina I would make the car backfire and give the thumbs up and salute, the way Maverick did in the film, just before the aircraft was catapulted from the aircraft carrier.

If I forgot my hat I could always get out and give her a kiss which had much the same effect: two very embarrassed teenage girls and two little boys fleeing into the classroom with Tina giving a little smile.

The girls liked going to our farm and driving the Land Rover. One day I was driving it in town with Sarah and having a drink or eating something. I ran out of hands turning a corner and asked Sarah to change the gears. She fiddled around and couldn't do it. I asked why she couldn't manage the gear change after driving the Land Rover in a very rough paddock and she said "Kirstin always changes the gears."

Kirstin was and still is a very caring and loving big sister to her siblings and so is Sarah. Kirstin's nickname was "Bruce Bullfart" and Sarah's "Lady Primrose Veronica Pickle Wart". Those names paint a very good picture.

Perhaps the best thing that happened for us was the wonderful relationship with my parents. We must have spent every Christmas with them, mostly in Port Lincoln because of my work commitments but sometimes in Adelaide. Their generosity and love to us all was unforgettable and they demonstrated a relationship with each other that many seek but few achieve.

When the girls moved to Adelaide and stayed in rented houses with their friends they knew Nana and Papa were always there for them, a great relief for us.

Amway was good for Leonore and she learnt to be a good public speaker this led a couple in the group to ask her to enter the Mrs Australia Quest in 1988. That she did and was very successful with her fundraising and in her public appearances. I have no doubt she would have won but when she was interviewed and asked how she would manage with a daughter doing matriculation the next year she blinked!

Leonore was involved with the Red Cross and in 1988 or 89 they decided to open a formal branch in Port Lincoln and started an Humanities Services Fund to pay for this. Leonore and I helped the local auxiliary to raise $50,000 for this purpose.

The other thing I was involved in was fishing at Coffin Bay for whiting as mentioned but also in Port Lincoln where we had bigger fish to fry called White Pointers. We as a family became very friendly with Chris and Christine Stone who had a superbly named service station and fishing tackle shop that they called "The Gas Catch." One of our interests was game fishing and together with some friends we bought a 28 foot long game fishing boat. We had a lot of fun and caught lots of fish on our overnight expeditions but never a White Pointer. Chris did, but from another boat. We managed with some other people to rekindle the game fishing in Port Lincoln with the "Home of the White Pointer" tournament which was a great success. The trophy for this tournament should be remembered.

In the early 1980s three men started Constantia furniture. These guys were Master Craftsmen in their fields a rare combination in the world. They made the speaker's table in the national Parliament House and Ken Martin, one of the founding members is a world recognised sculptor. To mention but a few of his art works: they are the statues of Barrie Robran, Ken Farmer, 'Boof" Lehmann and Gillespie at the Adelaide Oval and the wonderful race horse Makybe Diva on the foreshore in Port Lincoln. We were in a position to buy some of their furniture when they started out and became good friends and still are with Ken.

Earlier I mentioned that I knew the previous owner of our house, Brian Lamshed and also knew a mate of his Rory Dredge whose father was Colonel Dredge. When we moved into our house there was an elephant's foot with a piece of wood attached to it so it could be used as a table. I was told it came from Colonel Dredge, but I do not know the details or even if that is true.

I thought of burying it in respect for the poor bloody animal but procrastinated for long enough to have an idea— what about using it as a perpetual trophy for the Home of the White Pointer tournament. Done. The Constantia boys whipped up a top quality display cabinet and there it was good to go. The guy who won the tournament was a wandering cockney professional motor bike rider and when this well- hidden trophy was unveiled the term speechless, said it all.

After five years or so the boat had major mechanical problems and the other owners lost interest or had left Port Lincoln and I went back to whiting fishing.

Chris however used this experience to launch into a very successful game fishing career here and overseas. He also became involved politically and administratively in the fishing industry so that was a good outcome and he still has the elephant's foot that I will grab from him--maybe. I planned to display this at the book launch but felt uncomfortable so did not—things change.

The 1980s did not start well but by the end of the decade things were much better. In the late 1980s we were driving back from a trip to Western Australia and about 200km from Port Lincoln nearing Elliston I had a feeling that I was home.

The travelling throughout Eyre Peninsula when I was going to be a politician, visiting hospitals with Gary Phillips, having a farm about half way to Elliston and many friends who farmed away from Port Lincoln made me start to think about health and welfare of a larger area than just Port Lincoln.

Our children had grown up. Kirstin was 19 and studying nursing in Adelaide, Sarah 17 and in year 11, Tim 11 and Peter 9. The girls were quite successful at school. Kirstin received a medal at Government House for attaining full marks in her matriculation exams. Sarah did the same thing in due course.

In 1992 I worked as Medical Superintendent at the Alice Springs Hospital for six weeks and boy was that an eye opener, but that is another story

THE 1990S – well 1990-2002

There were two main features, the death of my parents and Leonore's mother in a 12 month period and my work and associated activities in what was probably the most enjoyable and challenging time of my career.

Mum and Dad's Golden Wedding anniversary was in August 1990 and predictably it was held at the Sturt Football Club. There were a lot of their old friends there, Leonore's parents, some friends of mine and our children.

Dad made a dignified and loving speech and in particular after beautiful words about Mum he said how they had been "Blessed with a son who cared." That meant a lot to me.

Our 19-year-old daughter Kirstin proposed the toast with great aplomb and love. She said some lovely things about them. In particular, how she hoped that she would have such a marriage as them. I am pleased to say that, nearly 30 years after that speech, Kirstin and her husband Andrew have certainly done that and their son, Jackson, proposed the toast to Leonore and me at our Golden Wedding in 2019.

My mother's 80th birthday was in 1991 and she and Dad shared it with us in Port Lincoln. Mum loved fish with a passion. Leonore and I caught 80 whiting, Kevin Enright's son Justin made a special trip to Coffin Bay to dive for some scallops, Bill Ford gave us some abalone, I caught some crabs that Leonore made into pate and John Taylor gave us a crayfish and some prawns. It was quite a meal. Dad also was 80 in 1991 and we celebrated with friends in Adelaide.

1994 was the next milestone. It was Leonore's and my 25th wedding anniversary. We had arranged a Murder Mystery weekend at the Bishops House in Peterborough on the last Saturday in June. The Friday night before we met the advance guard from Perth, a couple of my football mates, Alf Laslett and Allan Byers and their wives, the Stains and Mum and Dad at Clare It was quite heart-warming to see them all hanging off every word Dad said about football. The next day we drove to Peterborough and Mum and Dad went home to Adelaide.

This was a splendid event and in retrospect the last party of its kind we have held or attended with about 25 close and long time friends present. We were all in our forties. It was a watershed - the last of our youth and I guess we were lucky to stretch it that far. Within fifteen months my parents were both dead as was Leonore's mother nine months after that.

I have mentioned the demise of Mum and Dad at the start of this book and I was fortunate to spend the time with Mum under those circumstances and devote a small fraction of the time to her that she had done for me in my life.

In due course Mum came over here and was looked after in the Port Lincoln Hospital and the Matthew Flinders Nursing Home. The care she received was exemplary. It was so sad in that Mum loved a chat but the stroke damaged the right side of her body and she had no movement of her arm or leg, but worse for her she could not speak although she understood most things.

To Marie Woolford, a friend and nurse, and Steve Ballard, a friend and doctor colleague, thanks for what you did for Dad until he died relatively peacefully in my arms, I will not forget. To our son Peter who spent so much time with Dad and still has some scars—thanks so much mate.

One more thing. We decided to go to Leonore's brother's place in Adelaide for Christmas in 1995 and just as we were about to leave for Adelaide I was telephoned to be told that one of our cattle had strayed onto the road. A car hit it and the driver was killed.

There was no penalty to me but we certainly did not need that.

WORK

I was still at the hospital and The Investigator Clinic. Early in the decade a bunch of us decided to raise some money for the hospital.

We were encouraged and supported by the then Chairman of the Board Michael Burnside and the CEO Ian Matthews and DON Sandy Le Brun, local member of parliament Liz Penfold and many staff members had a Ball and a ball, sold manure, ran quiz nights and operated a bottom of the harbour scheme.

This last venture was the idea of Michael Burnside. The concrete slab for the boat ramp at the new Marina was moulded somehow into different size squares that people could buy for different amounts. When the Marina was inundated with water the concrete with the names of donors was at the bottom of the harbour like the nefarious schemes that have been promoted to save people tax a few years before. We raised $100,000 which was not a bad effort.

From 1985 for eight years I was a councillor for the City of Port Lincoln. From the mid-1990s to 2002 I was a member of the South Australian Medical Board and I believe the first country general practitioner to be so appointed. I also continued as a hospital surveyor for the ACHS.

In the early nineties there was concern by the Australian Government about the quality and the function of general practice in Australia. It was even mooted by a Minister of Health that the patients of single doctor practices may not be allowed to claim medicare benefits.

The concept of Divisions of General Practice was raised and 10 trial divisions were funded in 1992.

Divisions were to have several functions:

1 To be regionally based.

2 To allow and facilitate communications between general practitioners and other players in the heath arena such as hospitals, other health professionals and consumers.

3 To undertake projects in their geographical region involving general practitioners.

4 To provide Continuing Medical Education for their members.

5 To involve general practitioners in decisions about health in their area.

This concept I thought was absolutely what was needed in Australia and on Eyre Peninsula. There would be money coming into our area for various things not the least of which was for doctors to do projects outside the fee for service world.

There were some interesting attitudes about the source of

the funds that apparently came from the Medical Benefits Budget. When Medicare was introduced nearly 20 years before it was clearly and unequivocally promoted and sold as a scheme that would help patients pay the doctors' bills.

It was not long though that we were told by the Commonwealth to send them the bills and they would reimburse doctors directly. Phrases like "The fee we pay the doctors" by the public servants particularly and then the doctors themselves, saying that the budget for Divisions was "Their money". That was the last nail in the coffin for fee for service medicine as we knew it.

That could be the subject of another and very large book.

I thought that I had the interest, experience, the qualifications, the energy and the wider view that I have mentioned above to be successful at what was effectively change management. I had done that before.

I received encouragement from the CEO of the hospital Ian Matthews and at least some of the doctors in Port Lincoln. The Whyalla Hospital was keen to get the Eyre Peninsula Division of General Practice (EPDGP) in Whyalla but I had some support amongst the doctors there so I was elected as the General Practice Director of the EPDGP.

It was an exciting time and a management committee was set up with two doctors each from Port Lincoln, Whyalla and the rural area - there being a voting member and reserve.

At the suggestion of Dr Clive Auricht, who worked at Cleve we employed Kris Bascomb who had been his practice nurse/receptionist when he had worked at Elliston. She later became the Administration Manager and she and I were non-voting members of the board.

It all got under way on the 19th August 1993, my birthday. Kris and I set up the EPDGP downstairs in our house and I remember writing proposals late on Christmas Eve that year.

It was a blur for some time setting everything up but in particular seeking funding for projects. We soon grew out of our house, another two offices and finally the old nurses quarters at the Port Lincoln Hospital became our home and is now known as the Morton Building after the contributions made by Michael Burnside, me and the bequests by friends of Mum and Dad.

We developed and were funded for perhaps 10 projects over the years.

The Royal Australian College of General Practitioners (RACGP) wanted to develop standards for General Practice and set up a company called Australian General Practice Accreditation Limited (AGPAL) to do that. I became a director of that company. When those standards were developed, they needed to be trialled and the EPDGP got the job. I do not recall the total grant but the air fares were $50,000 for our surveyors to travel to various places in Australia.

I ran a project on Farm Injuries that had a budget of about $500,000 with Jane Mackereth, an intensive care nurse from Adelaide who had moved to Port Lincoln with her husband.

This was quite a complicated project and involved

participating in formal farmers groups such as a National and State Farmers Federation and setting up a reference group locally. I attended a Farm Injury Conferences in Wagga Wagga, Cairns and Saskatoon in Canada and in 1997 we ran a conference in Whyalla.

I was a guest speaker at several of these including Canada and we also attended and spoke at many meetings in Adelaide and one at Echuca in Victoria where we met the Victorian Coroner who encouraged our efforts, in particular our plan was to set up a register of farm injury related deaths, since one surprisingly did not exist.

As part of the project we had access to the South Australian Coroner's findings of deaths that required his attention such as accidents, suicides, murders and others. These were written by hand in large books and accessed by turning pages in those books. It was a Dickensian experience.

There was a funny side to this very serious matter. Later we tried to establish some sort of electronic system and approached various Commonwealth and State Departments to do this and were advised by a bureaucrat from somewhere to talk to the Victorian Coroner who had an interest in this area. Talk about going around in circles.

I mentioned earlier about contacts I had and this came to the fore in getting funding for this project. I found out that the Health Promotions people in the State and Federal Governments did not like doctors messing about on their turf. Goodness, how could doctors know anything about helping people in health matters? Attending gatherings of farmers and importantly their wives and running health checks was very much on our agenda.

The funding was held up and I happened to be at a meeting in Adelaide and at morning tea and approached Michael Armitage the SA Minister for Health who I knew reasonably well and he introduced me to the Federal Minister Michael Wooldridge and they were puzzled as both had signed off on this project. It was sorted out.

Perhaps a year later a nurse from Sydney contacted us about something and I arranged to meet the head of health promotions in the SA Health Department.

We had a pleasant three- way conversation about whatever it was and just before leaving I asked this lady why she had been against our Farm Injury project. She emphatically denied this but both her arms tightly folded and her legs crossed and uncrossed repeatedly did suggest otherwise.

The other thing that helped us was that I knew several people in farmers' organisations in Adelaide and locally, had a farm myself and had narrowly avoided an accidental death myself when I was hit in the face by a flying railway sleeper.

Jane was a huge plus. She had family connections through her husband with the Rehn Family as did I and even more importantly she could charm the crows out of a tree.

Farmers detest people, particularly those from bureaucracies, who tell them what to do on their farms, but we were seen as legitimate. The timing was good also because it was obvious that the tide was turning and rural folks were recognising that there were so many psychological and other health problems in their communities which needed attention, particularly in the field of suicide prevention.

A big factor is that many, if not most farmers were just too busy to attend meetings. One farmer told me that he rode a push bike from his house to and from his workshop, sheds etc. to save time and finally realised just how stressed he was when he pulled up alongside his diesel pump to fill up his bike.

Some people could not afford the fuel to attend functions. We had budgeted for some of these expenses so that helped

Last but not least Jane and I talked to some schools, with the parents' permission!

The male teacher introduced us as a doctor and a nurse and then asked the students who they thought had what job.

One little boy shot his hand up and said "He is the doctor". The teacher obviously looking for some PC indoctrination asked why the boy said that.

His answer was, "I play footy against his sons and he coaches their team. I know he is Doctor Morton!"

I mentioned that we ran the biennial Farm Injury Conference in Whyalla and invited a Canadian, James Dosman who was a world authority on the subject and that was very successful.

As part of that conference we arranged a session at

Tregalano a sheep station near Whyalla owned by a relative of Margaret Kretschmer a friend of ours form Port Lincoln and a member of the well known Nicholson family of pastoralists in that area who helped with this venture. A feature of this was a presentation by three close friends of ours who worked on the land in different areas and had been injured in their work places. They were Brian Murray, Noel Linsell and Oran Shardlow and their presentations were outstanding.

A couple of years later Dr Dosman invited me to a similar conference in Canada as mentioned and we were joined on this trip by Jack Hassell and his late wife Gwenda, farmers from Penola in South Australia and activists in injury prevention - and yes I knew him in another life. We met my oft mentioned friend Burley Vandergriff and his wife Loretta, who had flown into San Francisco from Colorado Springs to meet us and we spent a few days together. The highlight was watching the Blue Angels, the USAF aerobatic team strut their stuff over Alcatraz. Burley had been a jet fighter pilot so his comments certainly added to the experience.

Then Burley led us to Napa Valley the wine centre of America. After a discussion. I drove, Gwenda navigated and the rest of the team sat in the back. We needed all our wits about us as we crossed the Golden Gate Bridge at 0630 am all dark and foggy. My eyes were like lasers fixed on Burley's tail light and we managed. Again, we had a good time and resumed the same pattern on the way back to San Francisco to catch plane to Saskatoon.

I congratulated the navigator and myself on reaching the airport in good time but it was the wrong bloody airport and the right one was miles away but with good Aussie ingenuity we took the vacant emergency services left lane-just like home and fortunately were not picked up

So we made Saskatoon as planned where I spoke about the RFDS and the similarities of Australia and Canada with their major population centres in a relatively small area separated by long distances of sparsely populated and potentially hostile country. Toronto and Quebec and their distance from Vancouver is very similar to Sydney and Melbourne with Perth.

I chaired a "Hypothetical" about the effects of farm injuries on families that was developed by Lyn Fragar who was at the conference. I should have mentioned her before. She was the queen of farm injury work in Australia and had been for decades. She established Moree in NSW as the centre for this work and was a great mentor to me. I had secret dreams of doing something similar in Port Lincoln which is about the same size as Moree but with a much smaller surrounding population but for various reasons that did not happen. However Lyn actually got me accredited as a trainer of allied health professionals in the rehabilitation of injured farmers.

We would run courses in an Agricultural College such as Roseworthy in SA where we demonstrated shearing, farm machinery, beef and milking cattle handling, mechanical handling and workshops.

Another area that I addressed was driving cars on dirt roads. It is not uncommon for graduates to have only driven small cars and perhaps not very far and then find themselves in rural areas needing to drive big fast cars long distances for work and or educational activities, perhaps for the first time on dirt roads. This again is complicated but advanced driving courses are available and may well be essential as part of OHS practice nowadays.

I was paid now from the 'division' and the hospital and earning less from the clinic. It all just became too hard to fit into the practice arrangements so I was allowed to leave the "Investigator Clinic" and set up by myself in rooms owned by Peter Hawke, "my" physio therapist and good friend in 1996. Leonore turned 50 and her Mum had a stroke the day I started!

These arrangements are often fraught with difficulty but I am forever grateful for the ease in which this happened. At the time I still did on-call work but in 1998 I had some heart trouble and for a small yearly payment the other doctors covered me and my patients with after-hours services. That was very special and allowed me to throw myself almost full time into the EPDGP work that was about to expand even more.

In the midst of all these projects came the biggest of the lot known as the Coordinated Care Trial under the auspices of the council of Australian Governments (COAG).

Presumably because we were an established and enthusiastic group of people in a GP led organisation that had "runs on the board" we were approached by Peter MacDonald the Professor of Microbiology at Flinders University in Adelaide to become involved.

I had met him before and he was the brother-in-law of my ex colleague Chris Kennedy. He was not only a scientist and clinician he was a man who could design and implement system change. The details are hazy now but he told me that he had reorganised the health services in one of the states/countries that arose from the USSR and had plenty of money.

Closer to home he had worked out how much it cost to care for people with AIDS and managed to access these funds from the various State and Federal Departments to be available therefore making their short lives more bearable. Drugs for AIDS came later.

Peter had the ear of the CEO of the South Australian Health Commission, Ray Blight and of course Michael Armitage, the Minister for Health and the Premier Dean Brown. They all recognised that in Peter Harvey's (see later) words "Our ageing population and the increasing prevalence of chronic and complex health in the community was seen as a major threat to the sustainability of our way of life and our financial system and it still is" and they claimed that if this was not dealt with Adelaide would need another Royal Adelaide Hospital by 2020. That hospital has indeed has just been opened. Maybe they meant a second one.

We were asked to house the staff in the trial, provide transport, clerical staff, patients, IT people, nurses and indeed GPs. I was a member of the executive and very active in our division of general practice and the Mid North Division where our control groups with chronic disease lived. We actually recruited and managed the rural content of the whole trial.

The idea was to use data banks to work out how much was spent on specific patients for drugs (Pharmaceutical Benefits from the Commonwealth), doctors' fees (Medibank also Commonwealth) and Hospitalisation (SAHC) in a specific time.

We would access this money in real terms and use it to pay for care plans that existed such as routine Pap smears, diabetic eye checks or develop our own care plans over glasses of red from MacDonald's vineyard - and then measure and evaluate.

I do not think I will ever forget Peter explaining how this would work. It was called "An upfront draw down."

The main person I recruited was ex teacher Peter Harvey who became a great friend of mine and is truly one of the most interesting people I have ever met and a true Renaissance man.

Peter's family were deeply rooted in the soil but he was unable to continue this life because of economic circumstances and sought an education and living as a teacher and later a policeman for a time. His rather painful recollections of his abiding love of the very soil and soul of the land are painful for him.

The dissonance of his inability to make a living on the land and yet his very successful career professionally and financially in another field in this modern academic world. It is akin to the haunting words of Neil Diamond's song "I am I said" that I confess have often brought tears to my eyes when in a pensive mood. They are about his departure from his beloved New York where he was raised to a life in Los Angeles where he needed to go professionally.

The Greek Theatre where "Hot August Night" was recorded is in that city so maybe that says it all

The words are;

"I am New York city born and raised

But nowadays

I am lost between two shores

LA's fine but it ain't home

New York's home but it ain't mine no more."

Peter studied and taught maths, physics, chemistry and English. He is a writer of prose and poetry and loved music and wine and could make both. He rode motor bikes, is a runner, a share trader, had a plant nursery, was an excellent cook and a good father and husband of Jacinta and a left-wing intellectual who behaved in many ways like a right-wing person.

I should add that he is a kind and warm person and still

has or wishes he had roots in the soil and it was the poor health of rural people compared to their city counterparts that started him the road towards rural health equality. This road has led him to his current position of a Professor of Rural Health in Victoria.

I have the first chapter of the book he is writing on Rural Health and it is a most revealing and even inspirational. He does not mention being recruited by the EPDGP or and working in what was the home of the EDGP at the Port Lincoln Hospital.

Actually this is a bit tongue in cheek because it is not really relevant to his book but I have this feeling that a lot of what he achieved in engaging with health practitioners was made easier as he had the imprimatur of "belonging" to a GP run organisation.

His work also sat squarely with the aims of the Divisions of General Practice outlined above. I like to think that the health of rural people has been improved by the work we all did. I certainly know that the interest and awareness of farmers in farm safety has changed.

Anyway we muddled along and ultimately a great report came out that showed some measures improved with care planning, others didn't.

Nurses organised the implementation of the care plans and other projects we did. Many of the nurses enjoyed a change from shift work. No one ever seemed to grizzle and there was mutual respect forged in hospital clinical work between the doctors and nurses.

One outcome was that we cooperated with Pfizer, a multinational drug company, to extend the IT system we had developed for the trials to manage care plans and every GP in Australia received a copy as this now drives the Care Planning item numbers in the Medical Benefits Schedule.

I chaired that committee and being not very computer literate if I did not understand something it had to be re-done. A computer expert described the system we had developed for the trial as "A castle with no plans and no cement that somehow works". Sounded pretty good to me!

There were a couple of things that demonstrated Peter MacDonald's international standing. One was a couple of female professors in the health field from Harvard who visited Port Lincoln.

This was the time that Clinton was not having sex with Monica what's her name. Harvard and other so called liberal institutions were Clinton's heartland. Our visitors said "We know he is bad but don't think he is a crook". Surprisingly perhaps but consistent with that comment Clinton was re-elected.

Port Lincoln has an excellent air service that I used frequently and on a few occasions I flew to Adelaide and returned twice in a day. On one of these occasions it was to pick up another American Professor this time a male from San Francisco who wanted to know what Health Plus was doing. Sorry, I forgot, that was the trial group's name.

We got into a taxi and I asked the driver to "Take me home please" and he said "OK". Our friend from San Francisco thought I was quite famous but when he saw the size of the town he understood.

About this time in the late 1990s I was spending most of my time with the EPDGP and Health Plus and was given leave from the hospital but they decided this was unsatisfactory and understandably they wanted to reorganise things. That suited me fine and I was no longer their Medical Superintendent.

I mentioned I was on the Medical Board and that meant another trip to Adelaide once a month at least. My experience on that body suggested that there were few doctors that were evil, immoral, corrupt or incompetent but those that were tended to be recidivists and I knew a couple of them which saddened me.

I wrote a paper called 'Herding Cats" about managing doctors which was published in the Family Physician Journal and did a few other things such as trialling some on-line medical education with James Cook University plus I was on several national and state committees to do with divisions and farm safety but the halcyon days of divisions had gone.

It had long been recognised that people who grew up or had positive experiences in the country, as I did, were the ones who returned from their studies and worked in the country.

To build on this concept to improve the recruitment and

retention of doctors in rural areas, which was becoming a crisis, a nationwide initiative was developed that in essence was that Medical Schools in the big cities developed departments of rural medicine with formal branches in regional or subregional centres such as Mount Isa, Kalgoorlie, Whyalla, Broken Hill and others.

Divisions were later merged into what were called Medicare Locals which I believe help with relocating doctors and continuing medical education. Ours was merged with Flinders and Far North and the Mid North Divisions that covered about two thirds of South Australia.

UNEXPECTED OUTCOMES FROM EPGDP

Before I finish this section there were some unexpected consequences of the EPDGP. Australian Universities follow the British in that a basic qualification is a Bachelor's degree and in medicine there are twin degrees in Medicine and Surgery. The term "Doctor" means teacher and has been a term of respect for centuries.

The next in the hierarchy of qualification is a Master's degree that usually involves research but can be by course work. Finally there is a Doctorate that definitely has to involve original research. Science and Art graduates get a PhD or Doctor of Philosophy to hang on their wall. The equivalent recognition for a Medical graduate is a MD or Doctor of Medicine.

Peter Harvey mentioned above collected a PhD that was a

prerequisite for his subsequent Professorial position.

David Mills a GP from Port Lincoln did a project on diabetes for which he was awarded an MD and Graham Fleming from Tumby achieved the same success with a project on youth suicide. Richard Watts another Port Lincoln GP also was awarded a MD but that was nothing to do with EPDGP.

An even greater achievement was that of Kris Bascomb who returned to the local high school and did year 12 and matriculated with very high points and went to university, studied and passed medicine and returned to Port Lincoln where she now is a very successful GP. She was very determined and did this with three children and a very supportive husband. I remember her telling me she went to high school wearing business clothes, heels and stocking - it was not a game.

Alex van Roijen a local lad with a degree in biology joined us as a project officer and later returned to university to complete a medical degree and is also a GP in Port Lincoln.

Last but not least Glenys Bisset who took over from Kris as Administration Manager and later managed a large division of general practice in Adelaide until the bureaucracy wore her down, studied and now practices as an exercise physiologist.

WINDING DOWN

Quite unrelated to this but remembering the people I worked

with for nine years reminded me of a funny incident. Pfizer, the drug company we worked with made Viagra and I arranged to get some samples for a friend and patient for obvious reasons.

I told him it would cost him some seafood and he duly gave me a bag of prawns that I took to Adelaide. The head of the Pfizer office in Adelaide was an attractive, well dressed and groomed business woman who I arranged to meet at the old Adelaide terminal when people could park their car by the front door and walk into the terminal to meet passengers.

This she did and we swapped parcels and she asked if I would like a ride into the city that I accepted. Just before I got into the car there were three or four of the nurses I worked with who I had not seen on the plane pointing and giggling. I could sense that going about my business was the lesser of two evils rather than trying to explain the connection between the rendezvous with a young, attractive woman and the trading of prawns for Viagra.

Apart from a very complicated working life after I lost both my parents in 1995 and Leonore her mother in 1996, I had an episode of angina and needed a stent in 1998. There were however some good things in the dying years of the 20th century and the dawning ones of the 21st.

Kirstin met Andrew Croser from Crystal Brook in the mid north of South Australia where he had successfully completed an apprenticeship as a diesel mechanic in his father's machinery business. Andrew had bigger plans and joined the army as a private and later entered Duntroon for officer training where he was awarded the Medal of Honour. They were married in 1997.

Their wedding reception was held at the Royal Adelaide Golf Club on a ferociously hot day. The worst of it was that the photographer lost his car keys and the wedding party was delayed for two hours. Fifty thirsty people from Port Lincoln and 50 from Crystal Brook at four schooners an hour is 400 schooners—well something like that.

Leonore's Dad was there so Kirstin had one of her much loved grandparents to share her day. They moved to Queanbeyan and later Sydney. In 2001 Andrew was sent to Timor the day after a little Jackson was born on the 26th April.

What a joy that was as Kirstin and Jackson spent six months with us in Port Lincoln and shared a large family party in the Flinders Ranges for Leonore's Dad's 90th birthday AND our dog Lexi was born in 2001.

I am sure all parents have a degree of anxiety about their children's personal relationships with the opposite sex whether married on not. God they are the most weasel words I have ever written.

Andrew had a week of leave about half way through his deployment in Timor and decided to spend it here in Port Lincoln. I mumbled and muttered to Kirstin about how we would understand if she and Andrew went to Coffin Bay to have some privacy blah blah - more weasel words. After a few days there was no move from their downstairs enclave towards Coffin Bay and when I raised the subject with Kirstin she said that Andrew was very happy downstairs, enjoyed Leonore's cooking and lighting a fire in the lounge every afternoon.

So that brings us to 2002. The Coordinated Care Trial eventually finished and so did I. The board decided that nine years was enough and someone else should have a turn. My practice had become very small as I had been away so much. As so often happens what seemed to be a dark cloud turned out to have a silver lining.

I was disappointed of course but fortunately saw an advertisement seeking doctors to work for the Australian Regular Army (ARA) at Robertson Barracks in Darwin.

We went to Darwin for a month in August 2002 for me to try out the job, leaving our heavily pregnant Lexi behind and returned home to supervise the birth, raising and selling of nine Labrador puppies, storage of possessions and house rental and headed to Darwin on the 30th December 2002.

CHAPTER TEN
THE NORTHERN TERRITORY – WHAT A PLACE

BACKGROUND

There were a number of reasons why we went to Darwin. Firstly I needed a job and an attractive one was waiting for me and I had realised that salaried jobs were so much simpler than private practice.

Darwin had always been part of my very being. Dad was there during the bombing and despite that particular experience he looked back fondly on his time in Darwin. I had respect for service men and women because of Dad's and my ideas of what was right and proper in the Australian ethos. And I had had deep involvement with the American, British and Australian Defence Forces in Woomera. Of course having a son in law in uniform was also a big influence.

Strangely perhaps we had lived, worked and travelled in the Kimberley and Alice Springs and holidayed in far north Queensland but had never actually been to Darwin. So that was also a motivator.

On the way to Darwin in our relatively new Mazda Dual Cab, loaded to the gunwales, we stopped at Glendambo, a favourite spot on the Stuart Highway, Alice Springs and later

Mataranka. It was special to stop at Mataranka. We had reached the wet tropics and there were even a few cattle in a paddock next door to our cabin to welcome us.

It was hot, green and humid and as we shared a drink or two and a meal one of us said "Well we have arrived". Despite the humidity we were energised rather than miserable.

When we were in Darwin in August we became friendly with Jetta and Chris Natt. Jetta was a nurse I worked with and Chris ran the AFL in Darwin. He was a well-known Port Adelaide footballer and was a mate of people we knew in Port Lincoln and of John Kalleske who played in the same Sturt team as me. Chris was a close friend of Bob Elix, also an ex Port Adelaide footballer who was a legend in Darwin not the least because he won Tattersalls lottery twice. His sister was Verity who I had known since teenage years so we were amongst friends and to cap it off Jetta and Chris offered us their granny flat until we could get settled. That was special.

WORK

I was appointed to 1 CER a Combat Engineer Regiment as their Regimental Medical Officer or RMO. This was much better than working at the medical centre where I had been before as I had the chance to build rapport and to socialise with soldiers and officers.

The very first day promptly at 0730 I was about to sit down and an officer came in, welcomed me and introduced himself as the Regimental Padre.

I thought that was nice, thanked him and sat down. His next words chilled me. He had been rung earlier by a very worried father of a soldier who had left Sydney the previous evening on a late flight "wanting to stab someone but no one in particular." Obviously this was potentially a very serious situation.

I saw this patient whose main complaint was a headache from trivial trauma when he was working as a soldier seconded to another agency.

I won't go into the details but he was eventually found unfit for service and discharged. I tried to be as neutral and even friendly as his discharge process progressed. The last conversation I had with him he told me he was going home and would be spending a lot of time living in the bush and we chatted about that. He looked at me at one stage and said "And I never killed that bloke the police said I did". I have worked and been in some rough places and seen the face of evil working in a prison for 20 years but never have I felt fear as I did with that guy.

Generally I enjoyed the work very much. They were a good bunch of people in the Regimental Aid Post or RAP and elsewhere. The civilian nurse was very experienced in bush nursing and very helpful to me.

The patients to a man wanted to get better and go back to work that made life in the main easy.

Paul Faber was a tough, fighting sergeant in charge of the RAP and we became friendly with him and his wife. Very observant readers may remember I tried to pull a tooth from a guy in Port Hedland. Paul knew that man.

The work of engineers is varied and interesting. The ranks are the same everywhere in the Army except there are variations in the names of the lowest rank eg "Private" for infantry and others, 'Trooper" for cavalry and 'Sapper" for engineers. The name "Sapper "derives from the practice of digging holes under castle walls to weaken or "sap" their strength a function that became much more effective when gunpowder was exploded in the tunnels.

Engineers deal with mines and other explosives such as IEDs and clear battle fields. The words 'Follow the Sapper" show the respect that other troops hold for them.

They also are the "tunnel rats". One Anzac Day I saw a rat being played with at a table, it was the mascot of their squadron. The Engineers earned immortality in Vietnam when they scuttled into and around bends in the Viet Cong tunnels and put explosives where they would do the most good. This was unlike the Americans who, I understand, chucked grenades down the shafts of the tunnels where the blast would dissipate and be much less effective.

The Engineers also had the sniffer dogs who could detect explosives. There was a Labrador or two and a spaniel of some sort and a Border Collie who had corporal's stripes on his work jacket - and didn't he know it. When his handler put on his coat he was all business and woe betide the other dogs if they misbehaved. A carton of beer fixed a weekend dog sitter on occasions.

The other well-known job they did was to erect steel bridges and other things by hand if necessary. There was an occasional female officer but otherwise the soldiers were all males and square in shape. One sapper was Kim Dorward from Port Lincoln whose family name adorned the oval where I had made 100 twenty-three years before.

The Engineers also have the capacity to clear debris and provide clean water and shelter in natural disasters.

Last but not least they had a combat role and they were carted here and there in Armoured Personal Carriers (APCs) or were even used as Use of Force personnel elsewhere.

I wrote an article about my role as a civilian doctor that was published in the Defence Department's Medical Journal. I intended to write that engineers were soldiers' first, engineers second and specialists third. I venture to say that to most non-military people the word "soldier" conjures up an "infantryman" and vice versa but of course in the army someone in the infantry has a very specific role whereas a soldier may be a singer, a driver or many other things. I used the word "infantry" instead of "soldier" in the quote by mistake.

The 1st Brigade Commander Brigadier, Ash Power, had a meeting with his Regimental Commanding Officers (COs) to discuss an exercise and when the role of infantry was raised he said something like "1 CER has that under control". When the Infantry and 1 CER COs heard that they were somewhat confused and when Ian Cumming the 1 CER CO questioned the Brigadier he replied "Well that is what your RMO had to say in a magazine" Clearly a man with a sense of humour and an attention to detail.

There was a lot of medical paper work for new arrivals and other formalities such as fitness classifications. The soldiers had to pass specific fitness tests and be immunised appropriately before being deployed.

Most of the consultations were easily dealt with but there was always the over-riding consideration that these young men underwent hard and sometimes dangerous training and when all was said and done they had to be ready to go to war at any time.

I was talking to two young sappers who were going to the Middle East somewhere to search for IEDs. It became apparent just how hard and dangerous this could be. For example they could be searching a roadside verge with their detectors and a bomb could be blown up in a place they could not see or reach with their detectors. I was quite distressed by that and doubt I would have enjoyed the front line.

The clinical work was mainly dealing with coughs and colds, minor injuries and more serious knee and shoulder problems from the various varieties of football played on Wednesday afternoons and scores of other reasons but psychological problems were relatively common.

One day I thought I was back in Port Lincoln where I had become a dab hand in removing all sorts of fish hooks from people mostly using just a piece of string.

A treble hook is well known to fishermen and is three barbs on a single shank.

They can be quite big even 10cm or more long with the barbs having a gap of two centimetres and they can they be made of high tensile steel.

How do I know this?

Easy, a soldier had one hanging from his ring finger. He had tied the hook to a rope and threw it over a gate to open the gate from a safe distance in case it was booby trapped.

Somehow it caught around his finger and encircled it under the skin. I checked the function of the nerves and blood vessels and injected a big dose of local anaesthetic. He was remarkably calm and relaxed.

The two barbs that were free and the shank needed to be cut so that the offending barb could be twisted and pushed so that the point perforated the skin and could be grasped with pliers and extracted. This was definitely not a job for a piece of string.

Of course being 1CER so there would be plenty of good sharp, strong tools around. Wrong. I grabbed a pair of pliers that looked like they came for a specials bin in a hardware store and tried to cut the shank and all I did was bend the pliers.

Someone produced another pair of pliers and pair of bolt cutters that must have had handles 75-80 cm long so we soon isolated the barb we wanted to push through the skin and pull out. Paul Faber the RAP sergeant had one pair of pliers and I the other and we had to use all our combined strength, one pulling and the other pushing, to remove the hook. The man did not flinch and kept denying it hurt. We eventually removed it and dressed his finger. He just wiggled that and his other fingers and thanked us. I told him it would probably be sore when the local anaesthetic wore off because we had used a lot of force. I told him to go to the medical centre if necessary overnight, but that he was to report at 0730 next day.

He duly did that and shook hands with his injured hand and wandered off happy as Larry. With his permission of course someone had taken a picture from his feet end with his hand on his lower abdomen and me standing at his hip closing the huge bolt cutters. He happened to be wearing red jocks that made a very good photograph in the magazine I referred to earlier.

Psychological presentations are common and often are managed by psychologists. Soldiers can self-refer so it is not always easy to know what is going on because the psychologists were very protective about their "clients" confidentiality even to doctors. I thought that strange. The question of confidentiality can be thorny and we did not have to tell anyone in the chain of command that someone had depression for example. I have been absurdly protective of patient information even not telling my wife when a friend had a baby even though it would be in the paper next day but on the other hand there are lines that I cross with police and army officers.

I had a patient who was depressed and instructed someone that he was not to fire weapons and followed it up pronto only to find out that he was not firing, just loading the weapons and giving them to someone else to fire. Perhaps an even more dangerous action. So the CO got to hear about that. There are all sorts of restrictions around deployment with medication and promotion so it is not a simple matter to manage depression and anxiety and be confidential.

We had a great ally in psychiatrist Jock McLaren a man of scary intelligence. He had a theory that the working model I have always had in my mind - that depression and anxiety are at opposite ends of a spectrum – is quite wrong and that depression is caused by unremitting anxiety. He has written a closely reasoned book about this that I have trouble refuting as I have been using anti-depressant medication for anxiety rather than the addictive Valium and its friends for decades. Jock used beta blockers, usually contraindicated, to treat depression so maybe he is right. He told me that he has written a much more controversial book –maybe I should get a copy.

We had a lot of knee trauma as mentioned and the majority of surgery was done by a particular surgeon. I think he had done 200 knee reconstructions in perhaps five years.

At the time there was controversy about whether tendon transplants from the patient or space age plastics were best to effectively hold the knee together.

I am not sure whether the surgeon spoke to me or vice versa but it seemed that there was an ideal opportunity to set up a world class trial to determine the better method. There would be data available from the time of operation that could be monitored for the rest of the soldier's life.

The logic is that soldiers are treated/monitored by the Department of Defence while serving and the Department of Veterans Affairs when they are discharged with any health problem or when they simply leave the services for any reason. Even if they had no health trouble records would allow them to be followed up by researchers.

How good and potentially easy is this to do: random allocation of method used, monitoring every five years by the DOD, while at work and when finished work by DVH. The resulting data to be used to judge which method was better.

"No, no, no," cried the DVH our data is confidential we are not going to tell the surgeon /doctors who treated our veteran how he she is getting along and help the surgeon do better operations.

We went up the chain of command and got nowhere. This seems so much contrary to the spirit and practice of clinical research let alone caring for people. That was more than 10 years ago and it still makes me angry and disappointed.

I did enjoy the work, the camaraderie, Anzac days where I sat with the CO, Mess dinners, again where the CO's driver picked me up and took me home and being part of the organisation.

It was interesting to observe the way of life of soldiers. Firstly there are more recruits from broken homes statistics would suggest.

The army is all about tough love. Soldiers are trained hard physically and emotionally. They are well paid compared to other people their age and a target for young women to whom they offer some glamour perhaps, certainly money and nice accommodation. It is a complex situation but summarised wonderfully when a sapper told me he was "Getting a bit sick of my missus leaving her kid with me and getting pissed with her mates". Enough said.

The Warrant Officers and Sergeants really cared for the soldiers and even did patrols in the pubs and clubs to ensure they were all right. They would rescue them if they were not.

Soldiers have a higher rate of relationship trouble than is average. They generally are moved to different jobs every two years and this can be very difficult for partners and children in many ways. Everyone knows about deployments to major war zones but there are other places they go that are dangerous.

A wake up came to everyone when I was working with 1CER. One of our medics was sent on a course, with a different Regiment, I suppose to get soldiers "heat hardened". By an incredible coincidence my wife and I were camping that weekend. It was 1630 when we put up our camper trailer tent. We could not get in the tent and arrange the four poles in one go, it took us four tries and we were used to heat. It was 42 degrees.

That day a soldier died from heat stroke despite having medics and ice around so it is a serious business. Soon after we visited our son who was working on a farm in Tasmania and the lonely little church where the soldier was buried was opposite their gate.

This really was taken seriously and is a big subject. The take home message is "Drink before you are thirsty and if you can drink a medium size glass of water in one go you are already dehydrated".

Even when not deployed they do so much training and work in Australia away from their home base that any soldier is quite likely to be away from home about half the time.

1CER had carpenters but at the time the mines were recruiting tradesmen with massive pay compared to the army. One carpenter told me he had only been in Darwin two months out of the two years he was attached to 1CER. The rest of the time he was working somewhere else.

There are a lot of services and support available to partners and the army tries to match service men and women as much as they can in their jobs, but no hanky panky on exercises thank you very much.

It is probably not well known but when soldiers are deployed on exercises, they may go for say three weeks or so and have no time off and certainly no alcohol. On overseas deployment that applies for six months. This is a bit different to the situation of many civilians who may spend a lot of time away from home in the middle of the week, but not so much at the weekends and who may well enjoy some pleasant company when away. It is a tough job no doubt about it.

It wasn't all serious, there were lighter moments. One day Robert Hill the Minister for Defence at the time visited Robertson Barracks. I must have been invited to the function because I was walking in his general direction when he left his car and I walked towards hm. Two guys wearing suits, sunglasses and hearing aids sort of headed in my direction but when Robert who I knew well enough from another life said "G' day Peter nice to see you etc" they relaxed. I did get some odd looks from others.

On the subject of lighter moments. Leonore and I were invited to the Officer's Ball by the CO, LTCOL Ian Cumming and asked to join his party. Ian and I became good friends and although this was nearly 14 years ago we still keep in touch and as recently as yesterday spoke on the telephone.

This Ball was splendid. It was held on the oval sized lawns between the magnificent white Naval Base that overlooked Darwin Harbour and the sea. We heard a lot of stories from the Commanding Officers and their wives we joined and were spell bound by the band, the dancing, the food and drink and the atmosphere.

The dress was formal that meant that the males wore their Dress Uniforms with decorations and the females their slinkiest dress without their decorations probably because there was nowhere to pin them.

It would be hard to find a more attractive and indeed beautiful, healthy fit people in the world apart from the bloody awful and large tattoos on many of the women.

I had a real fit of melancholy when I thought that if that had been in World War One, gender aside, they would have been the best people physically in Germany, Britain and Australia and the first killed.

And should they go to war that would still be a possible outcome for some.

Perhaps it was a response to subconscious thoughts about my father being there when Darwin was bombed.

Last but not least when the tsunami hit Aceh in 2004 1CER responded immediately and loaded every square inch of the transport ship with water purifying units, bulldozers, fuel, water, food, timber, medical supplies etc and of course the troops themselves - and off they went. I was called into work and was proud that I could help. We made sure that all the soldiers were fit to go and this meant vaccinating against the appropriate diseases and having the appropriate documentation with them.

They saw and did some terrible, ghastly things. From what I saw when they returned, the young people had handled the experience well, but some sergeants and corporals not so well. My thoughts were that they had wives and children and would have thought of them, but they had also had the job of hanging tough for the youngsters.

Last but not least when I left there was a farewell at morning tea and the Adjutant read a speech that I had written – true.

I replied and basically said how much I admired who they were and what they did and thanked them for allowing me to be part of their world.

I was very moved by the long applause that followed. It was easily the most applause I have ever had when I have made a speech privately or publically.

LIVING IN DARWIN

Darwin harbour was first seen by Lieutenant John Lort Stokes of HMS *Beagle* in 1839. The Captain of the ship Commander John Clements Wickham named it after his former shipmate, Charles Darwin. Darwin had been on the ship's previous voyage under the command of Captain FitzRoy.

The area was settled and the township was surveyed in 1869 and named Palmerston after the British Prime Minister by the redoubtable Goyder, the Surveyor General of South Australia. It was renamed Darwin in 1911.

The town by whatever name was part of NSW from 1825-1863, SA 1863-1911 and the Commonwealth after that. A little-known fact perhaps is that Fort Dundas was established on Melville Island 1824-1829, Fort Wellington at Port Essington 1827-1829 and Fort Victoria likewise 1838-1849 to foil the French plans to colonise Australia. Brisbane was established in 1824 and both Launceston and Hobart far earlier, in 1804.

The population of Darwin when we were there was about 100,000 being approximately 30,000 in each of Darwin itself, the satellite city of Palmerston and the surrounding area of Greater Darwin. In 2017 the population is 126,000 which is about 50% of the total Northern Territory population of 250,000. Alice Springs and surrounds have about 40,000 people. The remaining population of 70-80,000 are spread over 1.35 million square kilometres and altogether the Northern Territory has one of the lowest population densities on earth.

That being as it may we arrived in early January and after a few weeks with the Natts settled into a lovely house, that we later bought, adjoining the golf course near the airport. We were very lucky to get this place. There was a nice living area in the centre with large glass windows front and back that allowed any breeze to circulate. With a kitchen set off to one side and the three bedrooms and bathrooms on the other side behind a wall and passage. At the back was a large covered paved area swimming pool, lawn and the golf course. Very practical and comfortable.

Cyclone Tracy in 1974 had flattened the place and when it was rebuilt it was well designed. Every suburb had a shopping centre, where most if not all had a supermarket, chemist shop, post office, fast food outlet, petrol station and grog shop and hairdresser shop. Most of the suburbs had crescent shaped streets that were safer for pedestrians and children.

There was quite an emphasis on cultural events. The Darwin Symphony Orchestra took its wares to the people outside of Darwin and there were some great shows in the theatre such as a tribute to Sammy Davis, Frank Sinatra and Dean Martin and also Cat Stevens that we enjoyed. We saw more shows in three years in Darwin than 20 years in Port Lincoln.

Whenever living in Darwin is mentioned the catch cry goes up, "what about the humidity". I accept that it can be very uncomfortable if a house is not designed for it and we have met people, in Coffin Bay no less, who had lived and worked in Darwin for 20-30 years until finally they and their group gave up and moved south.

We managed though in that we embraced the change and enjoyed the outdoor life and we had a house and garden that was designed for the tropics. One of the great pleasures of my life was swimming and floating in the pool at night looking at the moon trough the palm trees. It was like being in a 1950s movie.

We rarely used the air conditioner except tuning it on about nine o'clock for two-three hours so our bedroom was always comfortable.

Our advice to the many people who have asked us when to visit is to do so at the end of the wet season. It is wet green and exciting and is different to the vast majority of Australia. And there is the "run off" - the best time to catch barramundi.

We made three trips to Kakadu at this time and I drove halfway to an army exercise at Mount Bundy in the first week of June and saw more caravans in that trip than the other three so there are less tourists and believe me that is a good thing. Another negative, certainly in August and later, is that it is hot, smoky from the burning off of the three-metre-high grass and dusty. I understand all about getting away from winter but the end of the wet is very special and the scenery, particularly water-falls is fantastic.

The Northern Territory coast line in the dry season is about 4,000km in length. In the wet it is 11,000km as the water spreads so far inland. I can't help thinking about the Norforce soldiers who have to patrol this ever-challenging area.

Our life could be typified by a little story. I worked from 0730 to 1600 so I was home at 1630 and that was it. I went to work did what I had to do and went home. I was asked if I wanted to be on the after-hours roster as it was quite lucrative but apart from helping out twice I declined.

I had spent a period of madness and sadness much of which was my own doing and I do not regret but it was wonderful to experience something different that I like to think of as a one-dimensional job compared to the life I had led for 23 years in Port Lincoln. Getting home at 1630 felt like I had the afternoon off.

To the story. Most nights before tea I sat outside with Lexi and had a beer or two and often some nuts that of course Lexi also wanted to eat.

I eventually taught her to wait while I threw a nut on the ground and to only fetch it when I winked. Our son Tim had Lexi's son and I proudly told him about this to be greeted by a somewhat grumpy son saying in an incredulous voice "So you get home early from work, drink beer and teach the dog to do tricks."

I replied "Yes do you have any problems with that" leaving "After what I have done in the last few years" hanging in the air. There was a pause and he replied "No I don't suppose".

I should have mentioned sooner but something had happened prior to arrival that had a major effect on our time in Darwin

We had planned go to the wedding of one of the Phippard children whom we had known all her life, in Perth and had planned to stay with Rod and Sue Smith when all the drama happened in Port Lincoln in late 2002.

I rang Sue and said that we would not be going to Perth as we were moving to Darwin. Sue is very deliberate when she answers a question in her very nice soft voice. I thought the phone wasn't working but eventually in a slightly strangled sort of voice she said "Peter we are moving to Darwin".

We had been friends with Rod and Sue since I worked with Sue and delivered Emily their daughter at Woomera in 1975. I cannot resist this. Tim I mentioned before and his family now live in Shepparton and likewise Emily and her family and they are friends.

Rod was appointed as head of the IT section in the Health Department and Sue worked as a midwife. We shared lots of things such as weekends away exploring the surrounding areas, bird watching, fishing, dinners, fish and chips on the beach at sunset and so on. Rod had been in the Air Force and even Staff College so he was well up with what I was doing.

My 60th birthday was in August 2003 and with the help of Sue and Rod, Pam and Brian Murray from Clare, and from Adelaide Phillip and Chris Stain and Phillip's dad, Jack, Peter and Tanya Buttery and John Reece, my best man and his late wife Ann and a super surprise was our daughter Kirstin who had flown from Sydney with her two-year-old son Jackson and newborn Patrick.

Except for the Bagshaws and Phippards and of course our other children these were the most important people in my life.

A highlight of the celebration was a fishing trip and the look on Brian Murray's face as he pulled in a 10kgm Black Kingfish and afterwards. He was gobsmacked.

I mentioned before that Dad was in Darwin during the bombing. I remember him telling me that he had been the adjutant to the RAAF Commanding Officer (CO) at the time and when the Japanese bombed Dad and the CO dived into a slit trench. Sadly the CO jumped out of the trench with a machine gun and was predictably killed. After I left Darwin I read Dad's description of that day and the man killed was none other than Wing Commander Archibald Tindal after who the RAAF base at Katherine, opened in 1942, is named. Therein lies another story about one of the most exciting things Leonore and I have ever done.

Emily Smith had a long-time friend who was married to an RAAF pilot who flew Hornet jets at Tindal and indeed elsewhere in action. This girl had caught up with Sue and somehow we organised a trip the RAAF Base. I had a security clearance obviously so that must have helped.

We met this chap and he organised for us to "fly" a Hornet simulator.

We had to go through the air crew area and I noticed a pilot hand in a Glock, I think, pistol. They all carried them in case they had to eject and landed on or near a crocodile.

We entered a hangar and on the floor was bolted the simulator, basically a cockpit mock-up on an assembly that could move the cockpit in all sorts of directions.

I climbed a ladder and sat in the cockpit with an instructor who stood outside and explained the various controls. I was reasonably familiar with the throttle, joystick, brakes and rudder having done some flight training and I had held the steering wheel of RFDS planes at times. The flaps were separate and shared a very small space with the machine gun button so I left that well alone.

Anyway away I went and had a miraculous escape from a crash. I was too tall to see the top part of the Heads up Display or "HUD". This was fixed and the simulator was set up to appear as if one was in Sydney. It was amazingly realistic and bloody fast. I managed to get the 'plane' off the ground and fly 300 feet above the Bridge.

The instructor asked me to slow down as I had reached Mach1.5 i.e. one a half times the speed of sound - that is I think about 1100 mph- and I had taken out all the windows in the Sydney CBD - naturally I said "Sorry".

They monitored the exercise and although the graphs of my descent and flight path to line up the runway were wobbly I got the plane onto the strip at the right place and the right speed so that was very pleasing. Leonore also did well.

LEONORE'S LIFE IN DARWIN

This was inexorably mixed up with mine of course but she joined an organisation called the Ionians and also was employed by the National Trust.

The Ionians was established by Elizabeth Mc Donald in Launceston in October 1946 as a "Friendship club for women on the move."

The name was derived from Hellenic people who settled in an area of Attica called Ionia and brought their art and culture with them. It has a double meaning in that with Doric and Corinthian, Ionic is one of the three styles of Greek columns in classical architecture. So it has both a literal and figurative meaning: a supporting structure.

I suspect that the early members were dragged to Darwin by their Commonwealth Public servant husbands knowing no one, much like Leonore, and enjoyed, also like Leonore, their membership very much. Our friend Jetta Natt introduced Leonore to the club.

The club was primarily social but included what could be called educational outings and talks by consular officials and senior Australian government officials.

Whenever I think of Ionians I recall an evening at the Indonesian Consulate when a good time was had by all including Ted Egan. Now he was an interesting and lovely bloke. He was a singer, song writer and story teller and had lived in the Territory all his life and was very involved in all aspects of life, in particular with aboriginal people. He was 72 or 73 at the time and recounted how few of the aboriginal people he played football with were still alive. He was a true champion of their cause.

In what many people saw as a controversial move he was appointed to the position equivalent to that of State Governor, a duty he carried out with tact and aplomb. He entertained us at the Indonesian Consulate and it was great fun.

To digress to the subject of handkerchiefs an item of apparel I use for many things other than nose blowing. Our three-year-old grandson wiping a rock at the Cullen Bay beach with a hanky, spreading it on the rock and then sitting on it to eat his fish and chips says it all.

On the night at the Consulate I found another use. Leonore was interested in Argyll diamonds: rather beautiful pink stones found only in the Kimberley I believe. She had been discussing them with a lady who sold them. This lady was at the party and was adorned with a beautiful necklace of a gold chain with a thumping great Argyll diamond. Leonore introduced me and asked if we could look at the diamond. Now that sounds simple but let me paint a picture. I am 190 cm tall and this lady seemed about a foot shorter than me, chubby chatting and cheerful, with a large bosom pushed up into and out of her bodice. Nestling there was this huge diamond that she was proudly demonstrating to me. Quite frankly I was embarrassed and did not know what to do, so I whipped out a nice clean hanky and gently covered her cleavage so I could concentrate on the diamond that I rested on the hanky. She thought it was a hell of a joke as did Leonore.

Leonore worked for the National Trust for almost three years and we met a lot of interesting people and went to interesting places and with foreknowledge got a lot more out of various excursions than we would have otherwise.

There was and still are many relics of World War Two. There were many air strips that were graded dirt next to the Stuart Highway where bombers were out of range of Japanese fighters and some more sophisticated than others. We visited one where there was a concrete pit where they could bolt air craft engines on a bench and allow the propeller to turn in the pit.

We also visited the remains of the Newcastle Waters pub at the start or end of the Marranji Track a notorious and very dangerous track for man and beast. The drovers were said to celebrate the completion of this journey by drinking Ranken Bombs: a glass of rum with a splash of port.

And there was Grove Hill and Pine Creek of gold mining fame and so on.

The place we visited most was one of the Benny Burnett designed houses built for the senior officials in the 1930s on cliffs near Cullen bay and now overlooking the casino.

This had been restored and was the pride of the National Trust and a sort of living museum as well as their workplace. On Sunday afternoons they served high tea of delicate sandwiches, cake and tea in teapots in the beautiful tropical garden. It was easy to drift off into the imagined world of long ago. The bullet holes in the fence from Japanese aircraft added to that atmosphere.

We saw Kris Kristofferson perform at the casino and he told an interesting story. He was a Rhodes Scholar and had been offered the position of Professor of English Literature at West Point but had rejected that life to be a song writer.

He supported this by flying helicopters to and from oil rigs in the Gulf of Mexico. One day his boss asked him to write a song about a Bobby McGee, who just happened to be his secretary. Boy that beats flowers any day. The rest is history and explains the wording of that song as Baton Rouge and New Orleans went by on his journey.

The only bad thing about the National Trust was that they had a giant mango tree and Leonore perhaps ate too many and has developed an allergy to them and, as is common with allergies, even minute quantities upset her.

Last but very much not least about Leonore: her Uncle Leonard Scott was a pilot in the RAAF and was captured and executed by the Japanese during the war as an alleged spy with three fellow pilots. This was the subject of a film "Blood Oath" about the war crimes of those brutal bastards.

We went to a commemorative service about the bombing in a large tent on the foreshore where there is a wall with plaques about the various units and theatres of war. There was an impeccably dressed elderly lady and man in front of us and when the wreaths were laid they moved to the plaque commemorating Ambon that was Len's base.

When they returned Leonore asked if they happened to know Len Scott. The man's answer was, "I was drinking scotch with him the night the Japs came"!

OTHER PLACES AND THINGS

I had read about Darwin and the Northern Territory as long as I could remember certainly from school days when I well remember many books by Ion Iddriess and later "The Territory" and the "Great Australian Loneliness" by Ernestine Hill, "We of the Never Never" by Jeannie Gunn: truly bibles for interested people as is "Far Country" by Allan Powell which I read at the time we lived in Darwin.

There were a lot of things that came together for us. Leonore's work and indeed mine, our interest in the outback, my dreams about magic places such as the three Alligator

Rivers, Kakadu, Katherine, Arnhem Land, Darwin itself and the relatively nearby Kimberly. The list is endless.

We liked history, travel, fishing, camping, photography and travel. We had a four- wheel drive dual cab ute and in 2004 bought a camper trailer. There were two other things that made this mixture gel. They were the presence of Rod and Sue in Darwin and their company on so many of our jaunts and the fact that I had started writing magazine articles about the outdoors in the late 1990s.

The travel and writing reinforced each other. When we were planning a trip I would read about the history and other aspects of our destination and when travelling to and from somewhere I would be more observant and interested if I was planning an article.

As I am writing about this my thoughts turn to just how much we did and the fact that there were just the two of us made it easy, but it has just struck me that I was not on call and readers may recall that for many years I was on call two weekends out of three in Port Lincoln. Viva la difference!

Some highlights in no particular order.

I was due to have a shoulder reconstruction so we decided to treat ourselves to a quiet weekend at the crocodile shaped hotel at Kakadu.

Apart from having to change a wheel on the way, not good for a crook shoulder, we had an uneventful trip and a nice dinner after which we frolicked with a couple of younger women who were having a weekend without their husbands.

The next night we decided to eat in our room and we actually sat in the open doorway and could put our hands out into the torrential rain but it was so vertical we did not get wet at all.

We had Territory mates' rates so the accommodation was cheap but they had missed that second meal that I mentioned to them but it was all too hard so they did not charge us.

My surgery was very successful and interesting in that the surgeon, anaesthetist, assistant and patient were all in the same year of medicine at the University of Adelaide.

We went fishing with professional guide and owner of the boat ramp "two minute" Tony at Shoal Bay, relatively close to Darwin. He got that name because he knew the tides so well. It was a relatively shallow area that had to be crossed to get into the Howard River where we usually fished.

The very first time Leonore and I fished with Tony we took a 12 foot boat into the Howard River. We went to a particular bend in the river where there must have been eight or ten boats in about 100metres of 20-30 metre wide river. Some were tied up with the driver fishing from the bank. Tony pulled up alongside one bloke, jumped out and tied up our boat and told the bloke to move as this was his spot ---and he did. Most impressive, but it got better. I thought I was well kitted out with my ancient Abu 7000 reel and Super Barra 10 foot rod, instead of the little reels and six foot rods others were using. I handed my rod to Leonore. Tony put a live bait on the treble hook and Leonore dropped it right at her feet into the water and it was not long before she hooked a nice barra, the only one caught. It wasn't the only time that Tony got me to move my bait a metre or less so that I would catch a fish.

Another time we had two boats and I drove one and we were really pushing to get home as the tide was racing out. I hit the bottom but had enough knowledge of little boats to ignore that and go faster. Depending on the tide cycle getting stuck could mean waiting six hours or even days.

To walk across sand bars and into the mangroves would not be nice. We often saw crocodiles either in person or the damage they had done to our crab pots. I forgot to mention that we would put out crab pots on our way to fishing spots and pull out the pots on the way home. We never retuned empty handed and the bird life was splendid.

There are things that can happen quickly when fishing in those waters, apart from the ever-present hazards of big fish flopping around with big hooks in their mouths or elsewhere.

I was with Tony one day in a very narrow aptly named Scrubby Creek and in places we had to pull ourselves past a tree by hand. At one place we did that and had maybe 30-40m of clear water about 3-4 m wide. I expected Tony to increase power but he just went slowly. The next thing a crocodile 3-metres or more long wriggled along the bank and launched itself into the water close to a metre below it. If we had accelerated maybe we would have been occupying the same space. I wasn't afraid because it was obviously going to miss us but lying in bed that night I was sweating a bit because maybe it would have sunk the boat and we would have had to make our way through mangroves with night and a rising tide approaching and I had no idea where we would head for.

I met a Wayne "Buffalo" Ross once who may have been the premier barramundi fisherman in the world and had a pleasant chat about his catches and life in the Territory, I was quite in awe of him and somehow Coffin Bay came up and he said how lovely it was and he wanted to retire there. Grass is greener----!

Arnhem Land is known as the stone country for obvious reasons and a great feature of that plateau in the waterfalls. Jim Jim falls near Kakadu is a great tourist attraction and we flew over it once. There is a large cube shaped rock at the top that looks about the size of a car but apparently is the size of a house.

Gumlon near Pine Creek and Edith Falls near Katherine are nice places. Waterfalls have carved their paths through the rock and formed pools where people swim and camp. We climbed to the top of the Gumlon Falls and the effect of the rain and water on the granite at the top is truly awesome.

One feature in the chaos was a hole about the size of a domestic rainwater tank that the water had just gouged out and granite rocks that have been scored like a fork does to a cucumber from rain or stones or perhaps both.

Back to the camping ground and the pool where I saw a man swimming with this son and I asked him about crocodiles. He pointed out some polystyrene floats that the rangers had put out. Bitten floats meant crocodiles and no bites no crocs!

The East Alligator River flood plains at sunset are a beautiful and tranquil place and together with the art work on the cave walls and rocks leave no doubt in one's mind - or perhaps heart is a better term - of the long occupancy of this land.

The paintings mean many things but one message is to keep away from the river. That is excellent health advice, not because of crocodiles but because of the mosquitoes with their capacity to kill humans by malaria and other diseases.

The World Heritage listing of Kakadu reflects the wonder of the place. The birds, animals, scenery and ambience make it a place to visit most of the year. In this wonderful place, the aboriginals recognise six or seven seasons. In "Triumph of the Nomads" Geoffrey Blainey discusses the richness of the food supply and how women could gather adequate food in a few hours so that they and their friends and the children had plenty of time for relaxation, stories and play.

He also adds that if an aboriginal person from this area had been taken to Britain in the 1800s he would have been sorry for the meagre variety of food. Blainey noted that Scottish shepherds often subsisted on oats, being near to starvation.

We visited Kakadu four times as I recall and twice passed through it on the way to Cobourg Peninsula, once with our sons. I caught a whopping Giant Trevally that we threw back. We each had a camera but no one had any film. No fish, no pictures, therefore I did not catch anything was the rule.

A highlight of the trip was exploring the ruins of Fort Victoria. How people managed there I do not know. Our guide, a white bloke, didn't wear shoes and could walk over oyster shells and other such debris.

On our way home we left before daylight and in the half light I watched the left side of the narrow track. Leonore jumped or yelled and I looked to my right and there was a buffalo running on a collision course and I felt that if I braked the sand would stop me instantly and not only would the buffalo hit the car his horns were squarely aimed at my window. I could not do a full left turn because of the trees. We did a sort of waltz step. I did a gentle left turn and the buffalo turned inside me and disengaged with us. That was scary.

The Peninsula is shaped like a finger pointing towards Darwin and encloses Port Essington. For centuries people from various parts of South East Asia (often lumped together as Malaccas) visited this and other areas and traded knives, alcohol, tools, cloth and so forth in return for the right to dive for trepan aka sea cucumber which is used in cooking and as an aphrodisiac, and for pearl shell and pearls.

This was a valuable trade for all and extended as far as South Australia. Tamarind trees still mark some places and their green colour is in stark contrast to the blue grey of gum tress. One of the groups of people who visited were the Bugis and from this derived the threat to children about the bogey man getting them-apparently

Our founding fathers when implementing the White Australia Policy messed this up. If I remember correctly these people would travel with the north- west trade winds and the end of the wet season and return with the south easterly winds at the end of the dry season.

To effectively prevent the non-white people coming they had to get a licence in Darwin and to get there they had to travel into the wind so that was the end of a practice that enriched aboriginal life and was of significant economic benefit. If a ship was to go to Sydney in the dry season it was quicker to go via Singapore and Perth than to beat into the wind apparently.

We went to Katherine more than once and camped for a couple of weeks in the Kimberley - that was nice but there were more dramas when an engine mounting broke. But this was fixed at Drysdale Stations and we hitched a ride with Ian and Lyn Phippard to a fishing camp at One Tree Beach that was a disappointment.

We picked up the car all good to go and headed back to Darwin and en route turned into Katherine to go to the butcher, got back in the car, started it, did a u turn to head back to Darwin and that was it. The fuel pump had died. We had top cover with our Automobile Association and spent a couple of days relaxing and then headed back to Darwin.

Soon after this we decided it was time to move on and

other than "we were not going to stay forever" there was nothing wrong but I think I was keen to get back into medical administration because although I performed at a high standard with the army, it was a very narrow field and with all the other things I had done for more than 10 years I was past being a full GP looking after sick babies, old people, complex medical problems and emergencies.

I had an interview at Alice Springs Hospital and believe that I would have got the position, but I could tell it was not for me. Then I applied for a new position as Regional Director of the Pilbara based in Port Hedland. This was right up my alley as they say and I was offered the job. I asked them if I could have some time to think about it as we were still deciding whether to sell Mum and Dad's house or not and they were happy with that. Being a nice chap I said "If you find someone else I won't hold you to it", which of course they did and I didn't.

Soon after I successfully applied for a 12-month locum Medical Superintendent's job at the Gladstone Hospital in Queensland and we were soon on our way and arrived on Good Friday.

CHAPTER ELEVEN
GLADSTONE

We left Darwin about a week before Easter in 2006 and were delighted with the decision we had made to leave Port Lincoln. We were better off physically, mentally and financially than we had been and were looking forward to the new challenge of living and working in Queensland for a year.

It is a straight forward drive just head south from Darwin for 1000km, turn left at Three Ways, a few km north of Tennant Creek, and head east to Rockhampton, turn right and head for Gladstone. Simple enough but it is 3084 km. (Sydney to Perth is 3993). Technically we travelled from Darwin to Gladstone via the Stuart, Barkly, Lansborough and Capricorn Highways all names that ring with history. As an aside we passed through the Barkly Tablelands the home of Alexandria and Brunette Downs and other huge cattle stations.

We diverted to Boulia which added about 100km to the journey. We enjoyed the story of the Min Min lights and the laid back community. The locals reckon that the Min Min light finds you not the other way around. The light and sound show was well worth the detour. The main street was wide enough to turn a bullock wagon around.

Between Boulia and the Diamantina River is a town called Middleton where we met a Lester Cain who had organised the recreation of the Winton to Boulia Cobb and Co coach journey in 2001 celebrated in a book "The nine pillars of Cobb and Co" by Dick Gledhill. Lester wandered around in the early morning frost without shoes getting things ready. Someone said "He is not only tough he is the tungsten bastard" and of course that stuck.

There was drought behind us but the country we had passed through was in good heart. We saw more bush turkeys than in all the outback journeys we have made and dancing Brolgas that were very beautiful indeed.

Between Boulia and Winton the road crosses the Diamantina River and vice versa. It was not serious but we were caught between two of the many channels of that river that were running over the road, well it is the Channel Country after all. The road was shut and discretion being the better part of valour we camped literally on the road. It was a strange and haunting feeling to be there with the river in flood as Leonore's grandfather had drowned in that very river flooding 300 km or more south near Birdsville 86 years before.

We found that journey fascinating even in drought. The road through Camooweal, Mount Isa, Cloncurry, Winton, Longreach, Blackall, Barcaldine, Emerald, Rockhampton and Gladstone is a link between the past, the present and the future of Queensland and Australia itself.

Mt Isa has supposedly the biggest lead, silver, copper and zinc mine in the world. Dinosaurs lived along the way at Winton and Muttaburra, the ALP started up that way and the RFDS at Cloncurry.

Longreach has a jet aircraft celebrating the origin of Queensland and Northern Territory Airlines - aka Qantas of course. Also at Longreach is the Australian Stockman's Hall of Fame built literally by RM Williams and others. Waltzing Matilda was written at Winton by "Banjo Patterson", an enormous cattle industry feeds into Rockhampton and untold amounts of coal and gas leave Australia through Gladstone and Mackay and tourism is very important as well.

This area provides about 20% of Queensland's export income and there are 2,500,000 cattle within 250 km of Rockhampton—mind blowing

It would be easy to write a whole book about this journey. It traverses a part of Australia that has contributed an enormous amount to our culture, history, folk lore, literature, economy and future.

This is a big, big country but there are still things that happen on a human scale or even smaller. There is a town called Tambo south of Barcaldine that we had visited before and it has an unusual if not unique enterprise. A dedicated and worried group of women got together in the 1990s to do something about the parlous state of its wool dependent economy.

Talk about necessity being the mother of invention. They

made Teddy Bears stuffed with wool and dressed them in a variety of bush clothing. They had birth certificates, newsletters and became a folk lore item.

We bought one at the time and I assumed was for our daughter who had some teddies including one my mother and nana traipsed though Adelaide to get for me when I was a baby. "No" said my dearly beloved "He is for me" and he still sits next to my teddy on a cane chair that also was mine as a little chap.

We took a few days and thoroughly enjoyed the trip and will go back again, but to work. The lady who was to act as my Personal Assistant, Bonnie de Boer kindly arranged a picnic with a few people to welcome me, that was nice and together with our spouses we became good mates and they later spent time with us in Port Lincoln.

The Hospital had about 50 beds with six or eight junior and four or five senior doctors. They were an interesting group. All the juniors were from Iran and India and the seniors, apart from one from Burma the others were Australian, one of whose uncle I knew unrelated to medicine.

These senior doctors and the Medical Superintendent was one of them were the sort of doctors I wanted to be and perhaps, for a time, was heading in that direction. They could deal with virtually any emergency, looked after intensive care, gave anaesthetics, delivered babies and included Caesarean sections by some.

They were a great team and outstanding support for the

junior doctors. I was reasonably involved in that we met every morning for handover. I do not recall anyone ever doing anything wrong.

One Indian doctor whose first name was Sunil, after Sunil Gavaskar, the cricketer was in the top 1or 2% of 45,000 applicants for medical school. He designed computer programs for a hobby.

I can't help laughing, *with* not *at*, the romantic experience of another young doctor from India. He returned to India to complete the formalities of an arranged marriage. I do not know how long this had existed. He was all excited and off he went happy with the idea of the forthcoming nuptials.

However true love rarely runs smoothly because flies can get in the ointment and indeed they did. He did whatever he had to do and at some point met the bride's dad who must have known what was happening and tacitly agreed but asked our bloke where he planned to live with his beloved. "Australia" he said "That is where I work and live you clown you know that damn well" Well I think that is what he said but he was speaking Hindi when he told me, Dad's reply was of four words "No you are not". Game set and match but soon a new game was in play. Our hero checked out the little black book and lots of other things and turned up back in Oz accompanied by a different bride.

She was nice and I am proud to say that Leonore helped her settle in as she had done many times before for other people in other places.

My work was not terribly hard but involved endless checking of job applications from the sub-continent and the middle-east mainly.

At that time Australia was heavily dependent on overseas trained doctors. All the applications were perfect as expected but referees had to be followed up that was hard with the time zone differences.

The 500-pound gorilla in the room was the history of Dr Patel in Bundaberg. He was found to be incompetent, dishonest and incapable of performing some of the surgery he did and was initially found guilty of the manslaughter of three patients and sentenced to jail for two years. This conviction was overturned but he was banned forever from practising in Australia. He went to Bundaberg, having lied about his registration overseas, in 2003. The action against him started in 2005 and ran from 2005 to 2015.

The Department of Health and the regulatory body were in turmoil over this. I was told by my boss "Do not trust us" and the senior doctors told me the same thing that doctors had been sued by the Department and had incurred large legal bills. I must admit I didn't lose much sleep but another thing happened that indicated deep concern in the department.

I arrived at Easter time. I was told that salaries would rise by 30% as from July 1st but I would get paid the extra straight away. A mate of the incumbent rang from Ballarat where he had the same job as me and asked whether this manna from heaven was true.

I was paid substantially more than him, probably about 30%.

Ballarat has five times the number of beds as Gladstone and anyone who knows anything about hospitals would know that this would be ten times the problems or even more.

I remember one doctor who had something negative about him on the net to do with prescribing narcotics, always a red light.

I checked it out and found that the poor man had a wife with cancer and they lived way out in the boondocks in Wyoming and he was giving her the necessary medication under supervision with the regulatory agency fully aware. All clear.

Another example made me get up and have a cup of tea so that I did not beat my head on the computer. In 2006 my ilk and I were sent instructions to ask anyone, giving references or acting as a referee for a job applicant, if they were having or had had any sexual relations with the person they were supporting.

This was because of a recent case where a job applicant and referee committed what I surmise was fraud.

The case involved a nurse, female I understood, who applied and may have been appointed, for a Director of Nursing job, presumably in a small hospital. Registration as a midwife is often, if not always, a requirement for such a position even if obstetrics is not a planned service.

Some bloke who was sharing her bed declared that she was a midwife and acted as a referee but she was not. My frustration was at how stupid it was for the authorities to assume that, if someone had made a false declaration, they would retract it if asked the question. It begs the question of what is a sexual relationship, how long, where when and so on. I wrote this last sentence three days after raising the subject above when I was driven to the solace of a cup of tea and believe me I just made another one, this time reinforced by three chocolate biscuits!

I have belaboured this, I confess, but guess what? A male specialist obstetrician applied for a job in Gladstone naming a female referee. Yours truly, rang the referee, apologised profusely and popped the question. Her answer was twofold. "I am with him and a group of interns so I cannot comment and if I could do you really think I would." Her reply was "right on the money" as I expected.

Apart from being gormlessly stupid where do you draw the boundaries? And the question needs to be asked to everyone old, young, male or female.

WHAT DID WE DO OUTSIDE WORK?

Leonore, as she did in Darwin, joined the local quilters and met some wonderful people from the rural areas and the city when they met at a nearby township called Calliope, sometimes at a member's home.

She also met a neighbour at Tai Chi whose husband

became sick of dairy farming and re-joined his previous profession of helicopter mechanic and worked on the oil rig choppers at an airstrip or base in the far north of Western Australia named after World War Two fighter pilot and ace "Bluey" Truscott who after Clive "Killer' Caldwell was Australia's most successful fighter pilot.

We saw a little of Bonnie and her husband Bill and had visitors such as the Smiths from Darwin, Phillip and Chris from Adelaide who kindly pulled our boat all the way from Port Lincoln - and we only used it a few times.

The water was not scary but uncomfortable as after all the Pacific is an ocean. We needed a bigger boat to get out to sea or a smaller one to poke around in the shallows. Our daughter Sarah's in-laws, who we know well, called in as did our other daughter Kirstin and her family. Her husband had a boat the same name as mine but a good deal older and bloody well faster than mine.

We visited all the nearby attractions, such as Boyne Valley and, climbed Mount Larcom. Sometimes we camped and at other times it was day trips.

We thoroughly enjoyed Rockhampton and went there several times

The Cattle Expo held in May every two or three years was extraordinary and people came from near and far including hundreds from overseas. There was a huge fibre glass statue of a Brahman Bull on the roundabout at the entrance to Rockhampton that said it all. Lesser breeds had their statues in the back streets.

They certainly love cattle and there even is a pub with a small bull riding arena, seriously, we have been there and it was owned by Lee Kernigan at the time. We did not see the bull riding live but did see videos.

The bulls just bucked the riders off looked at them and walked back into their pens for a snack. The phrase "Ho Hum," whatever it is in bull talk, came to mind but it was great to be there.

I heard a story from someone about the wife of a doctor who lived in Rockhampton. She loved the place because every time she went down the street she was the slimmest, prettiest and best dressed woman she saw. The locals were like the Brahmans, larger than life.

One thing I really liked about Rockhampton was Quay Street. There is a row of 20 or so buildings each with a National Trust certification and is the largest number of joined buildings in Australia to achieve that distinction.

These were built partly to service the Mt Morgan, a famous and very rich gold mine, other prosperous ventures and the expectation that Rockhampton would become the capital of the anticipated state of North Queensland. Perhaps Rockhampton being known as a place of "Sin, sickness and sorrow" more truly reflected the lot of people than the street, river and land scapes of Quay Street magnificent though they are.

The reason that the port was not further inland is given by

its name. Hampton means river and it has a reef of rock across it.

We celebrated Leonore's 60th birthday with a weekend trip to Heron Island. A beautiful seafood meal was a highlight. I told our son it was the best seafood meal we have ever had. He said "That's a big call dad after the meals we have had at Port Lincoln and Coffin Bay"—and indeed it was!

We did some snorkelling that was a lovely experience seeing all sorts of sea creatures so close.

Heron Island is obviously a very important place for research as there are University facilities on site and it often features on television and brings back nice memories.

A thing about Gladstone we never thought about was the huge size and variety of timber in that area and Queensland in general. At the time we were planning on building at Coffin Bay and were interested in outdoor furniture.

We met a guy and his partner south of Gladstone who made a magnificent, big, but not bulky, table for us. It is made of a single piece of wood 3000 x 1300mm from a tree that originally supported a flying fox across the Coliseum Creek. His partner "Sprocket", a very feminine lady I might add, made the wrought iron legs complete with her trademark. It was "Red Gum" but maybe technically "Sydney Blue Gum" a truly beautiful piece of wood

We also brought home three pieces of spotted gum about 5000 x 1000 x100mm for our kitchen that never happened and only sold it recently—now that is downsizing.

We arranged to spend Christmas with our daughter and family who lived in Singleton in the Hunter Valley. We left at 0730 on the 23/12/2006. Leonore had made a quilt for one of the children and as we drove out the gate she started "binding" the quilt i.e. hand sewing tiny stitches around the edge of the quilt, maybe a total of four to five metres.

She finished it after 900km or so. I thought that's good we will be at Kirstin's house soon and I will have clocked up 1000 km in a day – that is never easy. Wrong. "You will not turn up a day early at another woman's house at Christmas time". "OK I will ring her." Stony silence. Turned into a motel where we had a super dinner of lamb shanks in Gunnedah the Koala Capital of the world and I had to face the reality that my lovely cute daughter had turned into 'another woman'.

We rendezvoused with our other daughter and husband and our younger son at Kirstin's and went to Port Stephens for a few days, a place I had always wanted to go and wasn't disappointed.

We had a great Christmas and returned to Gladstone and essentially packed up and left in a few weeks after a nice farewell that Bonnie organised.

On the way home we stayed with my great mates Dick and Trish Bagshaw at Maleny, now there is a place I could live. We also stayed with Greg and Leanne Jenke at Coffs Harbour. I had worked with Greg at the Port Lincoln Hospital where he was the finance officer. He left Port Lincoln to take up another position and became very successful managing private hospitals and at the time he was looking after Coffs Harbour, Armidale and Port Macquarie hospitals—other places I could live.

We meandered around Armidale, Tamworth and Walcha where I sought and found the grave of Nat Buchanan the premier drover and one of Australia's 200 greatest achievers.

We also visited our daughter again in Singleton where they had severe floods e.g. up to the cross bars of the local rugby goal posts and much worse.

This coincided with their 10th wedding anniversary. I was given a bottle of Grange Hermitage, regarded by most as Australia's best red wine. Seemed like an excellent time to try it. Andrew is in the army and he was instructing young soldiers and this means that the instructor instructs for 10-12 hours a day and then the soldiers go to bed but the instructor has to write reports, record scores and start early.

We had a nice dinner and he knew about the wine and was drinking coffee to try and wake up but alas he could not. Kirstin was disappointed but I was pleased to have his share, well some of it.

They lived on the western side of town so we were not inconvenienced by the floods and headed to Adelaide via the Dubbo Zoo. That was another highlight of our travels and I had an article published about it. Well worth a visit - a must actually.

We had to return home via Adelaide to see Leonore's dad and go to a wedding, on Yorke Peninsula, where out older son

Tim was the best man. We stopped for fuel at Murraytown and the garage man asked me to reverse a couple of feet.

This I did and heard a crash. Our towing assembly had fallen off. The arm of the tow ball was attached through a panel at the back of the car to the chassis by a piece of metal 5mm thick. I just could not believe it that such an important part was so thin. If that had broken when we were travelling at speed or on a dirt road it could been all over. The man fixed it thankfully.

Anyway we headed to Adelaide where a truck side swiped Leonore. So I used the remains of my windfall wages to get a diesel Mazda BT 50 that our "best man son" still drives.

If anyone is interested the petrol engine vehicle car used from 15-25l/100km and the diesel 10+ to 15l/100km. Loads varied from empty to pulling the same camper trailer with a full load of 1400k.

Home was the order of the day after the wedding and a couple of days relaxing.

CHAPTER TWELVE
EXCITEMENT AND WONDER
BUT SADNESS APLENTY – 2007-2009

We arrived home in Port Lincoln in March 2007 after a prolonged but very pleasant rambling journey from Gladstone. We saw some great places and great people.

We were fortunate to have had tenants in our house and while there had been a few problems there was nothing major but the garden had been neglected particularly the lawns.

We had planned to replace our beach house at Coffin Bay but there was a house for sale we liked so our plans changed and we pulled out all stops to get our much-loved old house ready for sale. This we did and about a year later when everything looked nice we held an auction that was an absolute flop.

We made a trip to Western Australia in 2007. Instead of turning right at Norseman we travelled due west on a dirt road and the wild flowers were absolutely and utterly amazing and made it a very pleasant excursion indeed. There was a lovely display of the unique flowers of this area at the Ravensthorpe Tourist Centre that was a lovely place to shelter from some torrential rain.

The main reason for our trip was to see an un-well Ian Longmire who lived in Esperance and farmed nearby. He was Dick Bagshaw's cousin and like Dick he had a maternal grandmother with the name of Morton from Ayrshire where my great-great grandfather came from but we have never managed to make the connection. I knew Ian and his wife well thanks to the time I had intermittently spent in the south east from the age of 16 to 24.

Ian was an absolute stalwart of Rotary in Esperance where he had lived for many years and various other places prior to that. He asked me to address a Rotary meeting and I did. I spoke about the fact that doctors who chose to live and work in the country most likely had been brought up in the country or had had very positive experiences there.

I went on to explain that I was of the latter group and Ian had introduced me to the life of a farmer which was mostly about driving around in old cars, drinking beer from longnecks and then throwing them out the car window and hitting white posts and I added that the only spanner he had ever used was a shifter.

The crowd roared with laughter and poor Ian went as red as beetroot. He was a Rotary luminary and clearly very embarrassed but his denials were useless. Actually, it wasn't far from the truth, I had observed both.

I have mentioned a "Bikey" Tor who chopped down the door of Ian's cottage with a chain saw 40 years previously. He had also moved to Esperance. He saw me in a shop and said

"G'day, remember me?" I said that I did and how could I forget the chain saw bit and he tried to deny it claiming it was another place, another door and another time. It was a habit of his I found out later.

Another good thing about the trip was meeting a Damian Schlink who had been a boyfriend of our younger daughter Sarah. He was very nice to me and said how much he enjoyed my company and was grateful for what I had taught him. I was quite chuffed for a split second and then he finished the sentence with "You taught me to eat smelly cheese and drink red wine". I remembered both, particularly the cheese that I had asked him to pick up one Sunday night from the local deli. It was blue vein that was so old it was brown and boy was it strong. He asked Leonore for some bread and jam to take the taste away.

Another pleasant reunion was with Chris Friend and his wife who I also knew well. Chris and I were in the same year of medicine and he actually came to Broome when I was there and worked at Kununurra and Esperance for the rest of career and indeed life as he died a year or two later.

As always in Western Australia we saw the Phippards and Smiths who lived reasonably close to each other and Dick Coxon my pilot mate who lived south of Perth in the Rockingham caravan park. He was also ill and in a bad way. Dick was a good, trusting, kind and generous man but like many people the cards he was dealt in his life were not good ones. It was the last time I saw him.

A good thing was that I met my cousin Maryanne's children. I was very close to Mary when we were little and as teenagers but I had not seen her for close to 40 years. She was a beautiful tall, Grace Kelly look alike, as a girl and still was. She kindly invited her two daughters who I had not met to change that. They were tall willowy blondes in their late twenties. One of them said "It is nice having a tall uncle" and I replied something like "Yes you two are tall. How tall are you five feet eight or nine?" The reply was, "I am five feet eleven she is six feet one". Actually the genes for all of us, including our children, came from our maternal grandmother in the main.

Another highlight of going to Perth was that Ian and a mate of his, Phillip Perkins, I had known for years were planning a trip to Zambia in 2008. Phillips daughter's father-in-law was well known by Ian and others in the mining world and had a mine in Zambia and a Zambezi Lodge for tourists. We put our names down quick and smart.

We returned across the Nullarbor and saw the whales at the head of the Great Australian Bight for the first time. This is a nice place managed by the local aboriginal people and very special to see the cows and their calves so closely. The mothers with their calves would swim right to the foot of the cliffs and then swim along the cliffs as if they were so proud of their calves that they wanted to show everybody.

The calves and mothers were black and white much like Friesian cows. At some stage of their lives, perhaps when adults, the patterns become fixed and they could be registered and monitored with photographs as can Friesian cows!

I knew a John Rogers from Coffin Bay who was a pilot and took scientists from the CSIRO to watch and monitor these whales for 20 years, three weeks at a time. He told me that he had never seen whales wag their tails, broach, or any of the other 'cute" things they do, in the open ocean. They only did it when there were people around. We watched a particular whale swim, with her calf, from as far out in the ocean as we could see, directly to 50 metres or less from the cliff where there was a viewing platform, as mentioned, with people present. Apparently their vision, designed to work in deep and dark water, is very good at spotting tiny little creatures called people a long way away.

2007 drifted along with both of us spending a lot of time cleaning and polishing the house and doing what we could to improve the garden. It took 12 months to fix the front lawn, it was so dry.

We also had to maintain our shack at Coffin Bay and we had a 120 acre property about 10km away from Port Lincoln that always needed something mended or fed or watered. Our great mate and neighbour Noel Linsell had attended to this while we were away.

I joined a new activity with some blokes I had met in the Division days and another two or three people and that was to make wine from grapes we picked where we could. It really worked well and we used nothing else except the grapes. We did it for five years or so but we wanted to get bigger and more sophisticated that meant more money. Graham Berry the instigator now has enough of his own grapes and still makes wine.

Sadly as 2007 ended so did the life of our daughter's mother-in-law, Jan Holden who had been sick for some time, who I knew at university.

2008 – A SAD, INTERSTING AND EXCITING YEAR

I have written about John Paltridge who I used to work for on his farm during university holidays in the south east. John, Dick Bagshaw, Ian Longmire, Ray Driver, Bill Dawe, Jack Hassell and others had a profound influence on the way I saw the world and the decision I made to live my life in rural Australia.

John was one of the hardiest and most courageous men I have met, and he dealt with major financial, marital and health problems in a manner few others could have done. Suffice it to say that for years he suffered an inexorable, incurable illness but continued to run his farm from a wheelchair and mini-moke with his tools and other gear on the garage floor so he could reach them from his wheelchair.

I kept in touch with him by phone and email and went to see him now and then and when the end came, Leonore and I stayed with Ray Driver in Keith and went to the funeral together on May 14th 2008.

John's sons Jimmy and Lawrie, both of whom I remember as little boys, were there with their families. Jimmy is a big player in the world of international racehorse transport and lives at Newmarket a major racing centre in the United Kingdom. We had spoken before the funeral and he appreciated the little I had done for his father.

The funeral was very sad with a lot people seriously distressed. The program card had a photograph on the front with John wearing sunglasses, a straw cowboy hat tilted back and speaking into a microphone with the caption, Stockman, Horseman and Gentleman, it said it all.

On the back page was the last verse of "The sick stockrider" a very moving poem by Adam Lindsay Gordon. Some of those words were:

"Let me slumber in the hollow where the wattle blossoms wave,

With never stone or rail to fence my bed:

Should the sturdy station children pull the bush flowers on my grave,

I may chance to hear them romping overhead"

It moved me then as it has now and I whispered to Leonore that with the raw emotions being vented how hard it would be to read it but no-one did and the service moved on to the graveside and Jimmy asked me if I would read it.

I was fine by then and managed all right after I made a little speech introducing myself because most people would not have known me. I acknowledged the debt I owed John and the others I mentioned above who had played such a major role in my life.

It was an honour and a privilege to be asked to read this most evocative poem at the graveside of such a wonderful man.

I had another little reminder that part of me will be forever in that world when I saw the grave of Dick Bagshaw's sister who had been killed in a car crash in Greece in the late 1970s, maybe 30 years before and I attended her funeral as well. She would have been in her early thirties.

Jimmy later thanked me because as unemotional as he had appeared he said that reading that poem would have undone him.

Back at the golf club later Jimmy introduced us to his English wife and their two daughters and thanked me and added that if we ever went to England to stay with them in what had been a house where the Bishop of the day lived and where the Queen stayed when she went to Newmarket.

As it happened we had thought about going to England on our way home from Zambia as our son was working on a farm in Essex so that settled it. We would visit England and stay with the Paltridges.

In a very happy frame of mind we went home with Ray Driver, who had just retired to Keith from managing a property where he was recognised as a real expert with Hereford cattle. I asked him how he was going and he said he was good but when he had his annual check-up the doctor said that he was anaemic. My heart sank because to be anaemic for no apparent reason at 65 was cancer until proven otherwise - and it was and he was dead in a little more than three months.

I had done a little bit of work doing employment medicals for some companies and being on standby at Woomera, my old stamping ground, where people were doing things that were by definition dangerous but our overseas trip was looming.

Just to put the icing on the cake John and Ria Versteeg friends of ours from Coffin Bay, planned on buying a boat and travelling around the canals of Holland and France. They were extremely knowledgeable about all aspects of such a trip and we were lucky to be invited to travel with them for a week.

It gets better. I was best friends with a Robert Angel from age 10 until my twenties when I was his best man. He came to our engagement party in 1969 but not our wedding as he had started on an odyssey with "Big Oil" as they say and once was in charge of Mobil for Southern Africa.

He owned a twelfth share of a game park in South Africa called Waterbuck Lodge and we were able to accompany him there the week before the Zambia adventure. It all stitched together in due course.

There was another little jaunt in the offing. Alan Evans a GP from Port Lincoln had left to work in Alice Springs for an organisation that employed and organised general practitioners and some specialists and nurses to regularly visit a dozen or more aboriginal communities in Central Australia. I did a locum for him for six weeks from late May to early July. The organisation included arranging flights to and from these communities. The doctors and nurses stayed four days on these visits. We were also responsible for tasking the RFDS aircraft that actually belonged to the Port Augusta section. This is a huge area more than half the Northern Territory.

My role was purely administration as I considered myself well past being able to look after a sick baby or severe trauma that is so common in these situations. There was one exception and that is that while in Alice Springs and later from Port Lincoln I did what was known as the Barkly run, a monthly trip to the cattle stations on the Barkly Tablelands to do medical clinics.

This was a fantastic experience and was from Monday to Friday and the plane had a standard schedule to five or six stations with flexibility to alter that schedule if necessary. This was big time cowboy and cowgirl, sorry Jackeroo and Jilleroo country. Some of the biggest cattle stations in the world are Alexandria and Brunette Downs. The basic stock was Braham cattle but one of them produced cattle with seven different breeds in the mix. I suppose they met the needs of the Japanese Ox market or some other niche.

A fellow by the name of Harry Readford started Brunette Downs with a mob of cattle and the title of manager in 1883.

Before this he had earned undying fame for finding a way to take a mob of 1000 stolen cattle and a white stud bull from Bowen Downs, in the centre of Queensland, 3000 km to Marree in South Australia via what became the Strzelecki Track. The bull was said to be worth 500 pounds or $1000 probably 20 years wages or S2M today and was found in his possession. He was found innocent obviously because the Jury found his discovery of another place to take their cattle a good not a bad thing.

The character of Captain Starlight in "Robbery Under Arms" was modelled on him. He did spend time in gaol for horse stealing and when old and perhaps unwell he turned up at Brunette Downs to be told "It's a nice day for a ride Harry" so he went for a ride. He apparently drowned in Corella Creek about 50 km from the home stead and he was an excellent swimmer. The manager of Brunette Downs was going to show me the grave but they decided to employ someone from Alice Springs not fly me from port Lincoln that was fair enough.

We returned to Port Lincoln July 10th and headed for South Africa a week later.

AFRICA, A FORUNATE AND EXTRAORDINARY EXPERIENCE
We had an uneventful but long trip to Johannesburg where Robert was waiting at the airport. We had not seen each other since 1969 almost 40 years but it was not long before the years slipped away. He lived in a very big house with a guard and alarms and it was fascinating to hear him talk about his

career and the people he knew from many walks of life. He was quite close to Mr Mandela who had shared some philosophical insights with him. In 1999 Robert was in Adelaide for the Christmas period to see his mother and sister and I asked if he would come to a rather special party we were having for Y2K. He could not as he was expected at Mr Mandela's party at Robben Island where he had been incarcerated for 20 or more years.

Robert was a cricket tragic and estimated he had seen 50% of the Tests Australia had played in the previous 30 years. He returned to Australia to live a few years ago and I am sure he has pushed that number over the 50% mark now.

It was not long before we headed north to his property Waterbuck Lodge for a week

There were four cabins each quite private and beautiful and furnished and fitted out just like what I suppose one would expect. The shower had a clear glass window and a Kudu, a deer like animal maybe 75% the size of a horse wandered by about five metres away while I was having a shower.

There was only Robert and us, with a guide and a driver. It was absolutely an amazing privilege, not only what we saw but how they went about their business.

It was like being in a movie. The land was relatively flat with bush not unlike Australia in size and shapes and colour. We rode in an open 4WD vehicle with the back seats elevated so it was very comfortable and great for photography. The main animals we saw were zebras and lots of birds and the odd Kudu. I did not know it, but leopards like our friends the whales and their bovine counter parts and perhaps goats have unique patterns in their coats.

There was method in what they were doing that I will mention later. The next day we went to a different area and were shown some hippos wallowing in a water hole.

I gave a quiet whistle and was told not to do that. They were wild animals and had got used to square brown things with some monkeys in them running around going brroomm broommm. They did not know that these monkeys whistled. Such a sound may be enough to make them run away.

We ate outside at night inside what was a small version of a village stockade for protection. There was a concrete bench about a foot high and a fire was lit on the top and food cooked in various ways. With the night noises, starry sky, nice food and wine it was very easy to doze off after what had been a pleasant, exciting but tiring day.

I am over simplifying this a little as we actually went out twice, early in the morning and late afternoon and like the animals had a siesta. Once the guides heard a lion growling at night. He was hiding in quite a thick patch of scrub that we inched our way through to be close enough to take photos with just the camera flashes and torches. A fantastic sight.

One afternoon I saw a grey animal run across the track quite fast and I got a very blurred picture.

The guide told me it was a Honey Badger and that was the

title of a book I read in the 1950s or 60s by Robert Ruark. The animal fought and could even kill a lion by running underneath a male and castrating it or near enough and causing it to bleed to death. The book was about women who were rising in the ranks of American business. It must have made a hell of an impression on me.

Next day it was elephants. One chased us and came very close indeed. They were just so special close up. Robert explained that the guide watched how people reacted and in particular followed instructions and that determined where they would be taken. We must have passed the test. Rob asked if we were good with big animals and if one counts cattle I suppose we were used to being in skin contact with them.

We were certainly close to elephants and later Cape Buffalo but stayed in the vehicle. Then we were taken seriously close to a lioness 15meters from us eating a kill next to a tree. She was on our right with a big tree directly in front of us. To get out in a hurry we would have had to reverse through some light scrub and then forward with the right hand down and so miss the tree next to lioness. Her nearly full-grown daughter was stalking her getting closer and closer.

I don't think that the guide thought that she would attack but he was concerned that they might fight and with two such big animals so close that could spill over and affect us. He gave us two instructions. "Take pictures if you wish but DO NOT

STAND UP AND DO NOT YELL." He may have had his rifle unsheathed I am not sure. The daughter got closer and closer. She reached mum who stood up gave her a lick and walked way and left the kill to her. Unforgettable stuff.

The other lion action was similar in a way. We saw a lioness and two big offspring "tell" them to walk through a rectangular area of bush. And we drove to a track where we anticipated that they would come out. She appeared, crossed the track and waited and soon one cub appeared and sort of acknowledged mum and walked on. The other one must have been another 10 minutes and mum was getting angry or anxious. She must have heard something because she crouched down in some straw-coloured grass perhaps 30-40 cm high and she was invisible to the naked eye, binoculars or a camera and we must have been maybe 30 m away. Daughter/son appeared and as soon as mum saw her/him she sprung and administered a hiding and wandered off after the first one.

I mentioned birds, and we saw some vultures that had only left the hooves and some bones of a Kudu that lions had killed. Twelve hours and virtually nothing was left. They descended like a cloud rather than a flock.

There were some very pretty birds and a little guy we loved. He was a Kamikaze bird. In his courtship dance he would fly around maybe 100 feet above the ground and literally stall in flight deliberately and fall to the ground completely out of control then stop the stall about a metre from the ground and turn it into a dive and zoom away almost hitting the ground. Clearly the chicks thought he was very cool. I was just thinking writing this that he was probably so light that he would not hurt himself if he did fall to the ground - good one Kami!

We then drove to Johannesburg and Rob took us to the airport next day where we joined our Australian friends and we flew to Livingstone. There was an immaculate old DC6 piston engine aircraft apparently functioning that brought back memories to people my vintage as we grew up with DC 3s 4s and 6s before jets in the mid to late 1960s. DC = Douglas Corporation.

We stayed for two days in Livingstone and checked out Victoria Falls which is as magnificent and awe inspiring as I had imagined. Monkeys perched anywhere near the entrance to our rooms to pinch food, zebras wandered at will and I took some great pictures of their unique coats. Best of all though were the two giraffes, male and female. No matter how many seen on TV or in a zoo their size and majesty are over whelming and they regarded the gardens of the Royal Livingstone Hotel as their patch.

If I had known that their kicks can kill a lion maybe I would not have gone so close with my camera but they knew I was harmless - I hope.

The people, the animals and the falls were spell binding but there was a little treat to come and that was lunch at the giraffe's hotel. This was the re-creation of one aspect of the

British Colonial days of what was once Northern Rhodesia and that was lunch in a splendid ornate dining room with our meal served by local people on magnificent silverware. When the waitresses had everything in place they whipped the silver lids from the dishes simultaneously, laughing as they did so.

It was nice and perhaps consistent with the fact that Livingstone was one of the very few, perhaps only two, places in Africa to retain their names from colonial times because of the respect they had for Dr Livingstone in their country. I suppose the same can be said of Victoria Falls.

Next was a light aircraft trip to Royal Zambezi Lodge (RZI) and again this was stunning. A beautiful central building adjacent to tented rooms with their verandahs on the very edge of the Zambesi River.

When we first arrived and drove to the reception area there was a huge elephant wandering around a bit like a bull eating someone's front lawn while you knocked on the door but it was wild. We never heard him or any other elephants near us but there were elephants or hippo tracks right next to our verandah where they had gone for a drink. Hippos wander on land to feed and leave the young in the water maybe with an "aunty" to stay behind and care for them. One night we were all having a beer on the main verandah when there was a huge ruckus of two hippos fighting in the water only a few metres from us. Later that night a man showed me a hippo tooth. They have four, two in the upper jaw and two in the lower. The tooth was about 35 x5 x 1cm but when they shut their mouths their teeth rubbed together in such a way that they were razor sharp. The biggest one he had seen was a metre long. A surgeon told me once that the biggest cause of deaths from things in the wild was being hit with falling coconuts - the next were hippos. They cannot swim and actually walk along the bottom and when two tonne of hippo comes up for breath he can go where he likes and not many boats will stop that - and just imagine the jaws.

The view from our cabin particularly at dawn was simply wonderful. The Zambezi River is the fourth biggest in Africa and fits Kipling's description of another river the "Great, green, greasy Limpopo" is very apt. One of us took a picture one morning with many hippos, crocodiles and birds visible. Later the 20-30 of us had a competition of the best out of maybe 10,000 pictures and this won.

We went on the water, on the land, to a village, had dinner on as island and had beautiful meals, caught fish and saw lots of animals including wart hogs. We all got on well and as our group were the only people there and there was never a cross word. I was perhaps the keenest photographer and when we boarded the vehicle, I was just given the front seat. How nice was that? We got a super deal and initially beer and wine were part of the deal, but whisky and champagne were flowing and I saw no money changing hands.

Were we cared for and protected, subtle, but yes we were. There were poachers and obviously wild animals. They were not conspicuous but there were big strong guys obviously patrolling the grounds and they carried fearsome weapons that were a cross between a club and a sword of very hard wood. We had a meal on an island mid river and I walked away for a wee and one of the staff quietly accompanied me. I also remember back at Robert's place when we stopped for gins and tonics it would always be in a clearing with no bushes for 1-200 metres and the driver always looking outward from the groups and quietly circling.

One day at RZI we went on a walk. The guide carried a loaded .308 rifle. Before anyone could get a licence to take people out like this they had to have shot four buffalo and four elephants in a real world dangerous situation not a cull. He then told me that an elephant's skull was two feet thick and it was no use shooting until the elephant put his head down to charge or the bullet would just ricochet. "When do they put their heads down?" I asked. "Twenty five to thirty metres away" was his reply.

The real world revealed itself another day. The driver stopped the vehicle. We knew there was an elephant shot dead nearby so maybe he was extra alert but he saw the track of a poacher. These guys wore lace up boots with heavy rubber tread soles. The poachers put their feet into plastic bags to disguise their particular tracks. What does an experienced professional tracker think when he sees these sort of tracks. Mmmm a poacher.

They radioed the game rangers and very soon they

appeared. There were three young guys with rifles and a tough looking bloke that could have been a sergeant in a past life with a UZI machine gun and they were ready to go and did.

Poachers were a huge problem. I was told that in Zimbabwe they were shot on sight but Zambia was a democracy and demanded due process, reports and review of arrests, evidence etc. particularly if deaths occurred. If rangers were found to have done something wrong and put up in gaol it would have been a quick death or a slow one from AIDS. I was also told that since that edict there had been a number of skirmishes after which the reports offered that "There had been gunfire exchanged with poachers and a number of weapons were recovered."

Oh I did a bit of doctoring. One of our gang was quite ill and I managed to keep him hydrated until he recovered, rang Robert Angel once and fixed an appointment for him in Cape Town with a specialist when we went on our various ways. The bugger did not turn up.

We headed for London, walked through an open gate in the terminal, were met by Leonore's brother Simon and his wife and stayed with them for a couple of days and then went to Paris in a train under the English Channel to a major station where Leonore had her wallet pinched and after a great deal of messing around found ourselves one station short of where we were to meet our friends, the Versteegs, with the boat and it was dark. A passenger who had left the train with us rectified this by driving us to our rendezvous where we joined our friends at Chatillon, had a nice cup of cocoa and went to bed.

Next morning we embarked on another unique, exciting and pleasant adventure. John and Ria were both Dutch but brought up in Australia and had worked for years and travelled extensively in Europe. Over the next few days we travelled on the Loire River to the heart of Paris.

It was all about a big river, fleets of pleasure and commercial craft, little houses, massive houses and those in between, greenery, lovely flowers, crops, trees and above all nice food, wine, company and tranquillity. The locks in the river were easily traversed and were quite old. One was built in 1600, amazing.

Ria and John are very pleasant, informative and polite companions and we enjoyed their company of itself but also the layer they added to the sights and sounds, the river traffic and France itself.

Very soon we adopted the French breakfast idea of leaving the boat every morning and buying baguettes and whatever else we needed. Somewhere we saw a statue of Henri Becquerel a man who I remembered as sharing the Nobel prize with Marie Curie and her husband. It was really quite special to see that.

Eventually the Loire River joined the Seine with its far heavier traffic and eventually we moored in the heart of Paris and visited Fontainebleau and Notre Dame. It would have been nice to spend more time but we thoroughly enjoyed such a different world.

So London on the train to Kings Cross station on 12th August and then Cambridge where we were met by James aka Jimmy in Australia Paltridge and taken to his house in Newmarket. This was a lovely old home and we were warmly welcomed by his lovely wife Mary, two girls and a boy.

We had an early night and the next day Jimmy showed us around Newmarket. We literally walked amongst the horses as they went from their stables to the training area. This was a state-of-the-art facility where they had prepared five or six tracks a furlong or about 200m long with different characteristics such as wet, dry, grassy, sandy, hard to imitate the nature of any track where they might race. I am not sure how many times they covered the distance but the training was all about keeping the horses fresh and interested not worn out. Jimmy likened them to three-year-old children in this respect. We also had a brief look at the National Stud. Jim's business was transporting race horses all over the world and he spent a lot of time in France where he had many business contacts and somehow managed to get by with his schoolboy French. His wife later told us how annoyed she was because she had studied at the Sorbonne and spoke perfect French, but Jim's racing contacts where always asking her to repeat herself. Perhaps university French was different to racecourse French.

That evening we had a lovely meal with beautiful wines

and Jim made the comment that a lot of French people did not like the big heavy Australian wines like Grange. Later he opened a Penfold's red and told me it was from my neck of the woods. It was very good indeed. I thought it was too obvious that it was a Grange and suggested it was from Coonawarra near where he had lived but it was a Grange so I missed my chance to be a star. Jim told me he remembered my being a good cricketer and drinking lots of beer but did not seem to remember me working 10-12 hours a day for his dad - funny that.

The next day we went to Cambridge itself and we hired a classic old boat polled by a student. It was like we had jumped into an 18th century poem. Cambridge University was founded in 1209. I tried to imagine the legions of students, heroes, villains, prime ministers, aristocrats, royalty, spies and soldiers that had passed though these streets and buildings. The corpus of knowledge, wisdom discovery and invention produced, made, built or discovered must be impossible to measure and here we were. It was a wonderful place for lovers of history, science and tradition to glide through in a simple wooden skiff.

We had lunch there and later Leonore had a meander through some lanes and countryside and looked at old buildings and in the evening we were Jim and Mary's guests at a lovely local restaurant.

At some time I mentioned that Peter was working on a farm in England and had been a jackeroo near Jim's old home and had gone to Marcus Oldham College and Jim said he had gone there as well and did the horse course and I think funded a scholarship or some sort of endowment.

He said he would like to meet Peter. Next day he threw me the keys of a Volvo station wagon to have a look around the general area and bring Peter back to their house in a couple of days.

Leonore and I went to the Duckford museum where there are many famous and interesting things particularly aeroplanes. I was fascinated by a USA B bomber, a reasonably recent aeroplane. Its wings were its fuel tanks and on the ground they leaked. When it was flying the lift and the heat from air friction and lift stopped the leaks. I wonder if they anticipated that. If they did it was a hell of sales story.

We met Peter at the farm in Essex where he lived and had dinner with his Kiwi co-workers. Next day we had a look at a rocky beach bought some Dover Sole, a lovely fish we ate later and headed back to James's house.

It happened to be my birthday on the 19th August and Jim and Mary really turned it on. We had a wonderful selection of French wines and nice food.

Later came a wonderful birthday present. Jim set plans for Peter to be manager of his late father's farm that was such a big influence on my life. That happened eventually and the circle was completed.

Jim left no stone unturned for us and next morning his driver took us to the airport and we headed home in time to go to Ray Driver's funeral in a few days at Keith where a huge crowd assembled.

It was a very sad occasion but I took something from the day. I was talking to Bill Dawe and said just how important that group were to me in my formative years. Bill said "Well you were one of us" and that has meant a lot to me.

On the subject of deaths Dick Coxon had died in June and Leonore's sister died in December.

There were however some good things that happened. We were approached to sell our little farm near Port Lincoln and did so at a nice profit that stood us well in the years to come.

2009 – A NICE YEAR-A GOOD JOB – IN DARWIN

Phillip Saunders, yet another of the South Australian Football gang who played for Sturt, was the South Australian manager for Health Services Australia, the descendent of the Commonwealth Department of Health and now part of Medibank Private I assume. They needed a doctor in their Darwin Office and he contacted his mate Chris Natt, the guy that was so good to me in Darwin, to see if he knew any likely people. Bingo I got the call.

Travel Medicine was a very important part of their role so I found myself working in Adelaide for a week or two learning the ropes because it has become a sub specialty in medicine.

We packed up our goods and chattels including the dog and coincidentally headed for Darwin, from Coffin Bay almost the same date as seven years before. Leonore noticed something wrong with the connection between the two Anderson plugs, one at the back of the car and one in the front of the camper trailer. This is a separate circuit to run the camper refrigerator from a second battery in the car. I was rushing around like a mad thing and mumbled something because the Engel was full of meat and fish. We stopped at Glemdambo and the food seemed ok when we left the next morning for Alice Springs but the following morning it was decidedly soft. The fact that there was no wire connecting the two Anderson plugs explained it. A large serve of humble pie for breakfast and we were on our way.

Phillip had organised some wonderful accommodation right on the water at Bayview in one of two luxury town houses each of two stories complete with plunge pool so that was excellent. Chris and Jetta Natt lived almost next door.

Health Services Australia had several roles. There was Travel Medicine, Rehabilitation, Vaccinations and many medical examinations for a variety of reasons such as:

Pre-employment for nurses to work at the Darwin Hospital, many from Zambia and Zimbabwe.

Fitness for deployment of families of Defence personnel and those who use explosives they are required to have medical certification every so often. This in my experience had been a form about the size of my hand with fingers extended with a place for BP and "Is the person fit for handling explosives". Not much more. A guy came in and on my day sheet was the reason for consultation. This was very soon after I started maybe even the first day. I assume he worked in a mine or similar and asked why he used explosives. His comment was along the lines of, "Sometimes I want to go somewhere where someone is trying to stop me, sometimes I want to stop people hurting me. Other times I practice blowing things up". My eyes were like organ stops, I thought that we had a very serious situation here. He must have picked up my vibes and gave me a bit of a smile and said, "I am in the police Tactical Response Unit mate". All sounded quite logical and reasonable when I knew that.

There were use force personnel also on Customs and Fishing Patrol boats who were part of the poacher patrols in the far Southern Ocean. I had to seek advice on medical conditions from the doctors who were experts on Antarctica occasionally.

Some of these guys did hours of pumping iron a day because they were there 'just in case'. One guy had been badly injured in a Black Hawk helicopter crash and had done a huge rehabilitation program that he continued whatever else he was doing. I asked him to do a few push ups as that is a good measure of upper limb function and started to write up his paper work. I was interrupted by him asking "How many push ups do you want me to do?" He was doing repetitive one arm push ups at the time he asked the question.

Conversely another guy was a seaman and the term "Old salt' would aptly describe him. He too served in these boats and I mentioned how fit and strong these "gunslingers" were.

He replied with a depth of feeling "Yair we call 'em larva lights, pretty to look at but no bloody good for anything else".

And then there were the Sky Marshalls who flew, armed and incognito on passenger flights.

I was asked one day if I was interested in being a "go to" person as they sometimes needed a very quick answer as to whether someone was "mad or bad". Sounded interesting, for about a nano-second, until the reality sunk in. We discussed it and I made a few calls, as they say, because we did have a duty to help these people and I found some people that could and would help. I asked him to get his commanding officer to contact me but I did not hear any more.

Road train drivers were in our net as well. Two, three and four trailer rigs were driven and there were very strict rules and a lot of stories came with their drivers.

Medicals for mine workers, usually FIFO people were interesting and the results, as seen on TV, varied from financial and personal success to a total mess. One man I remember was a paramedic or nurse who worked at a mine site, a fit looking and pleasant man with many detailed tattoos. We chatted about tattoos and avoiding the risk of Hep C and AIDS by insisting on an unopened ink and so on. He made a comment that I found most interesting in that his tattoos he compared to a business man wearing a Rolex watch. The cost was about the same and demonstrated on his body where the next tattoos were planned and what they would be when he had the cash.

Things moved along at a pleasant rate with work but there was a reorganisation. Perth, not Adelaide was now the head office and a couple of senior female office people turned up and went through the office reorganising envelopes and forms etc. I think one was the operations manager and on reflection seemed to have great pleasure in telling me she had sacked Phillip who employed me.

I have a great affection for Western Australians but they are very parochial and she was the worst I have ever heard. I mentioned, sympathetically I thought, how sad, hard, hurtful, disappointing and so on it must have been for them with the drug meltdown of Ben Cousins for football fans and him. "It was unfair, he didn't do anything wrong and if he did they all do it and what about Buddy Franklin?" She went on and on for days - talk about denial.

Our boss was a mid-30s tall woman, an exercise physiologist who perhaps by definition had a slim muscular figure or should it be physique. She brought a picture of herself taken the previous weekend when she went Heli – fishing, predictably that is when a helicopter takes people when they cannot get to a fishing spot any other way. She was standing in some swampy looking place, hat, torn off shorts and shirt sleeves with a .308 rifle across her right shoulder and a .45 pistol in a holster on a cartridge belt loosely around her hips and in her left hand held a huge knife. Oh, she had a foot on a pig, about the size of a Volkswagen, with tusks six inches long—some fisher woman.

I went to a company shin dig in Melbourne and the head physiotherapist for the company was Damian Lawrence, a Port Lincoln lad, I had lent my anatomy books when he was studying.

I met a lot of interesting people including a chap that sent us all the updates from the United Nations about epidemics.

We picked up a lot of our old friends from Ionians and added more so that was nice.

We also went fishing and crabbing successfully with Bob Morris, who had taken over Tony's business and generally enjoyed the atmosphere and places we had been before.

The clinical work was generally straight forward but I did find 20 or so people that had positive skin tests for TB, diabetes, deafness, cardiac arrhythmias and finally a girl with yellow hands from sun tanning lotion, that I had not seen before.

One person wanted cannabis for the pain of vaccinations. Now that was an interesting try.

A guy who was to be a bodyguard for the Prime Minister's wife who planned to climb Mount Kilimanjaro needed some vaccinations as did a lady who had walked across Spain and was heading for Nepal.

A train driver had some hearing loss in his left ear that I told him was due to engine noise with his head out the window, "No no mate it was the dets" "Eh" I said, "The bloody detonators. The gangers used to put on the rails to let us know they were working ahead, before radios, hell it gave you a fright and the bastards were bloody loud".

All sorts of people were coming in or out of Australia. In one day I saw a Brazilian teacher, an English Vet coming in, an Australian surgeon going out heading for Pershawar, a Chinese who danced in a night club for exercise and a 106kg woman who had been 140kg with five of her own and five foster children, a noble soul indeed.

A Zulu man told me that Shaku the Zulu warrior king killed many of the Zimbabwean people and President Mugabe was still taking vengeance on Zulu people. Not the sort of thing you hear about most days.

Oh yes there was a small group of Nepalese people. Darwin people would be blessed if those guys started restaurants.

There were many stories indeed in what sounded like a boring job it was definitely not that it was a great window on the passing parade of life.

Another role I had was quite unexpected. The Commonwealth Health Department was important historically and the Chief Medical Officer a Senior Public Servant who represented the department at all manner of meetings. The last meetings still held were monthly in one department or another and I was invited to them. Nibbles and drinks were served and a tour of the facility and talk about the role and function on a Friday night was pleasant and interesting. I was most impressed that the Australian Post Office had filled up their trucks with freight such as wine, then got bigger and bigger trucks and paid $300m per year tax – amazing.

I was particularly pleased that a Dr Dennis Sansbury worked part time. He must have been in his 80s but was as sharp as a tack and loved a drink and a chat.

He worked in Darwin for the Commonwealth Health Department when it really was alive and kicking and had a huge role in the vaccination of people and other things, maybe even leprosy management. I loved talking to him and picking his brains.

Something that was altogether different and I am glad I had some experiences with old people, nursing homes and so on and that I was Chairman of the Guardianship Board. This is a very powerful body and can take control over the affairs of people who cannot manage their own affairs. They may be of any age, but realistically the majority are elderly people at the end of life.

My recollection is that the majority of hearings were about aboriginal people taking control of their relatives' money.

This brings me to another matter and that was known as, "The Intervention" introduced by the Howard Government in 2007 "To address allegations of rampant child sexual abuse and neglect in Northern Territory Aboriginal Communities." There were said to be 600 soldiers involved and I am sure Federal Police as well.

One of my duties was to speak to such groups to explain that they were effectively going into third world conditions and to take care of their personal hygiene one aspect of which was to always wear shoes. For example stepping where dogs have defaecated is likely to cause hookworm in the gut through the unshod feet - always wear shoes/boots.

I looked at the internet to check when this was introduced and was stunned to read that there had been no prosecutions under this act. I just cannot believe it. To more pleasant things. We became friendly with Lynne, a nurse I worked with and Jim her husband who had a hell of a story and a story from hell all in one. They went to a cattle station somewhere near Borroloola over 900km away for Christmas in 1974 and when they heard about the cyclone they headed for home, in a MG A, a small open sports car.

Along the way a kangaroo hit the metal windscreen frame and broke it and that caused a serious injury to the top of Jim's head. Lynne somehow stopped the car and drove them to Katherine where Jim was admitted to wait for transport to somewhere because Darwin was out and of course all the emergency planes evacuating Darwin were full. Eventually a Hercules picked them up and took them to Sydney.

Jim finished up ok and worked a normal job so that is the good news. The other good news was that Hospital in Sydney employed Lynne to look after him and her fellow nurses helped her with money, clothes and so on. The bad thing was that when she returned to their flat, the painting of her at her 21st birthday was hanging in the next door flat but not for long. Later when she cleaned the car she found the piece of bone that had been ripped from Jim's head.

We had a wonderful weekend camping with them and they told us many stories about the Territory in the 1970s before all the National Parks and rules.

Jim had asked me if I was used to driving in sand and I was and said so but forgot that I had never pulled a rather heavy camper through it, so after I got bogged and he pulled me out, we set up the camp and settled down.

Jim smoked roll your own cigarettes that he rolled loosely with a large pinch or two of some very aromatic tobacco that reminded that 30 years ago exactly, I had stopped smoking a pipe but years before when working on farms and in shearing sheds I used to smoke "rollies" similar to Jim.

He also had a bottle of upmarket Bundaberg Rum. I doubt if Leonore and I had had drunk more than one or two bottles of rum in the 30 years we had lived in Port Lincoln and that included cooking. This rum was delicious on ice, maybe it was the coke that I didn't like. I had two or three rums and the same number of cigarettes the most of either I had in 30 years.

A year later I did a locum in Gladstone and found out that Bundaberg like Johnnie Walker with whisky; selling bottles of rum ranging from $40-200 a bottle and people queued at the distillery for some releases. Funny for a Queenslander the guy recommended Apple something from Jamaica and we have had a couple of bottles of that.

June 28th 2009 was our 40th wedding anniversary and we

went to Melbourne and later the Grampians where we had a wonderful time with our family and friends. We are very fond of that part of Australia and this party made us even more so. A feature was 25 dozen oysters that, courtesy of Joel Davies and our son miraculously found their way from Port Lincoln and I had some crabs and or barramundi from Darwin so we were well set.

We returned to Melbourne and had the most wonderful surprise when our children pushed us into a hire car and sent us off to see Simon and Garfunkel whose songs such as "Sounds of Silence", "Bridge over trouble Waters" and many others were key songs of ours in our early married years.

I used to sing "Bridge over troubled waters" to our elder daughter when a child and later she told me she thought I was going to throw her off a bridge. This was the story of my life, great ideas but poor execution.

It was the best show we have attended and it was particularly poignant as they had only recently got together after a gap of 10 years I think it was and may have been their first tour or even concert. They certainly seemed to enjoy themselves and bounced off each other. Paul Simon's joy and even pride were evident when Art Garfunkel made the last high note in BOTW-he melted. It was truly fabulous and a thoughtful gesture to really round off the celebration with our four children, friends and three grandchildren. Now we have 10 grandchildren and look out 2019 for the Golden Anniversary God willing.

The year moved on as they do and we thought we would treat ourselves to a holiday. It was obvious from work and socially that Darwinians went to Asia like people in Adelaide and Sydney go to Melbourne and thought nothing of it. Jetta Natt was an expert on Bali, I heard about all sorts of places from work and other people, we read widely so we knew a lot about the ins and outs, where to go and so on.

While we were procrastinating Phil and Chris Stain caught the train from Adelaide to Darwin because they had never seen a wet season and we drove to Kakadu. It certainly was wet. We had to stop several times it was so heavy. We stayed in a cabin and quite enjoyed it. On the way home we had a look at a few places but it was too wet to go far. We found a canvas type SCALA brand hat somewhere that Leonore still wears in the garden.

Phillip and Chris left the next day on the train and the day after that returned, the train having reversed from somewhere because of floods. Perhaps the next got through and there were two trains parked in Darwin the most carriages since or maybe more than the first train.

And what happened about our proposed trip? We got analysis paralysis. It was all too hard so we booked our car and dog on the train. One or another was supposed to be free but the other was $500. The nice thing was that Lyn and Ian Phippard flew to Darwin and later in January took the train to Adelaide with us and flew home to Perth. The trip was good with stops at Katherine and Alice Springs but we had been to both places. I certainly would encourage people who have not been to those places to take the train trip.

Oh and by the way there was no pig or knife in the picture of our own Lara Croft but I bet she wished there was.

CHAPTER THIRTEEN
2010 – WOOMERA, SYDNEY AND SURGERY

We arrived home from Darwin and the end of January and stayed with Pam and Brian Murray at Clare and as always enjoyed their company.

As before our garden needed a lot of care and I well remember our "Shiny Leaf" or "Coprosma" hedge that was three metres high and three metres wide taking many hours work to get it to a manageable size.

I was keen but not over anxious about working and did some work in Port Lincoln, Whyalla and Arno Bay with a nursing friend who had a business doing pre-employment medicals, and other services for industry. Our big hope was that we would become the providers of choice for what was going to be the next big thing, iron ore mining. In late 2017 the last of five or six of the prospective miners gave up the idea.

I did some fitness for work medicals for Jobfit on Eyre Peninsula, Woomera and even Gladstone where big things were happening in the gas mining, transport and export as well as the other large industries associated with aluminium, coal and railways. It was only for a week or two but I enjoyed it.

I enjoyed meeting a big strong young bloke from Cloncurry and that screams "Cattle." On his form in the "Recreation?" section he had written "bull rider" woefully misspelt.

I said something about the spelling and his reply was wonderful. He said "I can't read or write too good but gimme me a shovel and I'll wear the bastard out in half a day" Andrew our son-in-law used to ride bulls so I asked this guy a bit about it.

He said that everyone sooner or later would be bucked off by a bull no matter how good they were.

I also worked at Woomera a few times for a week or so standing by while dangerous things happened. There was a nurse there, from the army reserves, who had worked many times with my surgeon mate Peter Malycha in Adelaide. We had a few cups of tea and chats together and once I asked her thoughts about the recent publicity about females going into full combat roles.

Her answer was crystal clear, "With periods and hormones, no way, and if we were captured the boys would come and get us when they shouldn't." She was pretty and petite and I asked another attractive female in the RAAF the same question and her comment was that the males and females were all professional and inappropriate rescue attempts would not be made. My friend in Woomera was on a tank leaning on the gun and I asked her to sing "If I could turn back time."

If that is not familiar check out Cher singing it on a US battleship!

The only other job I had was as a consultant to Workcover. I had a lot of experience with injured people, their rehabilitation, interactions with their employer and treating doctors from the 1980s throughout my career and as recently as my previous job in 2009.

I responded to an advertisement and was interviewed in Adelaide. It was very strange because, as a country general practitioner, I was endowed with the status of a movie star or perhaps a Martian.

My job was to ring doctors who Workcover wanted to speak to; in most cases to question why they had or had not done something that Workcover wanted them to do or not do or, in short, give them a hard time.

I knew the contempt doctors held for Workcover so I was very diplomatic when speaking to doctors, busy or not busy. I think I lasted one or maybe two days and was told that I was not suitable. I had failed to speak to enough doctors. For someone who has been criticised many times for being abrupt and to the point this was peculiar to say the least. I was disappointed for the rest of the day but it was an environment and organisation where I would not have been happy. I did not have a negative opinion of Workcover because in the past I had many positive experiences but this was no longer the case.

Maybe I worked for two months in 2010 but apart from working in the garden I did a lot of fishing at Coffin Bay and some crabbing at Cowell. Our older son Tim, now married, had worked in Port Lincoln, in the field of workplace relations and moved to Whyalla to work for One Steel, now Arrum.

It was nice to have him around because with boarding school, university, working in Adelaide and travel we had not seen much of him.

Even with Whyalla 200plus km away it was not too hard to meet there Cowell, or Port Lincoln and it was always a welcome stop on the journey to or from Adelaide or further east.

We visited friends in Adelaide and Yorke Peninsula and roamed around the Flinders Ranges and took the cover picture of this book in Warren Gorge near Quorn.

A very special trip was to visit our daughter and family then of three boys and a girl in Sydney. Andrew, her husband, is an army officer and he invited me to join him at the Anzac Day service at the Holdsworthy Army Base where he worked.

We had to leave their home at 3.00am because of the distance and he had to be there early. When we arrived it was still dark and raining.

We had to wait while 15-20 soldiers went past. Every one of them spoke to Andrew and the way they looked and said, "G'day boss", "Morning sir" was not said in any sense obsequiously, but with respect and eye contact and Andrew replied in a similar manner. I can't say I was surprised but boy

I was impressed. I have been around long enough to know that respect cannot be bought or demanded it can only be earned.

The return trip via Melbourne was new for us as we travelled along the coast all the way and saw Nowra where Andrew was posted in late 2017, Ulladulla, Bateman's Bay, Narooma, Merimbula, Lakes Entrance and so on and entered Melbourne through the Yarra Valley.

We stayed with my cousin Bill Mitchell at Merimbula. His twin was at Dad's funeral but like their sister in Perth I had not seen him since the 1960s. We had a pleasant evening together and reminisced about days gone by and left the next day. He actually lived in Canberra and sometime later Kirstin and Andrew moved nearby and they met a few times.

Later that year I developed severe pain radiating down my arms caused by a neck problem. The long and the short of it was that I had a plate put in my neck to fuse a couple of vertebrae. It was all relatively simple but I had a reasonably objective measure of the effects of anaesthesia on the brain. Before that I used to do the harder Sudoku puzzles in The Australian and would get eight out of ten correct. After the operation I cannot remember how many I got out but I gave up for years and only started again a couple of years ago. I kept a rough count last year and I got 50/90. Nearly eight years have passed since then and my memory is not as good but the immediate inability to perform as well surely means something. Between 2002 and 2010 I had two shoulder and two spinal operations so maybe there has been some additive effect. Another measure was I rang my nurse mate Jane and told her about my operation about a month later. She reminded me that she had visited me in hospital. I did not remember.

So upward and onward, the next big thing for us was Christmas with the whole family coming to Coffin Bay and it came with a special treat. We were to meet son Peter's brand new light o' love Patricia, in the Coffin Bay vernacular she was a 30cm long whiting, or to be brief a "keeper", and her mum.

CHAPTER FOURTEEN
2011 – GOOD AND BAD IN SPADES

GOOD STUFF

Leonore and I stayed at Coffin Bay for two weeks which was most enjoyable and perhaps the longest we had stayed there for several years. We had a number of friends there and there was always fishing and walking to occupy us.

Peter and Patricia announced their engagement on the 28th January that was no surprise to anyone but joyfully received by all.

I read a lot as usual and probably from 2002 when we went to Darwin to 2016 read 50 books a year sometimes more. 2017 and 2018 has seen a great reduction in this because I am on the other side of the page so to speak. In the last 20 years I have had about 25 articles published in outdoor magazines so writing a book, actually two, is a natural progression I suppose.

There were various jobs possibilities but nothing came to fruition so we continued to garden and also to work on plans for our proposed house at Coffin Bay.

In March we kept an agreement to go walking in the Ottway Ranges south west of Geelong with Terry and Judy

Holden our son in law's father and step mother, a couple we knew well and liked. This we did and had a great time and returned to Sarah and Nick's house in Melbourne to say farewell to them and their little boy Max. Sarah was heavily pregnant at the time.

LUCA'S PREMATURE BIRTH

We headed for home via Adelaide and Leonore's dad had something wrong in his world so Leonore stayed with him and I drove to Whyalla and stayed with Tim and Lisa. The next day I just did not want to go home and asked Lisa if I could stay another night. I just felt bad, anxious and strange. That night Sarah had a 10-week premature baby so at least I was 200km closer to Melbourne than I might have been. I drove to Adelaide, picked up Leonore and went to Melbourne.

It is a blur but Sarah was lucky to get to the local hospital and was transferred to the Austin Hospital, literally the opposite side of Melbourne from where they lived near Point Cook. I will never forget the look on Sarah's face two weeks later when she first held this little mite on her lap. It was the eternal look of a mother's love for her child. Soon after birth the baby had had four intravenous lines put in him and two tubes in his chest to help inflate his collapsed lungs so Sarah had not been able to cuddle him before. I felt like I would have been more use in a nuclear submarine that in that intensive care unit.

The good news is that he, Luca, was 1.8kg and significantly

bigger than the 500g babies there and he recovered but it was tough going.

After Sarah came home she had to go to the hospital twice a day to feed Luca and we obviously helped with the driving. It seemed an age but after three weeks Luca was transferred to Werribee Hospital, a relative "stone's throw" from Sarah's home and we came home via Peter's place near Naracoorte. Luca was kept at Werribee for a further four weeks but had to return for five days after episodes of apnoea but after that he went home and was fine.

SOME MORE GOOD STUFF

It was a tough time. Leonore rose to the occasion, as always. I was hopeless but two good things came from it. One was that I spent a lot of time with Max, Luca's brother and I think our relationship is better for that time. Secondly, I realised just how much the mothers of premature babies have to do and spend to manage their babies. Since them I have donated some money to an organisation "Life's Little Treasures" supporting the mothers of these precious children.

Later I worked at Woomera again and Tim and Lisa and their little girl, Laila, visited and we had a great time. The Sturt Peas were extraordinarily abundant and we have some lovely pictures of Laila and the dogs almost hidden by them.

MEETING A TAIPAN

After they visited we searched unsuccessfully for some

Aboriginal paintings and another day had a very surprising find when we took Lexi for a walk along a path on the side of a dry creek. She was ahead of me and Leonore behind who said "Is that a snake you have just passed by?" I grabbed Lexi who was old and had cataracts and gave her to Leonore to hold. Sure enough there was about six inches of a snake tail near the path quite still. I nearly picked it up but something told me not to, perhaps because it was shiny black.

I squatted down and could only tell it was moving by a occasional blade of grass moving. I could also now see it was a fair size. Estimating now I would think that it was bigger than I could get my thumb and middle finger around. It had big diamond shaped scales if I recall and with the size I thought at one stage it might have been a python. When I looked closely the belly was flat on the ground and the tiny muscles contracting and relaxing to move it along reminded me of caterpillar legs. When I stood up its head was visible. It was more than a metre long and it had a large head with a forehead. Photographs and enquiries later confirmed my second guess. It was a taipan.

NORMAL PERIOD

For the next month or so we were back to normal, whatever that may have been. We had an offer for our house but the potential buyer could not get finance. Tim and Lisa came here and we went fishing and then they moved to Gove where Tim had a new job. We looked after his dog Barney who was our dog Lexi's son so that was good fun and again worked in Woomera.

We arrived home in late May and our attention turned to two important events. One was Leonore's dad Michael Sullivan's 100th birthday to be celebrated on July 16th and the other an exciting trip through the Kimberley and then to Burketown and home leaving on the 18th July.

PAPA SULLIVAN 100 NOT OUT

Papa's birthday was really good. Michael Sullivan when young had film star looks and he still did and was very slim from his lifelong walking habit. There was a big crowd and he made an excellent speech. Sadly his beloved wife Jean, eldest son and eldest daughter Susan had predeceased him. Susan, a nun, only six months before but a sister nun of hers read the telegrams so that was something I suppose.

Michael was the oldest member of the Adelaide Oval and the South Australian Cricket Association put Michel Sullivan 100 NO (Not Out) on the real scoreboard, a nice gesture and much appreciated by Michael and his family.

Michael had played a French Horn in the Adelaide Symphony Orchestra in his youth and Leonore's remaining sister Jacqueline had organised a young man and woman who played that instrument in the current orchestra and were, I think, romantically linked so it was a really pleasant interlude when they played for him and his pleasure was obvious. I actually thought he was going to have a blow but no such luck.

I was later telling an army musician about this and he said that the French Horn was the hardest of that type of instruments to play because of all the coils.

On 18th June we drove to Quorn and met Ria and John Versteeg our friends from Coffin Bay and our hosts on the wonderful cruise on the Loire and Seine River a year before.

OUR BIG TRIP

John and Ria were seasoned travellers but had never done anything like this long camping trip before so they beefed up their Prada's shock absorbers as did I with our Mazda BT50. We had our camper trailer and they borrowed their son's. We shared the cost of a Satellite phone and collected lots of tools, glues, medical supplies and so on and away we went. We all liked food and wine so the girls precooked and froze some meals so it was a nice mix of camp and frozen food. John had pre ordered a case of champagne to be delivered somewhere up ahead.

So it was all systems go on the 19th June and we left Quorn.

We did not want to take the easy way and drive up the bitumen Stuart Highway to Katherine and turn left into the Kimberly. We wanted to go via the Oodnadatta Track and then to the Binns Track that ran from Mount Dare in the Northern Territory to Alice Springs roughly parallel with the Stuart Highway but through the Simpson Desert parallel with the dunes and other adventurous spots.

We managed this quite easily with a swim in a mound

spring on the way but John had car trouble at Alice Springs that took a few days to get sorted out. The Binns Track took a circuitous route east, north and west to rejoin the Stuart Highway but floods had closed that section so we by passed that and went up the Stuart Highway as far as Dunmurra and picked up Binns track where it headed north.

I had never worried about CB radios apart from a trip with the boys to play with when they were young but John was keen that we should keep in contact so we both had sets and in the next part of our trip I was glad of that. We were nearing the legendary Victoria River Downs universally known as VRD once the largest station in the world at nearly 16000 square miles now "only" the fifth biggest in the Northern Territory at 3440 square miles.

John called on the radio and said that a road train was coming. This was from VRD and was the first of eight semi-trailers each pulling three trailers made up of two decks of cattle. We happily pulled off the road and let them go past one after another. They were noisy, we were covered in manure flavoured dust that blotted out the sky but it was exhilarating. It was the sight, sounds and smell of the land we had come so far to experience. It was the real thing.

We continued north and then west on the main road between Katherine and Kununurra and stopped for a few days at Gregory National Park. This is highly recommended, there are Stromatolites that are fossilised cyanobacteria, aka blue green algae the first living things to photosynthesise ie produce oxygen.

Tofa dams were also interesting and are formed when calcite is broken down by the carbonate rich waters of the wet seasons.

Poor old John had trouble with his car and other things I haven't mentioned before but misfortune overtook him again. He had a good looking pair of boots with the name of a tractor company and both soles became separated from the boots, one on the walk out from the camp and the other on the way back. I had something in my pocket and fixed the first but the second he had to hobble. Talk about planned obsolescence.

We did the other things in this part of the world, had a look at Timber Creek, Kununurra, the bird watchers' paradise of Parry's farm near Wyndham and Mitchell Falls via a safe trip on the Gibb River Road.

My good luck in this part of the world where things go wrong continued.

We returned from Mitchell Falls and pulled up at the diesel bowser at Drysdale River Station and while I was filling the tank I noticed people staring and pointing at the other side of the car. I had picked up steel splinter from a grader and the back offside wheel was deflating. Easy fixed at what was essentially a service rather than a cattle station.

From there we drove to Katherine and went our separate ways as we had planned to cross the 700km of Arnhem Land to visit our son Tim who had moved to Gove only a few weeks before.

This we did successfully and had a nice time with them and a good look around the area. On the return trip our bull bar looked like it was going to fall off so I took it off. Once again it was held to the car by two pieces of thin metal, smaller than my palm, with holes drilled in them to act as a crumple zone. A pleasant young bloke pulled up and did most of the work. His wife was with him and she was Tim's boss to be.

Bull bars are unwieldy things but I managed to tie it onto a blanket on the roof and it rode happily to the welder man in Katherine.

We joined up with John and Ria and headed south to Mataranka where we enjoyed a relax in the hot springs pool that had been built for the RAAF offices during World War Two, still in excellent shape.

The other attraction there are the real graves, some had been moved, of the people Jeanie Gunn immortalised in "We of the never never" and a copy of the Elsie Homestead where they all had lived and or worked. It is a haunting, solemn and beautiful place indeed.

My thoughts are that reading this book and those by Ernestine Hill and others add a depth of understanding or appreciation about the people who pioneered the Northern Territory that is hard to achieve otherwise.

The next move was to join the 3700km long Savannah Way that joins Cairns to Broome and head for Borroloola along the Roper River. This road is a ribbon of history. There are unlimited camping and fishing spots. Two places that we found absolutely magnificent for different reasons were Butterfly Gorge and the Lost City between Roper Bar and Borroloola. Borroloola is not to be missed for its past and its present as a jumping off point for the Gulf fishing grounds if that is your pleasure

This was a meander through some magnificent country and historic places but we did have some method in our madness. We had arranged to stay at Armraynald, a cattle station south of Burketown and on the Albert River.

Jim Longmire the brother of my late friend Ian worked there. I had run into him when I was in Darwin and he was working at a cattle station west of Katherine and we had kept in touch. Armraynald was a big place and it was fascinating to once see 500 or more cattle walking in a line on the brow of a hill into the sunset. I tried throwing lures into the Albert River but there were no safe spots I could see where I could get close to what was a dry season river. I have been in a couple of cyclones but the damage I saw from the wet season storm or perhaps a cyclone was hard to describe. Huge trees had been tossed around like sticks into odd places or piled on top of each other. If they were somewhere that interfered with management it would have needed large machines to move them.

We spent three days there and that included an obligatory visit to the Burketown pub that was predictably interesting as was the fact that it burnt down not long after we were there.

The time to go was upon us, we headed home and John and Ria kept going east to the Queensland coast where they had some friends so they had another 800 km to go before they turned the Prado's nose for home.

We wandered home avoiding Birdsville because the Races were on and went to Naracoorte to pick up Lexi our dog who had been baby sat by Peter and Patricia and I was treated to a lovely fathers' day lunch. Finally we reached home on 9th September and were very happy to do so. I did a few weeks' harvest medicals and that was quite pleasant.

A SAD ENDING TO THE YEAR

In November we went to Adelaide and left our much-loved Lexi in a kennel we trusted in Port Lincoln. We arrived home about 5 o'clock and the kennels closed at 4-30. Next morning when they let her out she collapsed and they called the vet who rushed her to the surgery but she died from a twisted bowel that is not uncommon in big dogs.

We were devastated and felt so guilty. We could have easily been home by 4-30 and normally would have been but we fiddled around a lot on the way. Maybe it would not have helped but she must have been in pain and surely we would have heard her but who knows. Her son was next to her so just maybe that helped her.

CHAPTER FIFTEEN
TENNANT CREEK

In 2012 I was appointed locum Director of Medical Services at the Tennant Creek Hospital for four months from August to December.

The Chief Executive of the Tennant Creek Hospital was on sick leave but the outgoing DMS, who had been there for some years, was able to give me an excellent handover and the benefit of his experience. He did clinical and administrative work. The clinical staff while I was there were all locums apart from some regular visiting specialists. I only did administration as I was well past dealing with the complexity of the patients attending the emergency department although I did help out on occasions.

The locums were an interesting group. One was the guy who had given me the porno handcuffs for Christmas at Gladstone. They were excellent clinicians and about 60% were regulars and from various places with different backgrounds. My mate and others were essentially very skilled locum general practitioners. Others were studying to be or were employed as Emergency Medicine Specialists or other specialties and wanted a change, often the same time, each year. Some of the locums took two or three months a year to travel, ski, sail or whatever. They were well paid to work in Tennant Creek and other places that had such a burden of seriously injured or ill people.

The DMS told me that they used to do surgery under general anaesthesia but that had ceased and people were flown to Alice Springs. He was a very dedicated to the Aboriginal Community and even grew a house block sized vegetable garden in the hospital.

He planned to feed hospital patients with vegetables from the garden and when they experienced the pleasure of eating nice vegetables they might grow and eat their own. No! not allowed to feed patients in hospital with vegetables grown in the yard that may have had sprays on them, had to give them commercially grown products that were certain to have had chemicals on them.

The good news was that during my employment I was also in charge of the garden and benefitted from its fresh produce. Leonore was amazed how quickly she could dry tomatoes in the fierce sun. In a matter of hours she had large amounts of tomatoes that we were able to take home with us.

There was a young dietician working there in her first job who I thought showed a lot of get up and go to come from Melbourne to Tennant Creek. She had the idea of working with women's groups to grow vegetables for the same good reasons.

Leonore has a friend who is involved in the garden world

in Tasmania and through her I spoke to Tino Carnevale, a presenter on the ABC Gardening Australia TV show and he gave us some useful suggestions and information.

She was making some progress when I left Tennant Creek but I do not know the end result.

Like most outback hospitals the injuries from accidental or deliberate trauma, particularly associated with alcohol, in aboriginal people were frequent and severe.

I remember white people used to say that Aboriginal people could not handle alcohol with the implication that they could only drink a little and they would be drunk. Nothing could be further from the truth.

I was told by an expert in Alice Springs many years before that a carton of VB and a cask of Coolibah white wine is merely an appetiser for some aboriginal people not an impossible amount of alcohol to consume as it would be for most other people. The same person told me that a higher percentage of black people are teetotallers than white and I believe that.

There are a number of houses in Tennant Creek with signs indicating that alcohol is forbidden often with an unmarked police car nearby to enforce it.

Police would breathalyse aboriginal people in the bottle shop on their way out and if they blew over the limit, whatever that was, they would confiscate the alcohol.

My predecessor Tim did some statistics about violence in the Tennant Creek aboriginal population and it was some magnitude higher than the average in Australia. An internet search revealed that the murder rate in Tennant Creek is 50 times greater than the rest of Australia and 30 times greater than the national rate in the USA. The numbers are small but it certainly indicates a problem with in the aboriginal community and is similar in Katherine. There were 14 police officers in Tennant Creek in 1980 now there are 52. In a recent interview the Senior Police Officer was optimistic about the situation as there is less violence and the use of iron bars, machetes and the like in fights than there was in my time at Tennant Creek. A week or so after the above was written a two-year-old child was raped by an Aboriginal in Tennant Creek and Australian Story was about Gayle Woolford, a nurse, who was raped and murdered at Fregon in north-west of South Australia in March 23rd or 24th 2016. I am appalled to read that Safework SA refused to recognise this as a work-related death---they have now.

At the time of writing there have been several newspaper articles about the situation. One being "Silenced" abuse victims living in fear, where amongst other distressing information, Tors Clothier a paediatrician in Alice Springs, is quoted as thinking about a "seven-year-old child who was raped (some years ago) and died from her injuries" and his belief that few girls reach puberty without some sort of unwanted sexual activity. In the edition of 7th March 2018 THE AUSTRALIAN quotes previous Minister of Health Mal Brough, who implemented the Intervention initiative as saying effectively *that the situation was out of control and that some settlements should be closed echoing the sentiments of ex- Premier Barnett of Western Australia.*

The Royal Darwin Hospital has a major role in the response to disasters in Australia and over- seas. There is an emergency response group that can and does respond to disasters all over the world.

Some of this group came to Tennant Creek to provide training for doctors, ambulance officers, para-medics, fire and police officers and nurses. The scenario was a crashed car where they showed us how they secured the site, kept people safe, get into the car and got victims out, using the "jaws of life" and other emergency rescue equipment. The head nurse was a small lady who was at a decided advantage at getting into and out of places where big people like me could not.

They then talked about the hazards that they had experienced going to aboriginal communities or houses. They had even developed tactics to use. Such as if things went quiet to get to hell out of the direct line from the door as a spear might come through the door when it was opened. I am not a stranger to these stories but the way they spoke it was common. And it horrified me.

I had to do a report for the victims of crime tribunal on a 22-year-old aboriginal female who had three files of medical records each 10cm thick. They included records of pregnancy, drug and alcohol abuse and trauma.

The particular admission the tribunal was interested in

was when she was drinking with two female friends who turned on her and beat her up with a hammer including smashing her joints.

I am certainly not an expert on aboriginals but I have been involved with individuals, groups and organisations for a significant part of my career. There are hundreds or even thousands of good kind caring dedicated, black and white people devoting their careers to aboriginal health in its broadest sense.

I mentioned about the locums that we used. Recently I read an article in "Outback" magazine about the Tennant Creek Hospital and the doctors who were employed there full time.

They were working in and studying aboriginal health to help with becoming Fellows of the Royal Australian College of General Practitioners. I am proud to say that I had some part in the birth of that scheme working with the relevant bodies in Alice Springs and elsewhere during my time at Tennant Creek in 2012.

There certainly is progress in aboriginal health services but there are chasms between black and white in some areas. For example it is now February 2018 and there have been forests of newspapers devoted to the Australia Day debate with quite extreme views from some aboriginal activists.

An article by Grace Collier in The Weekend Australian newspaper of 15-16 January 2018 cites the government expenditure of $33 billion in 2015-16 on aboriginals or

$44,500 per person per year.

There about 670,000, or 3% of the population, aboriginal people in Australia estimated from the last census. This is about double the number in the 1960s and significantly higher than estimates of 2-300,000 before the white man arrived.

Many Australians think that the traffic is all one way. Australians have been renowned for giving people a fair go but from what I have seen and heard over the decades the perception is that it is all about take and little about give.

Unfortunately, the voices of aboriginals and organisations that represent them and the scores of nurses, doctors and others who work in aboriginal health are relatively silent in the caterwauling of the dissatisfied.

Let us also remember the 55-60 % or maybe more aboriginal people who do not drink, they protect their children and help their relatives, are wonderful artists, valuable employees and sports men and women.

In the time I have lived in Port Lincoln, an aboriginal organisation and health service have been established and flourished and an aboriginal football team now over 30 years old has been very successful and has produced many of the star AFL players of recent times. There now 72, a record number of aboriginals who are members of AFL teams. A telling statistic is that 156 aboriginal players have made their AFL debut since 1980 and that there were only 23 before that date.

Could Australian aboriginals come to make Australian Rules their own as black Americans have done with basketball? To quote George Bernard Shaw "You see things and say why? I dream of things that might be and say why not?"

Could a black leader arise in Australia who would lead the aboriginal community towards what they can do rather than demanding more and more money? Maybe, male and now female footballers could lead the charge because females are certainly suffering and in many places trying very hard to prevent this atrocious situation.

Success is no panacea for some successful aboriginals. David Gullpilli is the best-known aboriginal actor in Australia but he is frequently in trouble with police in Darwin on his forays between his white and tribal world. A police sergeant who lived in his community told me in Darwin that his fellow tribesmen beat him up occasionally just to show him he wasn't so special. I find that so sad.

Tribal mores also rule in a less dramatic way. A well-known Port Lincoln aboriginal man explained his dilemma of seemingly always having a house full of aboriginal people in this way. "You white fellas have first and second cousins we have fifth and sixth cousins and we have a responsibility to look after them."

Our aboriginal friends have fused Communism, Christianity and Darwinism, (social and biological) that has evolved over 50,000 years into a somewhat coherent whole that is their way and very much their burden.

The annual 'Closing the Gap" report was also released at the time of writing, 10 years after the project was introduced and although it has been the most successful of the annual reviews in that three out of the seven targets were on track for achievement the others are not, in particular the gap in school attendances.

The Australian editorial thunders about this under the heading "Entire nation must own Closing the Gap failures" and writes authoritatively about funding, state and federal roles and so on.

But nowhere in this editorial, or anywhere else have I read in recent times, has anyone addressed the role of parents in the education of children. I know about drunkenness, violence, petrol sniffing and school absenteeism. Petrol sniffing was endemic in the APY lands in South Australia a few years ago and I could not believe the television footage of children walking around with tins of petrol on strings around their necks from which they frequently sniffed with adults looking on. I believe that was sorted out with the introduction of a particular type of petrol without the horrifying side effects on the brain of ordinary petrol but there are still people with residual damage.

If kids are not going to school how can anyone, other than their parents, really change that?

Nepotism, fraud and mismanagement of funds are common in the whole chain of funding. The heads of clans frequently receive large amounts of cash to grease the wheels of project applications on "tribal" land. Where does that go?

Even a casual interest in the news reveals poor project management with debt written off, government funds not used or transferred to meet other needs and so on.

One of the great difficulties in this discussion is that any comment like I have made can be brushed aside as "racist". I am not trying to sheet blame but without acceptance of responsibility by the aboriginal industry to the people who live in aboriginal communities I cannot conceive how things will change.

Money is necessary, certainly, but I doubt chucking more at this situation will achieve anything.

I have thought and talked about this subject during the long preparation and writing of this book and at many points decided not to express an opinion but I owe it to my family to write as near the truth about my life as is practical.

Sadly my opinion is that aboriginal and white people live in two different worlds and neither side accepts that the other's is legitimate. Let us hope that at the contact points between us there can be enough cohesion to live in harmony, with respect and in a safe world. But there are some good things.

A mate of mine, Mathew Hutchinson, wrote this account of his time in Arnhem Land.

Living and working in Arnhem Land for nearly twenty years has been an amazing experience, from living and breathing another culture to going through a category four cyclone.

The amazing part of living in an Aboriginal community is gaining the knowledge of culture and beliefs from these wonderful people. I have been lucky enough to gain acceptance into their lives and thus I have been adopted into a family and given a "skin name".

A skin name is traditionally given to people who have the respect and acceptance of Indigenous people. Along with the name you can also be given a Totem. This totem will define the family and clan group that you are a part of. My Totem is the Shark, and my skin name is "Burralung Dammarandji". The first name Burralung means "calm salt water" that represents me very well as I lived and worked at sea for many years. Along with this also comes responsibility and cultural lore. For example the Indigenous lady who I work with and in my role was her supervisor; she now became my "Mari" which means Grandmother. So in our professional environment I was her boss but outside of work she was mine, and I was to give her the respect she was entitled to as an elder of the community.

This arrangement took some time for me to understand and also for us both to work out what was acceptable within the work place. Sometimes at meetings we were both attending my role as chair or facilitator was reversed pending on who was attending from community. I was extremely lucky that my "Mari" was an amazing woman and taught me the local customs and ways of culture. Even though I am now working at another community I am still a part of her life and family. Being adopted into a family and clan allowed me to transition into a new community with ease. Once the members of the new community understood my adoption and skin name I was accepted. I also gained more family relations in the new community. The totem I was given has allowed me to access traditional areas around the new community which would normally be off limits to "Balanda" white Australian.

I feel very privileged to work and live in Northern Australia. I have met some amazing people and experienced some elements of Aboriginal culture that very few White Australians will ever see. Life in a community is not easy at times, the wet season can isolate access into community for up to six months every year. Wet season also brings humidity of 98% for months, Food supplies are delivered by barge, the mail can take up to 2 weeks to arrive. We don't have all the luxuries of Western life, going to cafes, theatre and restaurants. We do however enjoy some of Australia's most untouched lands and unspoiled coastline, no traffic lights, and we can finish work and go and catch barramundi just ten minutes away. Community life is not for everyone but I am forever grateful is has been a part of my life.

Ed: Thank you for this Matthew. Your words and actions are a bright light in what is a dark world at the present time.

CHAPTER SIXTEEN
2013 – THE RAAF AND WAGGA WAGGA HOSPITAL

In early 2013 in response to an advertisement I was employed once more as a medical officer with the Australian Defence Forces at Salisbury north of Adelaide. It was at the Edinburgh RAAF base and an infantry regiment had been moved there from Robertson Barracks in Darwin as had part of 1 CER where I used to work. I think that they wanted the experts at finding explosives working much closer to the infantry. So I would be working with RAAF and Army personnel.

The security checks were much more thorough than when I worked in Darwin that I can't even remember but I must have had one. Terrorism has certainly changed our world. The forms must have taken an hour to complete. Main road Alice Springs for example was not an acceptable address!

The reason for this was to get a pass and to access computers and therein is a certain irony. I was issued a pass but my security clearance did not come through until I had left six months later. That suited me because I was able to use the familiar old pen and paper files. As it turned out the lack of access and therefore practice with using the computers may have saved me a lot of grief later.

On the subject of passes one of the guards was another Peter Morton who I had met and helped, in a small way, he and his wife to write our family history.

The medical centre was well equipped with about half a dozen civilian and one or two military doctors predictably some with Aviation Medicine qualifications. There was a hospital attached to the medical centre or perhaps vice versa. We all shared the on-call duties that were not onerous.

The Lyell McEwin Hospital was nearby so we did not see nasty accidents although I did see a man once who had flown back in a RAAF plane from the Middle East as part of his job and developed gastro enteritis and was quite unwell when I admitted him. He was a lovely bloke and when I reviewed him I asked why he had not made a fuss on the aircraft. He told a story that would apply to many other service people I suggest. He had wanted to be an aircraft mechanic in the RAAF and for whatever reason he was unsuccessful several times but eventually he was accepted. He said, "This is everything to me and I never complain about anything in case they throw me out."

I found the work interesting. I mentioned before that the patients I saw in Darwin were all male, mostly strong and injured at work mainly playing sport. There were also the usual common illnesses such as colds and flu.

They were posted for two years although many would come back when promoted so in a sense the majority of the patients were always the same age.

The RAAF patients were quite different, both genders and ages ranging from 18 to 50 plus. Some like my friend above could only be employed there because that is where the planes and radar sets etc. were.

I had one patient who with good reason had severe Depression and she told another doctor that I saved her life, she was that bad. Was it true? It may well have been.

We saw many couples with infertility. I had seen a lot of people in their "baby making" years and do not recall infertility being a huge problem but maybe my memory is playing tricks because we knew three couples well who adopted children and later had their own.

Maybe free medical care was a motivator for young couple to join the defence forces and the more young people the more infertility.

One of the paradoxes in medicine is that the patients who see specialists almost always have something serious or something that the patient's general practitioner cannot manage, whereas the patients a general practitioner sees - unless it is relatively obvious - often do not have anything seriously wrong but may have. GPs have to be aware that amongst the myriads of "sparrows" we see, "Birds of paradise" may pop up so our intellectual antennae must always be active.

I saw a man on a Friday complaining of dizziness and ringing in his ears which is quite a common condition of the inner ear and usually not harmful though unpleasant. He also complained of pain in his ear that was normal to examination. I explained to him what I thought it was but specifically said that pain was unusual and asked, well told him, to return the next morning.

The doctor who he saw was equally concerned said what I did and asked him to return the following day The third doctor did a CT scan and the man was found to have a cerebellar tumour and had prompt surgery performed. I think that indicates good medical management. Two of us were alert to the fact that something strange might be happening and made sure that the patient also knew and indeed it was.

One thing that was definitely not usual in my civilian or military work places was aircraft landing emergency callouts.

The RAAF had been flying the four turbo prop P3 Lockheed Orion since the late 1960s and these operate from Edinburgh patrolling all over the place. One day I was minding my business when a nurse ran past and said "C'mon you're the duty doctor come with me in the ambulance there is an aircraft landing alarm". I obeyed instructions and sat in the ambulance as the plane landed. This happened maybe once a month.

Maybe that is why I have just received a signal from Wing Commander Google to the effect that we are or should be in the middle of procuring eight Boeing P-8A Maritime Patrol and Response Aircraft with twin jet engines that have missiles, torpedoes and Triton Drones.

It is easy to be blasé working with military people because they talk and walk and eat and speak like the rest of us but they are involved in a world we can only glimpse from time to time.

A cheery, chubby, red haired flight lieutenant was a few minutes late for an appointment and I jokingly reprimanded him. He said 'Sorry but I had an aircraft on my screen". I thought that was no big deal as the P3s were landing and taking off all the time and said as much.

He said "No, it was a P3 in the Indian Ocean looking for people smugglers and I had to put in a report to Canberra"

He was the link effectively between the War Cabinet office and the plane. Made me sit up that's for sure.

We were fortunate to live in a house owned by an RAAF sergeant and apart from a giant TV and a complete series of the Jack Reacher books that I read it was in a lovely spot behind the "Old Spot Hotel" on the Main North Road.

I cannot remember a normal hotel with a better selection of wine and spirits. About 200 metres from the house we could walk into the Little Para River gorge. The river was a creek really but it had carved out a decent sized gorge that was made for our Labrador puppy. There were mushrooms everywhere that other people did not eat but we had a ball collecting, cooking and eating them. If they looked like a mushroom with pink to brown gills and smelled like a mushroom they probably were and we haven't been wrong yet.

Another place we found interesting and quite close was Kersbook.

I have referred to Mount Leonard as Leonore's family home. Her great-grandfather, great uncle and grandfather were from Kersbrook and were part- owners of that property that must have promised so much but caused so much pain when Leonore's grandfather was drowned in the Diamantina.

We looked though an old cemetery and saw the graves of some Scotts but did not know where they fitted as we did not have enough information with us at the time.

The next highlight of the year was on 11th July when Peter and Patricia had a daughter they called Skye and rounded our grandchildren to 10 and the total with adults to 20.

Then Tim's wife Lisa was naturalised and then, wait for it, we Leonore and I saw Don McLean. He introduced the show by referring to one of the great questions of our musical times when asked, "What is *American Pie* about? His answer, "It's about me never having to work again unless I choose." He was special.

The next couple of months were about designing our house to be, endless gardening at Port Lincoln and Coffin Bay. But relief of a kind was welcome when we headed for Wagga Wagga where I was to be Director of Medical Services for three months.

We stopped with Iain and Helen Simpson in Loxton on the way and Iain rang an old school friend Betty Anne Mawson and her husband "Blue" who they often visited in Wagga to let them know we were on our way.

I started work on the 4th November for three months to keep the seat warm for another doctor.

We liked Wagga Wagga. It was big and in a great part of Australia. With this job and another we spent almost a year there so saw the four seasons. It certainly was hot in the summer and cold in the winter but the heat was dry and the cold and frosty mornings turned into bright still days that to Leonore and m were close to ideal. We enjoyed the journey to and from Wagga and visited the nearby attractions such as the air show at Temora, Junee, and Bradman's birthplace of Cootamundra, Gundagi, and Tumut and so on.

Did I like the work? Yes, I did.

I had a number of tasks and the prime one I suppose was looking after the welfare, performance and training of interns and other junior doctors. Interns have a service role of course but they must complete their year to become registered as medical practitioners. Similarly other junior doctors may need to meet targets to enter training courses. Somehow the hospital had not organised rosters properly and there was a lot of anger about that. Fortunately I had some role in sorting that out mainly because I listened. There was an intern, Phillip Kirk - over 30 and ex navy. He was a calming influence and of great help.

I got on well with a few specialists who welcomed me and called into my office every now and them.

I was puzzled with the on-call roster. Even though there might have been several specialists in a given field there were occasions that no one was available and we had to employ a doctor from elsewhere or send patients to another hospital. This was not acceptable in my view for a major hospital that provided services for 300,000 people.

Accreditation was another role and I chaired the relevant committee.

Translated it meant that I sat there and a senior nurse ran the meeting after I opened and closed it.

There was a regional authority and I attended their meetings together with Kath Atkinson the Regional Medical offer who was a great help to me as were the Senior Doctors in the Emergency Department.

I cannot recall if there was a sub-committee of that group or another but it looked after the clinical privileging and accreditation of general practitioners who worked in the smaller hospitals. These meetings were by teleconferences and I would have liked to have done a trip around to meet these people but that did not happen.

The CEO was Dennis Thomas. His workload was phenomenal and I was actually quite pleased that he agreed to give me a reference if I asked.

I was recruited by David Campbell from Skilled Medical who had been a Senior Medical Administrator and said that "Wagga Wagga is a tough gig".

I had been home for two or three weeks when the person

whose seat I had kept warm rang me and said something along the lines of how hard Wagga was and he was not going to stay. Interesting!

Last but not least we flew to Gove for Christmas to see Tim, Lisa and their two children and predictably had a great time.

On the flight back we had to spend a few hours at Cairns and we caught up with Roy Hogben and his wife Tracy. He was a partner and good friend of mine in Port Lincoln so that was nice.

Before we leave Wagga. Ian Simpson's school friend Betty Anne looked after Phryne while we got ourselves organised in a house.

This was not successful as Phryne pinched their old Labrador's bed.

While we there a very chatty lady obviously a friend called in and talked about all sorts of places she was going with her husband. God she could have talked underwater with a mouth full of marbles.

About three or four months later Ian Simpson asked me if I had met the Governor General Peter Cosgrove. I had when our son-in-law was awarded the Sword of Honour at Duntroon as it so happened.

Iain then asked how I got on with Mrs Cosgrove. I was quite confused then he dropped it on me that Mrs Cosgrove was Betty Anne's chatty friend.

We left in mid- January and returned via Loxton and Stains

to Adelaide where our dog Phryne needed a knee reconstruction that was very successful.

Recommendation: Don't let young Labradors chase hares on ploughed ground.

CHAPTER SEVENTEEN
2014 – PORTLAND

The early part of 2014 revolved around getting our dog's knee surgery to heal and get strong, tidying up the garden and progressing the planning for a Coffin Bay house.

We made a terrible and expensive mistake with the house and when we asked a builder for an estimate it was $800,000. The plans were all in proportion but we had not realised that the house was so big. We literally went back to the drawing board.

In March Leonore's father died at 102 years old. Apart from the last 18 months in a nursing home he had been in good health and lived independently.

The funeral was in Adelaide on 3rd April and coincidentally we flew to Sydney the next day. We had invested heavily in Kimberley Diamonds and the shares had risen. We were invited to a gala function to raise money for the aboriginal community near their mine.

It was spectacular. Food, wine, dancing girls, band and singers amongst Sydney's best I imagine. It was way ahead of anything we had ever done but we felt we had earned it with all the places we had been for work in the previous 12 years.

Unfortunately the venture that promised so much fell over.

Next day we checked out the Maritime Museum at Daring Harbour and had a pleasant lunch and relaxing day. That night we had what really was one of the thrills of out married life. We attended a performance of Madame Butterfly on an inlet of Sydney Harbour. Apart from the woman in front of me waving around a set of binoculars that looked like they belonged on the bridge of a battleship the experience was faultless.

We returned home via Melbourne and saw Sarah and Nick and then flew to Portland where I had a successful interview for the position of Director of Medical Services at the local hospital for six months.

We went home, packed dog, goods and chattels and headed off via a day or two with Peter and Patricia in Lucindale to Portland.

I looked forward to this job as it was half way between Peter and Sarah's homes and a reasonable distance from both and they did visit once or twice. We liked the general area from my time in the south east and Warrnambool and the town and hospital were a nice size.

Portland was probably a little more than half the current size of Port Lincoln with a population of about 12-13,000 and reminded me of Port Lincoln when we moved there in 1979 and of course fishing was a major industry.

The Chief Executive Officer (CEO) welcomed me warmly when I arrived and said something really strange and to the effect of "Don't think you can put anything over me because you are a doctor and I am a nurse. I scored enough points in matriculation to be a doctor but my father wouldn't let me." She also couldn't stand anyone moving anything from its designated position on her desk.

She was a very capable and pleasant person and I don't recall any one who was unpleasant. The two main aspects of my job were to be responsible for the medical staff and to be involved with the relevant parts of the Hospital Accreditation Survey that was due later in the year. I also helped in the new Commonwealth funded Health Centre attached to the hospital seeing some patients on occasions.

We had a physician from Sri Lanka and he was joined by an Indian physician who I was able to help with his registration and specialist recognition. Prior to his arrival the incumbent physician shared the on-call duties with a general practitioner with skills in that area and the odd locum. I thought that the two physicians would be able to share the roster but no, they had signed up for no more than three nights a week.

My model for this was Port Lincoln, a much more isolated place than Portland, where a surgeon, the late Ian Fletcher and physician Rufus McLeay, were on-call virtually every day they were in Port Lincoln for almost thirty years.

When I asked the CEO to support this she gave me a kindly smile and said, "Peter you are a dinosaur". I discussed this very situation with Rufus prior to writing this book without mentioning her remarks and his reply was, "Yes I am a dinosaur." So I was in good company.

Christine, the CEO, was also philosophical about an anaesthetist from South Africa who cut short his agreed stay to take up another job.

Yes, we need overseas doctors and go to a lot of expense to get people who wish to live in a safer place or somewhere where they can have a higher standard of living. A junior doctor from India, working in Gladstone in 2006 told me his wages in India would have been $150 a month so it is annoying and disappointing when overseas doctors bite the hand that feeds or protects them.

The half dozen resident doctors, mostly females, were all from overseas apart from one from Australia. I cannot re call anyone causing trouble.

The Australian doctor was someone who really was "something else".

She was just in her 50s or I should say still in her 50s, just, if I recall correctly. She was a grandmother, ex teacher, professional fire fighter and forestry officer, slim, fit and a very nice lady who was a real asset to the hospital. She was doing general practice training and I am sure that she would have made a success of that job.

The Human Resource bloke was an ex RAAF aircraft mechanic and he had some great stories about life in and out of the RAAF but he had a disagreement with the Victorian Government and left and the only other male, the accountant also left soon after so I was the last male in the administration department and I was put into a smaller and then a shared office.

I looked up the hospital a year or two ago and there were no males but today the internet revealed that there is a male doing the same job I had.

I got out and about a bit to Hamilton, Heywood and Warrnambool and also tried to establish a business of doing pre-employment medicals for the industries in Portland at the Health Centre but that fell on deaf ears unfortunately. We did have a session on men's health so maybe that took off after I left. There is massive amount of money available for women's health but the Men's Health man in Portland could not even get an appointment to discuss the subject with the Minister for Health let alone funding for anything.

An emergency medicine specialist from Warrnambool kept an eye on the Emergency Department (ED) and I used to meet with him frequently.

I must confess I dropped the ball when it came to the handover process that was very important to accreditation surveyors.

With the changes in working conditions for hospital doctors a patient may be seen let us say at 0700 with a broken arm from a car accident. The patient is assessed by the night duty doctor who hands the patient over to the day doctor who orders an X-ray, takes whatever action is necessary, admits the patient to the ward and hands over to the ward doctor who later hands over to the night doctor. Relatives are encouraged to be present so everyone is kept informed.

We did not actually fail the survey but given a conditional pass subject to the handover process being reviewed in six months.

I mentioned Warrnambool Hospital that was now the "mother' hospital to Portland Hospital. When I was there in the 1970s Hamilton Hospital had that role.

I have mentioned this before but it really is a remarkable statistic. On the subject of Warrnambool Hospital Peter O'Brien was the current Director of Medical Services, a Daryl Pedler, who was working with Deakin University locally, had also held that position, as had I.

The three of us had also been general practitioners on Eyre Peninsula in South Australia, Peter in Wudinna and Daryl in Cummins---very long odds indeed.

We lived in an old three-storey house in the main street that had been a shop, a union office and goodness knows what else and was obviously decorated by someone who loved the sea. It was walking distance from all the essential things in life, bread, meat, vegetables, fruit, beer wine and drugs, from the chemist of course, the beach, sea and work for that matter.

Portland is a major exporter of wood chips from the pine forests between there and Mount Gambier and the trucks run for 20 hours a day leaving time for maintenance of equipment in the middle of the night.

The trucks, all with two trailers, are unloaded in a way I

have not seen before and never tired of watching. The trucks drove onto the jetty and were lifted with the front of the prime mover pointing to the sky to about 80 degrees. As it was heading skywards somehow the two trailers gates were opened and the chips in the top or front trailer ran into and through the rear or bottom trailer. The load of chips fell onto a belt running beneath the jetty and into a silo.

There were many old buildings made from basalt reflecting the volcanic geological history of the Warrnambool to Mount Gambier area. The coastal scenery is magnificent and the nearby Bridgwater Bay where a friend has a very special house. Cape Bridgewater is the highest cliff in Victoria and the place where currents rounding the Cape of Good Hope reach Australia.

The continental shelf is relatively close to Australia and presumably why Portland is an absolute mecca for people wanting to catch tuna when they are running in huge numbers. We went out once and hell it was rough. I caught a fish and fell head over tail fortunately all in the boat. There was a lad who had over indulged the night before and he knelt on the deck with his head on the gunwale for four hours.

Overall I enjoyed the job, the environment and the opportunity to see more of our family.

Later in the year I went to a Medical Conference in Adelaide that I enjoyed. We demolished our shack at Coffin Bay and at Christmas time the family came over and we stayed at a large rental property that was great and caught heaps of fish; a simple and good holiday except the children having to drive so far.

CHAPTER EIGHTEEN
A BRIDGE TOO FAR

I have not looked forward to writing this chapter that describes my last job and has an unpleasant ending. The title of the film about attacking the bridgehead over the Rhine River at Arnhem during the Allied Invasion of Europe in world War Two seems rather grand but I cannot get it out of mind.

I worked for the Australian Defence Forces (ADF) in Darwin, Edinburgh and lastly at Kapooka near Wagga Wagga. That statement is actually shorthand. I worked for agencies that provided health services to the ADF and in the last two jobs my employer was Aspen Medical.

In early 2015 I saw an advertisement for a medical officer at Kapooka. I was told that it was not an easy place to work but thought I would give it ago and started work there on 16th April. A positive aspect was that it was half way between Melbourne and Sydney where our daughters and their families lived.

We had a nice house, where we had lived when previously in Wagga Wagga and it was on the western side of what is quite a large city. Kapooka was about a 10-15 minute drive and I was given a car to use.

Kapooka was a training centre for all soldiers who entered the Australian Regular Army and there was a section for that purpose complete with its own medical centre.

The area where I was primarily employed dealt with the staff who trained the recruits. It is probably over simplifying things, but to some Non-Commissioned Officers (NCOs) and Officers Kapooka was a positive career move. To others it was a place to put personnel where they were under less pressure and not on active service, often to recover from psychological problems or to simply be occupied until claims for such problems could be resolved.

An interesting unit was a number of musicians, one of whom was a champion bugler who played at major functions. Part of the training of recruits was marching drill hence the band and it was quite haunting to hear the drums and other instruments playing for the marching soldiers on a frosty morning.

Leonore and I attended the Anzac Day dawn service and it poured. The doctors were treated as members of the public. I was disappointed in that because in Darwin we were very much part of the service and the later breakfast. It retrospect that was probably quite significant-we didn't matter much in Kapooka.

The base was a very pretty place to work with a golf course and open grasslands where kangaroos abounded.

Peter Manns, effectively the Senior Medical Officer, had

extensive experience as a remote general practitioner, eg he removed a melanoma from his own leg once. He was also extremely well versed in military medicine. He and his wife were very supportive of Leonore and me, both at and outside work.

Erwin Moore was an ex South African doctor who was also very patient with my computer fumbling and later we saw him and his wife Annelize socially. As an aside her mother visited them from South Africa and we invited them to our place for tea. I had a partner in Port Lincoln, Dick Schoeman, whose South African mother had come to our house for dinner 35 years before and I recalled him calling her "O'ma". I rang him and he affirmed it meant "Old Woman" and was a term of respect. When the Moores brought Annelize's mother to our place I threw open the door and said "Welcome O'ma". She was quite taken back but soon was calling me "O'pa.

About a month after we arrived I went to a major national General Practice Conference in Sydney and attended handpicked sessions relevant to my job as well as those of general interest such as the increasing work being done on gut bacteria.

One session was on infertility run by two 40-year-old females. It was very interesting indeed and as I have mentioned before quite a common presentation in military medicine. The two women were indeed experts and clearly very caring but I must say that I felt they revealed more than they should have about their own experiences and emotions in their personal situations. I have always been comfortable talking to men and women about personal things but to a 100 people audience, I am not so sure. Maybe it reassures a female audience that they are empathetic.

I also attended several sessions on mental illness run by a real pop star for want of a better name. He was a vigorous promoter of general practitioners and their roles in treating depression. He essentially said, "Don't think only surgeons and cardiologists can save lives, general practitioners can do that with aggressive use of anti-depressants medication. Psychologists have never saved anyone's life". Definitely a black and white man, no shades of grey with this bloke and it was music to my ears.

We enjoyed Wagga and visited many of the nearby attractions including spending a lovely, but cold, weekend in Tumut, Batlow and surrounds.

I thought I was doing alright at work and I had passed the dozen or more topics about how the army operated in the mandatory training.

I also passed the computer training but that was more by flukes than good management. The system was known a JEDI and was generally despised by all who used it and I was just hopeless.

Clinically I thought I was doing alright and even made friends of a couple of patients who had a connection with Naracoorte where my son worked and Peter Heysen, grandson of the painter, who I knew well.

Thinking back. I was off balance in some way. My inability with the computer made me angry and I found out later I had disadvantaged some patients by not providing some paperwork that I didn't know existed in time for them to attend a course that was important for their careers.

I mentioned psychology problems. The major one of course was Post Traumatic Stress Disorder or PTSD. I was comfortable dealing with this but some people seemed to want to get better but one guy just wanted certificates to not go to work when he had no real job anyway.

In civilian practice it is relatively easy: a doctor sees a patient, refers them to a specialist and follows up that patient for the period of that problem. I found it hard at Kapooka because I would become involved with someone and maybe recommend some medication and a certain course of action. And then they would disappear into a maze of other health professionals, Department of Veteran Affairs, counsellors, social workers and so on. I seemed to be off balance with the complexity of management.

I am not suggesting that I should manage everything but together with my inability to manage the computers I was a struggling and patients doctor swapped, understandably, as Erwin and Peter had been there for years.

I also worked at the RAAF base occasionally on the other side of Wagga and that was interesting for a change.

I had done some sessions at the recruit clinic and as usual had trouble with a different computer and the Nurse Unit

Manager eventually helped me but she was as abrasive in her manner as I can be.

After I had worked for about two or three months I had a significant cardiac irregularity that needed attention by a cardiologist and I was not allowed to drive until that was sorted out. Peter Mans kindly drove me too and from work - that was most appreciated.

Not long after this Aspen talked to Peter about me working at the recruit centre as the doctor who worked there was leaving and there were three of us at the main clinic when two was enough. Peter strongly recommended I did not work with that particular nurse.

Peter was the embodiment of patience and diplomacy and had been there for years and he told me he found her difficult.

Despite his recommendation I was transferred there and on day one I was in trouble. I could not get my computer to work at all. Another doctor tried to help but he was flat out. The senior nurse when I asked for help said something like "It's a bloody awful system everybody hates it, just get over it." I managed to somehow get some medication for a recruit with a cold from the pharmacy and gave it to her.

One of the nurses at the desk asked me to do a certificate for her to carry. I asked why because it was not prescription medicine and I had not given anyone else with their $50 boxes of cold medication from the pharmacist a certificate. But this girl was a recruit. I somewhat grumpily wrote out a chit.

The nurse came into my office and said that she didn't

appreciate me being so rude, grumpy or whatever and I apologised and I thought she had accepted my apology. Next thing the Nurse Unit Manager stormed into my room and roundly abused me. No apology was good enough for her.

I thought about this long and hard over the next day or so. I was not always the most popular doctor around the place but I do not recall anything like this rudeness that in the grand scheme of things was the sort of thing that can be defused by a simple apology.

I had always fought my own battles but thought that this nurse had crossed a line and I wrote to Aspen and complained about her conduct. Of course that resulted in a counter claim that I had only seen two patients and the other doctor had seen ten. No comment about the computer.

There was a formal interview with two people from Aspen and Peter Manns about my performance and they thought it unlikely I would be able to improve my computer skills in the three weeks left on my contract so perhaps it would be best if I took my holidays and left and this I did.

Of course I was hurt, angry and disappointed but the reality was that I could not cope with the computer system and, I confess, with the way the Army did some things.

I wrote a letter to the Major in charge of the health centre and apologised for my inadequacies and how I was very proud to have been formally involved with the Defence Forces for four years and less formally at Woomera for three years and said I was sad that things had ended this way. She wrote a gracious and courteous reply that I appreciated.

By the way, the cause of my computer malfunction was that I forgot to do what was necessary to log on to a different site, that is all I had to do and I suppose that reinforces that I was past my use by date.

It was my last job.

We left Wagga on the 17th October and via Tumut to camp at Talbingo a lovely place that was balm to my wounded spirits and from there to Jindabyne and to Mansfield through the magnificent Alps past Mt Kosciusko and through Corryong eventually to Mansfield via Yark and then to Melbourne.

A wonderful trip and there was method in our random journey and that was to scope out a place at Mansfield we had heard of and duly celebrated Leonore's 70th birthday there in May 2016.

One inconvenience was that there were a father and son who were armed and dangerous, loose in the area so our ideas of camping in isolated spots changed to camping in the guest room at our daughter's house in Melbourne.

After a few days there it was back to Beechworth and a camp by a creek and exploratory walks around one of the nicest places we have been. There are a number of places in Victoria that were rich enough to build beautiful buildings in the gold rush days and diversified enough to maintain them but were not so successful that they were replaced with supermarkets and hamburger places.

We then headed to our son's place in Shepparton and from there passed a significant milestone when we camped with them at a place called Gunbower between Echuca and Cohuna where there are wonderful wetlands and camping places. It was a little disturbing as shooting was allowed and whilst .22 rifles and shotguns were relatively safe unless at close range some high-powered rifles I heard were not. Boating, walks, campfires and their new tent were enjoyed by Lisa, Laila and Harry and turned out to be a good omen for the future.

We arrived home on 7th November so we took three weeks to get home, time that was well spent.

Sadly Ian Fletcher who had no peer as a country surgeon died soon after we arrived home. I was pleased I was able to join the very large crowd that attended his funeral service.

The rest of 2015 disappeared as usual with gardening, worrying about Coffin Bay, playing bridge again and little else. I was sorry about Kapooka but starting to realise and accept that almost certainly I had run my race.

Christmas and the New Year came and went but at the end of January our world changed and any regrets or sorrow about Kapooka disappeared. We had some serious stuff to deal with.

CHAPTER NINETEEN
2016 – OUR WORLD CHANGED

We were looking forward to some friends coming to our home for a traditional lamb roast on Australia Day 2016 when our son Tim rang and told us his little boy Harry had been admitted to the Royal Children's Hospital in Melbourne with Acute Lymphatic Leukaemia. He was three and a half and Laila, his sister, six.

We drove to Melbourne and later Shepparton where Tim and Lisa lived and were away from 23rd January until 17th March, although the last seven days were spent with our other son Peter and his wife Patricia in Naracoorte, and Leonore's brother and sister in Adelaide.

It was a terrible time for Tim and Lisa. Lisa had to stay in Melbourne with Harry and then even after they returned home there were still frequent visits to Melbourne for ongoing treatment such as Lumbar Punctures, IV chemotherapy and consultations with specialists. Even though I think I was calm about the situation I find it hard to remember the details.

I won't be so silly and say that I looked on the bright side as there was no bright side but there were some positive things. The type of leukaemia he has, had the best prognosis; they lived reasonably close to Melbourne; and the hospital was on the right side of the city for their visits from Shepparton. Sarah, our daughter lived in Melbourne and the hospital is perhaps the best in Australia.

Last but my no means least they had recently left Gove in the NT and Chinchilla in Queensland. Accessing treatment from those isolated towns would have been a nightmare. We saw our role as doing what we could to help in Shepparton so Lisa could concentrate on Harry. We took Laila to school and to various places in and out of Shepparton. I did a lot of work in the garden of their new home to help with their long-term plans for improving its ambience.

Later in the year when things had stabilised somewhat they were thinking about the medium-term treatment for Harry. I was with Tim and Lisa soon after he was first admitted to hospital and we were told his treatment may be eighteen months to two years. As time moved on Tim and I were thinking that 18 months is not too bad, that's only another eight or nine months. The treatment was always to be three years but the medical team are deliberately vague so that people are not overwhelmed with too much information. This I can understand.

We also returned to Shepparton in June 2016 for almost two months when Lisa had to take Harry to the Children's Hospital in Melbourne as part of his treatment regimen. Our dog Phryne, was in season and as we had planned to breed from her took her to a kennel in Mansfield to be mated which was unsuccessful.

There have been many times where Harry has made two steps forward and one step back. But time moves on. He is developing, physically and mentally, that is truly a blessing. Yes there are still hurdles to jump and Tim and Lisa will never be free of worry but things are pointing in the right direction.

I was feeling sad as I started writing about this and trying to remember details of when Harry first got sick and the times we were there when Lisa rang. She said "You would be proud of me. I just made a speech to 15-20 teachers about Harry's needs when he goes to school." I am indeed proud and it changed what I was going to write to a much more positive point of view and that phone call was just what did the trick.

I must place on record the pride and gratitude I have for Kirstin and Andrew, Sarah and Nick and Peter and Patricia, our children, their spouses and their children for the unfailing support that have given to Lisa, Tim, Laila and Harry in this journey that they are all sharing.

The last little fling in 2016 was presenting the PT Morton medal to the best and fairest player of the Sturt Football Club that happily had won the SANFL premiership that year, the first since 2002. There was a shadow hanging over that trip to Adelaide because we were heading to Sydney.

Our daughter Kirstin had been given a drug, flucloxacillin when she had a rare but known serious allergic reaction and that was drug-induced hepatitis. Like any other form of hepatitis it can be very serious.

When we saw her in hospital she was beyond yellow with jaundice, she was orange. She eventually had to take some very fancy medicine and has drunk little or no alcohol since.

We stayed in Sydney for more than three weeks fetching and carrying kids and groceries because above all, people with hepatitis need rest not running around after four children.

We arrived home early in November and got ready for the Coffin Bay family Christmas that duly happened without Tim and Lisa who, I forgot to say, really need to be within two hours of Melbourne.

There is a rumour that the custom of the children and families coming here on the even numbered Christmases has reached its use by date.

Last but not least I thought that I would remain a registered medical practitioner from 2016 to 2018 but there had been changes in what was required in October 2016.

By the time I was interested in working again in 2017 I could not meet those requirements so I happily cancelled my registration.

It was probably for the better and I have not once regretted it.

At the time of publication of this book on 23rd of April 2018, the good news is that Harry's treatment is now two thirds completed. He is now able to have his monthly treatment at the Shepparton Hospital which is steroids for a week each month as well as chemotherapy via a port which knocks him around. He does get ill every so often and needs antibiotics with or without admission to hospital.

CHAPTER TWENTY
REFLECTIONS – CHANGES IN MEDICINE

I am nearing 75 and I practiced medicine for almost 50 years until I retired in 2017. God willing my wife Leonore and I will celebrate our Golden Wedding next year in 2019. My paternal grandparents were a few years short of that mark but my maternal grandparents and parents reached that milestone. I doubt that three generations reaching it is common.

Wars, TB, cancer, childbirth, infectious diseases, smoking, car accidents and heart disease were all common causes of mortality in the two generations preceding mine. The last three agents of mortality were very prevalent in my generation but now happily much less common.

I was born into a world where anaesthetics, obstetrics and surgery were safe. Polio had been a significant problem but vaccinations, immunisation and public health had largely eliminated most infectious diseases. HIV-AIDS and hepatitis have become common in relatively recent times.

Road deaths were high at 3,000 per year in the 1960s for a population of less than 10 million but are now 1500 for 24 million. I have worn seat belts since 1960 and they were made compulsory in the early 1970s. Roads are better, air bags, car engineering, speed limits, random breath testing and perhaps community attitudes have all had a positive effect on reducing the death toll. Smoking has decreased and so consequently have the deaths from hypertension, heart and lung disease.

"Doctor in the House" written by Richard Gordon, an anaesthetist, who undoubtedly dreamed up his plots in the nether world of anaesthetics between boredom and sheer terror, well reflects my years at medical school in the 1960s.

I remember an evocative description of medical students in that book before final exams, running down the path through the garden of knowledge grabbing handfuls as they passed by.

The ambitious idea of describing the advances in knowledge since I graduated, in this chapter, is impossible and reminded me of that quotation. I pictured myself in a utility with a landing net that had holes in it driving through an orchard trying to grab fruit that was multiplying and accelerating away from me.

One of the very obvious changes has been the development and use of fibre optic endoscopes since the 1960s and 1970s.

These were used as a diagnostic tool in the respiratory tract and gastro intestinal tract, from both ends. These tools are able to take pictures, do biopsies and remove some lesions.

In the 1980s came a major change in abdominal and

gynaecological surgery. Once these were all open operations. In other words gall bladder removals, hysterectomies and so on all were done by making a hole in the abdominal wall and many required an assistant to hold retractors so the surgeon could access the relevant organ.

The major post-operative discomfort for patients was the cut in the abdominal wall. Whether the retractors caused damage I do not know but I hung onto plenty. It almost seemed overnight that this open surgery ceased and endoscopic surgery went from looking through natural body orifices to making their own way into the body through very small "key holes" that in terms of trauma and recovery were almost trivial. Soon most surgery was done this way. Part of the technology was that there was a camera that projected the view of the gall bladder or whatever it was onto a screen so the surgeon could manipulate the instruments while watching the screen.

We are now at the point where robots have entered the system because they have steadier and smaller "hands" than people.

Orthopaedics has advanced incredibly with scopes and other techniques, procedures and sophisticated rehabilitation. It is fair to illustrate with a simple sentence. Footballers in my father's day were ruined by cartilage injuries, in my day by cruciate injuries and nowadays they are likely to have arthroscopies almost as a routine and knee reconstructions are common and usually successful.

Associated with technical change day surgery became common with lighter anaesthetics and less trauma to patients so they could go home earlier than before. But there is a caveat to that as people from the country often do not know the ways of the big smoke and can be left standing on the footpath outside a hospital or day surgery suite with an overnight bag and not knowing where to go and how to get there. My wife worked with Red Cross and would arrange transport for people in that situation.

As an aside: all these new techniques reduced the opportunity for general practitioners to do surgery because we could not get access to the training and technology needed to use endoscopes.

Another major area for fibre optic scopes is in cardiology, particularly but not exclusively the introduction of stents. These are tiny tubes that are passed via a hole in the femoral artery into the aorta and then the relevant coronary artery which is partly or completely blocked. It creates a passage to allow blood to flow to the heart muscle.

Cataract surgery does not involve scopes but is done as a day procedure and I have just experienced how effective, comfortable and efficiently that can be done. A few hours at our local hospital, home with a patch that was removed the next morning and I could read the bottom line on the eye chart.

The progress from standard x-rays to CT Scans, the increased use of ultrasound, the miracle of MRIs and the interventions of radiologists who insert catheters into the tubes between the bladder and kidneys and explode renal stones with sound impulses are to me what Churchill said about Russia, "A riddle wrapped in a mystery, inside an enigma."

When I graduated partial gastrectomies were common in the management of duodenal and gastric ulcers. Gordon Ormandy, my surgical boss in Broken Hill, was an expert in that procedure. This operation removed large parts of the acid producing tissue of the stomach. That procedure is rarely done today.

At the time the only thing to heal ulcers was rest, cessation of smoking and perhaps a drug made from liquorice called carbenoxalone. In 1982 two Australians Barry Mitchell and Robin Warren discovered that Helicobacter Pylori bacteria, seen for years in the stomach, actually caused ulcers. This was an epochal discovery and they received the Nobel Prize in 2005. There were tests developed to detect these organisms that made diagnosis easier than endoscopies.

Regimens of different antibiotics were developed to treat these bacteria and together with Proton Pump Inhibitors, histamine blockers and other medications to reduce production or protect against the effects of gastric acid the problems and dangers of ulcers have been minimised.

These and endoscopic surgery also have had a big role in the management of gastro oesophageal reflux aka hiatus hernia in days gone by.

While on the subject of medical super stars in Australia, Professor Frazer developed a vaccine to prevent cervical cancer that was marketed in 2006. Since 2015 205 million doses have been distributed worldwide.

In Broken Hill I did tonsillectomies every Saturday morning. They are hardly ever done now and have gone the way of mastoid surgery perhaps due to the use or even over use of antibiotics.

Our generation of doctors were almost the first to have effective medication for a range of mental illness particularly Depression and Anxiety and these conditions are accepted much more in our society now and general practitioners have undoubtedly contributed to that situation.

Electronic transmissions of ECGs, x-rays, ultra sounds and pictures via telemedicine can be invaluable for isolated doctors in emergencies or unusual rashes.

On the subject of rashes, roacutane for bad acne would count as a significant advance as would steroid creams in the management of eczema.

Asthma is still a major problem and getting worse despite many new drugs mostly in the Ventolin or steroid group. We use much bigger and or more frequent doses of these agents and we monitor responses with peak flow and other measurements.

Feeling good is no indication that an asthmatic is well controlled. I looked after a 190 cm slim soldier with asthma and he passed all his tests and was fit for combat. I measured his peak expiratory flow and it was less than 300 instead of 600 l/sec and he felt fine. That is a picture of a young man who has a cold, goes out to a pub, smokes and has an asthma attack from which he may not recover not that this happened to my patient but that is the picture.

Constipation was a problem in post war Australia. My belief is that the new prosperity allowed people to eat meat and eggs every day and bacon if they wished. Dad had diverticulitis and was told not to eat fibre but by the 1970s fibre was part of the management. The work of Burkitt in Uganda suggested that a high fibre diet, by soaking up bile salts that were potentially carcinogenic, could reduce the risk of bowel cancer and of course it prevents constipation.

On the "Doc Martin" television show recently there was a patient who was clinically drunk and had a high blood alcohol despite denying drinking. The good doctor diagnosed that as being due to bacteria in the bowel acting on the food he ate and producing alcohol. I really sat up and took notice. Something I have never forgotten was an accident in the early 1980s in Port Lincoln when a truck hit a car and the car driver was killed and found to have a high blood alcohol. His wife was adamant he did not drink except maybe a glass of wine at Christmas. I believed her and followed this up with the police and got some weird answers such as the blood sample must have fermented or the wrong one had been tested.

I contacted my mate Pat Phillips, an endocrinologist in Adelaide, after the TV show. He said that specific bugs in the bowel given the right substrate (i.e. what the man ate) could and did produce alcohol in the gut. Pat actually had a patient with that very condition that he had dealt with and cured.

The fibre and bacteria in the bowel story has a long way to run and already seems to explain a variety of complaints. It may finish up being another "ulcer" story.

Another thing that has changed is the management of emergency injuries and illnesses. There is now a specialty of Emergency Medicine and some general practitioners have become expert in the skills, such as anaesthesia, in order to do this work in hospitals and outside. I have been closely involved with Royal Flying Doctor Service (RFDS) and their aircraft most of my career one way or another. They were sophisticated but what could be done in the air was limited.

In Port Lincoln we used to stabilise patients that could take hours or even days but nowadays an injured patient will have a primary and secondary survey of injuries and resuscitation. If required a much larger aircraft with a retrieval specialist and nurse will fly to Port Lincoln, take over the management of the patient and take them back to Adelaide. <u>However it must be recognised that aircraft are not always available so well-trained doctors and nurses must be available at rural hospitals.</u>

It has been said that advances in medicine from 1980 to 2000 would be greater than from 1900 to 1980. This may be hard to believe but certain things have certainly changed. Interventional cardiology and the whole gamut of endoscopic investigation and procedures have truly been revolutionary and we are on the cusp of robotics.

Some things that happen in medicine are dramatic such as the discovery that germs cause ulcers and the introduction of vaccines to prevent cervical cancer as mentioned above.

Many other things progress in a less dramatic fashion and one that illustrates this is the management of prematurity. When I did obstetrics in 1967 babies only 24 weeks old were considered to be unsalvageable but by the late 1970s they were surviving.

Most importantly these tiny babies did not show any damage from their difficult start and had met the normal milestones and had done well at school. I assume that progress has continued.

The management of ischaemic heart disease has changed with new drugs and a mixture of high technology interventions such as heart transplants, coronary artery grafting and the ready use of stents even as an emergency response to a cardiac arrest, as happened to a good friend of mine in late 2017.

Undoubtedly the clinical, therapeutic and public health attacks on high cholesterol, smoking, hypertension and obesity on certain groups have helped but other groups appear to be unaffected by these endeavours.

The progress in many respects has again been incremental. We have gone from parking someone who has had a heart attack in a private hospital room with not much more than rest and anecdotally a bottle of scotch, to monitoring in an intensive care unit to prevent or detect problems. This has made a huge difference in the survival of people with heart attacks. Similarly, the professional expertise of ambulance officers must never be forgotten.

I have only touched on the technical changes but there have also been some system changes such as the development of care plans for patients with chronic disease and Medicare item numbers to support this initiative.

An oddity I experienced when I worked in Woomera in the 1970s as a Commonwealth Medical Officer and a public servant to boot, has certainly disappeared, more the pity I have been tempted to think on some occasions! One of the many duties was to perform medical examinations to determine fitness or otherwise of applicants for specific jobs. If for example someone was applying to work on the counter at the Post Office they had to be presentable to the clients. I cannot remember how it was defined but bad acne for example could exclude a person from that position because of their appearance.

Illegal drugs I have not mentioned and they certainly are a major problem for society as a whole. I have not experienced "ice rage" as a clinician but as an administrator I am aware of the problems and maniacal strength of users. Many times I have seen nurses tell an injured drunk to sit down, across an open counter. That doesn't happen now.

I was lucky getting into medicine. I have a wife and

children who have been loyal to me. Our children are all happily married with a total of ten children of their own. I have survived some accidents that could have been fatal.

Professor Kamien from Western Australia wrote decades ago that longevity of general practitioners in rural Australia was influenced by activities outside of general practice. I have had other professional interests in medicine as an administrator and outside of medicine which has helped. Rural general practice was likely more financially rewarding due to the hours worked and expensive hobbies were possible. I have certainly seen that on Eyre Peninsula where doctors have owned farms, built aeroplanes, had successful and indeed unsuccessful business ventures, built and sailed yachts, played in bands and so on. Other examples are the three general practitioners who earned Doctorates in Medicine in Port Lincoln and Tumby Bay.

I fit in here somewhere with my administrative and general practice qualifications. After finishing work in Port Lincoln in 2002 I worked part of the time from 2003 to 2015. I was a general practitioner for the Australian Defence Forces for five years and a medical administrator for about three years.

And it all is getting harder but we won't go there.

One thing that I have treasured that may well not be available in the future is GPs doing obstetrics. Firstly women understandably may prefer to see a female doctor and secondly the town or hospital where a doctor works may no longer be allowed to deliver babies.

The other spin off that comes from delivering babies or indeed just being a general practitioner and seeing women is that one treats children and again that is part of the richness of general practice and usually a real joy.

Some male doctors see women as "tears and smears" but I have always enjoyed being a true general practitioner as best as I could and seeing old, young, male and female patients.

PERSONAL

To practise medicine is a privilege indeed. In essence people bare their bodies, minds and even souls to doctors and this is a sacred trust and few doctors ever betray that trust.

Medicine is also a profession with many nuances and variations in actual jobs. A wise Professor of Paediatrics, George Maxwell, once told our group of students that it was the broadest profession that there is and I am sure that is true. Research, administration, Defence Forces, public health, the clinical specialities such as medicine, surgery and sub specialities, cardiology, gastroenterology, urology and nephrology are probably beyond counting now. Radiology and other imaging, pathology, immunology, physical, rehabilitation medicine, paediatrics, forensics and of cause psychiatric medicine are more branches and job opportunities. Whoops I have forgotten general practice.

I must confess I am passionate about the benefits of

working in the country as a general practitioner.

Professionally there are more opportunities to deliver babies, give anaesthetics, do procedures such as managing simple fractures, suturing lacerations and more depending on interests and training.

An absolute corner stone of rural practice is having access to local hospitals and I cannot imagine practising without being able to do that. It allows a general practitioner to extend the scope of care to a patient and/or their family. Often people need to be admitted to hospitals but not necessarily to be seen by a specialist. Pneumonia, gastroenteritis, influenza, bad backs, migraines, work and sports injuries and an endless list of other conditions may need hospitalisation and can be managed by a general practitioner.

Medicine is not only about proper diagnoses. Sometimes people are simply distressed or unwell from the burdens of life and a couple of days in hospital may return them to their normal selves.

Another example is babies or small children who are hot and unwell in houses without air conditioning with worn out parents and siblings—been there done that as a doctor and as a parent! Overnight admission into air conditioning with good nurses who know all about crook bubs can do wonders.

It is the continuum of care that can be so rewarding to doctors and patients and their relatives. This is unlikely to occur in metropolitan areas and in large country towns nowadays.

On the subject of continuity, a colleague and close friend, Steve Ballard, coined the phrase "the intense intrusiveness of remote town practice". I understand that and one day I was rather rude to a patient who made some stupid comment about me eating a pie while I was rushing along in the main street between meetings but the benefits outweigh the disadvantages by huge margin.

We were welcomed to Port Lincoln by some old friends as mentioned and at the time it was almost a cashless society. Leonore would bring three dresses or clothes home on approval. I would book up things for the garden, farm or even at the pub.

I mentioned Bill Holland who seduced me with whiting to play cricket for Waybacks. People who I met at work were friendly and helpful outside the surgery so it was an easy place to live. There were only 10,000 people then and only one practice so it was common to meet people at work and at play.

I was lucky in that I cultivated an ability to remember people but usually I managed to forget why I had seen them at work.

I did have trouble coping with the ceaseless demands and the hospital became somewhat of a refuge for me where I assisted at operations and did the medical administration and various activities I mentioned.

It was an easy place to work and play and we are eternally grateful for the opportunity and friendships.

I would strongly advise young, or even not so young, doctors thinking about general practice to think very hard about rural practice. There are just so many rewards professionally and financially that are not found in urban practice.

Another factor is that that for a doctor or others there are more opportunities to meet politicians, business people, police, fishermen, farmers and others than if working in the suburbs. Of course doctors can become involved in their local communities anywhere but it is far easier in a country town to get someone to "give you a hand with something" than in the city.

As a matter of interest in a town of 10-20,000 people there is little in the way of goods and services that aren't available and it is just so much easier to get around. I had a shoulder reconstruction and could walk to work for example.

I was able to work away from my practice at different jobs and projects that urban doctors would find difficult because of the incessant demands of practice.

In particular a Farm Injury Project was tailor-made for me and attracted a lot of support. I was on several National committees and spoke at conferences locally, interstate and overseas and a member of the South Australian Medical Board. These opportunities and more, happened because I worked in a country town.

I made a decision in the mid-1990s that the work I did with the Division of General Practice benefited our local and regional community more than sitting in a surgery seeing patients. I was greatly helped by the Investigator Clinic doctors and allowed to leave the clinic and share rooms with my friend, Peter Hawke a physiotherapist. This lasted from 1996 to 2002. I had some health problems in that period and the Clinic covered me for after-hours work from that time. A kind and magnanimous gesture.

All good things come to an end though and my work with the Division ceased in 2002 and my practice was pleasant but not viable so I sought work elsewhere as described. I managed to be in the right place at the right time and had a gentle, wonderful and entertaining glide into retirement with Leonore and our black Labradors in Darwin, Gladstone Wagga Wagga, Portland, Alice Springs and Woomera.

My career has been a wonderful journey and made as easy as possible by the superb body of nurses I have worked with and despite some grumpiness at times there has only been one nurse I have found impossible to work with. I am tempted to name more nurses than I have in this book but I believe that many will know who I am writing about.

This is the third printing of this book and I am especially grateful to the nurses, old and young, who came to the launch, 16 years after I worked in Port Lincoln, it was terrific and very moving.

In my career I have worked about half time as a GP and/or a medical administrator and apart from six months in Adelaide always, in the country. An unexpected benefit of working in different places is that we have seen much more of our widely spread children and their families than would have been possible over the last 20 years than if we had stayed in Port Lincoln.

Thank you, Leonore, Kirstin, Sarah, Tim, Peter, your spouses and children for being who you are and with Mum and Dad, making me have such a fortunate life.

www.ingramcontent.com/pod-product-compliance
Lightning Source LLC
Chambersburg PA
CBHW051417290426
44109CB00016B/1327